OUR KATE

Other Novels by Catherine Cookson

Katie Mulholland
The Glass Virgin
The Dwelling Place

OUR KATE

AN AUTOBIOGRAPHY
BY

CATHERINE COOKSON

THE BOBBS-MERRILL COMPANY, INC.
INDIANAPOLIS / NEW YORK

THE BOBBS-MERRILL COMPANY, INC.
A Subsidiary of Howard W. Sams & Co., Inc.
Indianapolis/New York

Originally published by Macdonald & Co.
         (Publishers) Ltd., London, England
Library of Congress catalogue card number 74-161241
Manufactured in the United States of America

CONTENTS

CONTENTS

DEDICATION
To all bairns

To all bairns
Who own no name,
And who behind laughter-lighted face
Hide the shame
Of sin,
Which benefited their joy
Not a trace.

To all bairns
Who carry the weight of guilt
Of censure and law,
Who reach the Courts,
The Borstals,
The Homes;
Look not in them for flaw.

Nor yet in their mothers,
Who were bairns,
Or in their nameless fathers,
Who were bairns,
Right down the ages to times start.
But seek the flaw in good men,
Who make laws for bairns to keep.

And having looked,
And found,
Ask that this law
That breeds a stigma,
That reeks its stench on woman
And calls her offspring
Bastard,
Be changed.

Do not ask me how
The victim's vision is distorted,
For in her mind
She is still a bairn,
And the flyblow of a system.

AUTHOR'S NOTE

For obvious reasons some names, especially those of the inhabitants of the New Buildings, have been altered.

Part One

THE LONG CHILDHOOD

CHAPTER ONE

Now you're married I wish you joy,
First a girl and then a boy.
Seven years over,
Seven years after,
Now's the time to kiss and give over.

When I first danced around the lamp post and sang the above words I was about five years old. I was fifteen when I asked myself who had written them.

'Seven years over, seven years after, now's the time to kiss and give over.'

Eeh! they were bad words. Fancy saying things like that in a bairn's song.

'Now you're married I wish you joy. First a girl and then a boy.' That was all right; I liked that part because I wanted first a girl and then a boy. But above all things I wanted to get married. It was nothing to do with having a husband, nothing at all, I just wanted to be called Mrs, because our Kate wasn't called Mrs.

I was born in Number 5 Leam Lane, at the bottom of Simonside Bank, Tyne Dock. Tyne Dock is, or was at the time, just what it says, a dock on the river Tyne. Where the river flows into the North Sea the towns of North and South Shields stand, one on each bank. South Shields is connected with Tyne Dock; up river Jarrow, Hebburn, Pelaw, Felling and Gateshead all follow; on the other side of the river is North Shields, then follows Howdon, Wallsend, Willington Quay and Newcastle. Both banks were lined with shipyards, chemical works and factories.

Simonside Bank was just a cluster of houses within three minutes walk, under five great slime-dripping arches, of the actual dock gates; and yet we were on the verge of what was known as the country. A few minutes walk up the hill from our house were the big houses. There were about half-a-dozen of them, and above them a farm and a little country school and church.

The first group of houses on the left going up the bank was confined between two house-shops, one at each end. One was kept by the Lodges, the other by the Lawsons. In the middle was a public house. I never knew it called anything but 'Twenty-seven', because I understand there were only twenty-six staiths in the docks and the bar being a place where the men eventually docked became twenty-seven. Our house was next to the bar. On the opposite side were two houses and a blacksmith's shop.

Simonside Bank was shaped like a bent funnel, the broad end opening on to the main road between Tyne Dock and Jarrow. Where the funnel curved and narrowed sharply to mount the steep bank, there was, on the right hand side, a row of houses perched high on a terrace. On the left hand side, just beyond the Lodges' house and shop, was the gas-works, and directly above this, the Dixons' cottage.

The Dixons were people on a different social scale altogether from the McMullens. I was only once in their house, it was on a Saturday morning and I found myself sitting on a chamber in their front room. I had been carried there after my Uncle Jack had grabbed me by the hair and dashed me against a wall. Jack was eighteen and roaring mad drunk; he was fighting my step-grandfather, who was, if anything, more roaring and more mad than his only son. I must have tried to separate them – I was to do this very often during my childhood – and Jack had thrown me out of the way. They both loved me and would never have consciously hurt me. But there I was sitting on the chamber and crying my loudest, not because I'd nearly had my brains knocked out but because I was in the Dixons' lovely bedroom and I had wet my knickers.

On the high terrace, I remember only two families; the Richardsons, with daughters Sally and Polly, and one son; and the Watsons, with a son, Willy, and a daughter, Eva. It is Willy I remember playing with, in the gas gates as we called the rough space beyond the big gates that shut off the works and the gasometer itself. I used to run around the rim of the gasometer fascinated and frightened by the foot of water dividing it from the enormous tank. I rarely went beyond the gasometer itself, except one morning early, when I went with our Kate to the furnace and saw it being raked out, a great red terrifying mouth that belched a funny smell. It filled my mouth and clogged my nostrils and as we walked back to the house, Kate now carrying two buckets of hot cinders with which to start the wash-house pot, I told her that I felt the funny smell on my tongue. 'You're daft, bairn,' she said.

I have a pale memory of hanging over the wall of the gas gates and looking down on to the steep curving road of Simonside Bank. Opposite, against the high terrace wall that buttressed the bank, lay a bike, and somebody was lying on the road. It was a young lad who had come down the hill at speed and, attempting to round the curve too fast, had been thrown off his bike and hit the high wall. I think he died on the road, but I remember them saying that he cried for his mother and that she had been dead for years.

The Richardson girls grew up to be fine, well-dressed women. I can hear Kate skitting at their mother, always with the same phrase, 'If you talk properly you'll get nice clothes'. And why not? But in those days, to say anything like that turned you at once into an upstart. Yet underneath, Kate had the same desire for me, that I should talk nice, be different, and have nice clothes. I was full of admiration for the Richardson girls and they were always very nice to me.

But most people were nice to me. Yet I was always fighting against something I couldn't understand. Eventually I realised I was fighting against what people were thinking underneath the niceness, that I would go the way of my mother. Then they

11

would have said, 'Well, what can you expect? What chance did the lass have, I ask you?' It was this I fought against, their pity. I wanted to be looked up to, respected, even envied – not pitied.

One day when I was three, and walking through the arches from the Docks – from a very small child I was used to going about on my own – I saw someone coming towards me whom apparently I didn't want to meet for I crossed over the road and, turning my face to the blank, black wall, walked sideways until I was passed them, for I knew that if I couldn't see them they couldn't see me. I was to follow this pattern for many years; whenever I didn't want to face up to some reality, I would turn my face to a wall; and always I would see a picture, which became the focal point of my striving, because it presented to me a different way of life. It showed me a big house peopled by ladies and gentlemen, and surrounded by cars, horses and servants. Of course, I was in the picture, dead centre.

The people who lived above us in Leam Lane were called Angus. I remember them because of the cow. The cows being driven down from the farm at the top of the bank, probably on their way to the slaughter-house in South Shields, were frightened one day by the old rumbling tram that plied on the single-line track between Tyne Dock and Palmer's shipyard in Jarrow. One of them, tearing out from underneath the arches at all of five miles an hour, frightened the animals and they scattered round the back lane. One out of terror or curiosity came into our back yard, and finding Mrs Angus's staircase door open mounted the stairs.

The first indication the herdsman had of the whereabouts of the cow was Mrs Angus hanging out from the upstairs front window screaming blue murder. Had the cow decided to go straight down the narrow front stairs, which dropped from the six foot landing, speculation was ripe for years afterwards as to what course would have been taken to get it up again, but the cow, being a sensible creature, just left her visiting card, which covered the landing, turned round and went out the way she had come.

The story of the cow was repeated again and again and again over the years in our house. Anything with a trace of humour in it was squeezed to death, and even the dead remains were kept hanging and were laughed at.

The McMullens were either laughing or rowing.

Although rows were not a daily occurrence in the house – the money coming in was not sufficient to provide for such regular relaxation – they were certainly a weekly affair and put the stamp on the McMullens in the dockland area. Old John and young John were characters – fighting characters. But, of course, they were not alone.

Then there was my grandmother. She was a tall woman, with a round, somewhat flat face. Her hair was parted dead centre and pulled painfully tight into a knob on the back of her head. I can see her with an apron on and a shirt blouse which was always buttoned right up to the neck. I have a picture of her standing with me in the doorway of a house in William Black Street. She looked a hard woman; I think from what my mother told me she was, at least towards her. She was very old as I remember her, being in her middle fifties when I was about seven or eight. And when she went out she wore a bonnet and a big cape. She too loved me.

She had had five daughters by her first husband, my real grandfather, who was a very good man and a Brother in the Catholic Church at Jarrow. He died, in his early thirties, of consumption. There were no pensions in those days, so my grandmother and the five girls were kept for a time by my great-grandmother and grandfather, a respectable, highly esteemed couple, possessors of a small holding and lavish table. But my grandmother, still a young woman and wanting independence, married again. This time a dashing Irishman, John McMullen, who had served in India and who had just come out of the army with a bit of money – Perhaps the real reason she married him was to enable her to stop working in the Puddling Mills at Jarrow, where the owners supplied milk or beer at break to keep the women going. For here death met you early.

All I know of my step-grandfather's background is that he hailed from somewhere in the bog country of Ireland, was one of triplets, and had thirteen brothers. He could neither read nor write, but could tell you the price of all eatables. My mother remembers his other two triplets coming to visit him shortly after he had married my grandmother. She said she remembered them because they brought the girls a big bag of pomegranates, and the next morning they got their backsides smacked because

13

of the pomegranate stains on the bedclothes. It is interesting to recall that my mother had real bedclothes over her at that stage in her life for this luxury didn't last long under the care of John McMullen. Yet let me be fair to him, he was a good worker ... when he could get it. He would walk right from the top end of Jarrow to the docks, a matter of about six miles there and back, for one shift.

My mother tells me that she can remember my grandmother, together with her sisters, Mary, who was younger, and Sarah, who was older than her, doing this walk at ten o'clock at night to take their stepfather's supper to the dock gates. It would be twelve o'clock when they got back home, and this journey was often done in the snow, and at times bare-foot, for by now there was no one to provide the extras. Two of the girls died before they were fourteen and my mother used to say it was a blessing in disguise.

During one period of great depression – this was when my mother was a child – me granda worked in the workhouse, breaking stones at a shilling a day. The shilling was paid as a voucher which had to be taken to a grocery shop, and if anyone dared to ask the shopkeeper to put in a penn'orth of baccy he was likely to lose the voucher altogether.

Looking back, I see me granda acted according to his lights and values, and who is to blame him for his values when, for a ten-hour shift unloading iron ore boats, his trousers wet to the thighs, he got three shillings and six pence.

My aunt Sarah and my mother went into 'place' when they were twelve years old. Of course they had done work long before this, but it was mixed up with school – that is when they attended, for sending three children to school meant threepence a week and you could make a dinner for that with a penn'orth of pot stuff (vegetables), a penn'orth of peas, beans, and barley, and a penn'orth of pieces. What did it matter if there was sawdust sticking to the black congealed blood on the meat or that it was just a piece of the beast's lungs – it made a dinner.

They had also begged bread from door to door. I used to envy my mother having experienced these things because I longed for such poverty that there would be no money left for drink. My mother used to tell me of being sent out to beg for bread one day – she was not the only one begging at that time in Jarrow.

Her feet were bare and bleeding, the calves of her legs split with keens. At one house a compassionate woman took her in and gave her a pair of boots and stockings, and she went home, forgetting about the bread. Her delight in the boots, although her feet were paining even worse from their pressure on the keens, was short lived, for her mother took them immediately to the 'In and Out'. It was an appropriate name, for you would pawn, say, your man's suit on a Monday to meet the rent and if you hadn't the money to get it out on the Friday you would take in something else to help retrieve it. Brass candlesticks, mats, fire irons, even the stone dish you baked the bread in. One thing was always going in to get the other out.

My mother's first spell of actual service was in a house in Stanhope Road, Tyne Dock. I think they were butchers. There were four sons, and the washing was colossal. She couldn't reach the top of the poss-tub to wield the poss-stick, a great wooden beater on four legs, three to four foot high, so the woman had a stool made for her. She did all the housework, all the washing and all the ironing. She worked from half-past six in the morning until late at night, with half a day off a fortnight, and all for half-a-crown a week, usually subbed a month or two ahead. She stayed there a year. The tale of my mother's first place stayed in the front of my mind even as a child, and when I went into service I thought how lucky I was to be treated so differently. But only for a very short time.

I was born when Kate was twenty-four and the life she was made to endure because of me would have driven anyone less strong not only to drink but into the madhouse. The cruelty of the bigoted poor has to be witnessed to be believed. It has to be lived with to be understood.

When my mother, sick to depths of her soul, as I know now she was, had to come home from 'her place' and say she was going to have a baby, The Fathar, as he was always called, was for killing her – she had committed the unforgivable sin. Yet when I was born and she had milk fever and her breasts swelled to bursting, the fathar was supposed to have saved her life by sucking the milk from them. It seems incredible to me that she should have looked upon this act as something almost heroic for, remembering him as I do, I can see that he would have enjoyed this operation – he was a frustrated, licentious man.

15

His antidote against this, which the ailing health of me grandma could not alleviate, was drink and a dirty tongue, which he used against all women. Yet I must say that only on rare occasions did he let himself go in my presence, at least when he was sober. I feel grateful to him for this, for he had been known to make even the toughest women in the New Buildings blush.

As the years went on I think that of the two, me grandma was harder on Kate than the fathar, because, when coming home from place on her rare days off, if she'd attempt to take me in her arms me grandma would grab me from her, re-arrange my clothes and almost dust me down as if Kate's hands had contaminated me in some way.

At the time she met my father she was working in an inn in Lamesley. She was working in the bar, and had been for two or three years. Her sister, Mary, who was three years younger, was a housemaid, and a very haughty, hot-tempered housemaid at that. I am not quite sure of the name of the owners of the inn at that time but I do know that the daughter was Miss Jenny. Kate often spoke of her. Also of the pitmen who used to take the long trek past the inn to the mine, and on pay day, which was once a fortnight, have a blow up in the bar and a pay up for the odd pints that had gone on the slate. She must have been a favourite with them, for she was an attractive woman in those days, gay, warm, large-hearted.

My father, I understand, first set eyes on her when she served him in the saloon.

Kate never told me anything about him until six years before she died. It was my Aunt Mary who, when I was sixteen, gave me the sketchy outline of my beginnings and set up in my mind an inordinate pride, a sense of false superiority and a burning desire to meet this wonderful creature who had shocked me into being. This man. This gentleman. Oh, yes, he was a gentleman. My Aunt Mary stated this with emphasis. She had no love for her sister, Kate. Later in life when Kate became the object of her scorn, she still remained jealous of her, for people liked Kate, loved her in spite of everything. Mary did not have a nature that one could love, and when she imparted this news to me it was to hurt Kate, make me more ashamed of her. Yet deep in me I knew that my Aunt Mary wasn't a patch on 'Our Kate'. But Mary was often kind to me, it was only her scorn of

Kate that made me dislike her. Anyway, Mary said this gentleman went head over heels as soon as he saw Kate.

What did this gentleman do for a living?

Nobody has ever been able to tell me.

How did Mary know he was a gentleman?

Well, he wore a black coat with an astrakhan collar. He had a high hat and carried a silver mounted walking stick and black kid gloves, like 'The Silver King', she said. 'And he spoke different ... lovely.'

For two years the gentleman courted Kate. He did not come regularly but when he did he took her out, arranging his visits to her day off. She looked at no one else in the way she did at him. She was deeply in love. What did she expect from this association? She never said. But, knowing her level-headedness, I feel that she knew from the beginning that it was hopeless and therefore she kept him in his place, except for once; and once was enough. It seems pitiable to me at this distance that it wasn't until she was twenty-three that she first went with a man. I say first; it was the one and only time she had this kind of association with my father, and it's more pitiable still that she never had this association with anyone else until over sixteen years later when she married David McDermott, because she was of a loving nature. I can feel myself getting angry when I think that she was branded as a fallen woman – and you needed to make a mistake only once and give evidence of it in order to acquire this prefix in those days – whilst today girls still at school indulge in intimacy for kicks. If I hadn't stopped believing in God this injustice would surely have acted as a springboard against believing in a benevolent father, a controller of destinies, someone who has our welfare at heart, for such a deity must surely have had his favourites, and Kate wasn't one of them. Her taking to drink, her servitude to her mother and stepfather in a house hardly ever without lodgers, the persecution, through love, or lust, of her half-brother, the indignities and slights she had to put up with, the undermining and ruining of her moral fibre, can all be laid at the door of one ecstatic moment.

My bitterness on this point is not for myself because I realise now that in being part of 'the gentleman' – and I have my tongue in my cheek even as I write the word – I have a great deal to be thankful for, for he provided the norm at which I aimed. It was him in me that pushed and pulled me out of the drabness of my early existence. It was from him that I got the power to convey awareness, this painful sensitivity, without which what I sensed in others would have remained an untranscribable mass of feelings. Yet should I be thankful? Wouldn't it have been much easier for me if, having been born sixteen years later, I had inherited David McDermott's utter placidity? With this trait, and a touch of my mother's sense of humour, life would have been a straight line track, no sharp bends, no up hill pulls and . . . no summit.

I don't know when it was that the gasometer caught fire, but I do know that I was perched high on me Uncle Jack's knee. He was lying on his back on the saddle, giving me a shuggy, and I can remember the song he was singing. It was one I think he made up himself. It went like this:

> Father Chitmas soon will come
> Laden with all treasure.
> I would like a boat to sail,
> A rocky horse with a bushy tail,
> A doggy
> And a spade and pail.
> Katie wants a big
> BLACK PUD-DING.

He was singing this in an imitation of my clipped childish voice, hence Chitmas for Christmas. He could have been a grand fellow could me Uncle Jack. Even Kate said this. But there I was this night perched high on his knee, and I can hear myself shouting and pointing to 'the bonny fire'. The next thing I knew I was in me granda's arms and we were at the Sawmill Bridge, half-way up the road to East Jarrow; a good quarter of a mile distant.

The veering of the wind that night turned the flames away, and this, it was said, saved part of the town from destruction. My husband tells me now it wouldn't have blown up at all.

It would perhaps be untrue and very unkind if I thought that me granda ran all that way to save his own skin taking me as a cover, but he certainly left me grandma behind.

When I look back on incidents such as these I always see an ulterior motive. Perhaps I am wrong – I hope so.

I started at Simonside Protestant School before I was five years old. The teachers used to pass the door on their way up the hill to the school and they would take me with them. How I loved those teachers. Miss Curl and Miss Nesbitt; beloved Miss Nesbitt, but shattering Miss Nesbitt. She it was who first showed me up as a liar.

I must have been between five and six years old when we moved from Leam Lane to East Jarrow. We made the move on a flat cart. It would likely be Jacky Halliday's, for he was the coalman and the only one we knew who had a cart. And I remember I sat on the back, under the big arch of the mangle, swinging my legs.

East Jarrow lies between Tyne Dock and Jarrow. It is only about three-quarters of a mile from the dock gates and half-a-mile from Leam Lane.

The New Buildings as the two terraces and the three streets were called – and weren't new at all – faced the Jarrow Slakes, a huge timber seasoning pond into which the river Tyne came and went on its rise and fall. From the bottom of William Black Street, the street in which we went to live, you could look across the road – the same road with the single line tram track that connected Tyne Dock with Jarrow – across the Slakes, to the ships in the river, and beyond them to Howdon on the other side of the water.

Compared with Jarrow and Tyne Dock, East Jarrow was a paradise. As you went up William Black Street you were flanked on the left by black timbered palings behind which was a field of corn. Some years the field held potatoes or beet, according to the planning of the farmer, but most years it seemed to be corn. The farmhouse and main farm were opposite my school at Simonside and at the top of the street was an open space that took in the end of Philipson Street too. Beyond this was a railed-in field and a small market garden. The back doors of William Black Street and Philipson Street faced each other across a cobbled back lane, but whereas there were two families to a backyard in William Black Street, every house in Philipson Street had its own backyard, walled high on all sides. Opposite Philipson Street front was another open space and beyond that

19

a short street called Lancaster Street. At the end of these three streets ran the two terraces. The five streets formed a letter E – the two terraces being the upright, divided in the middle and facing the main road, while William Black Street was the bottom line, Philipson Street the middle, and Lancaster Street the fore-shortened top. And it was in this small community, in this chequered world, that I lived until I was twenty-two, in it, but not of it, accepted, yet rejected. Yet I did not reap my environ-ment so much from the community as from the kitchen in 10 William Black Street. The kitchen is the heart of the matter, for the kitchen was the axis about which revolved the lives of those nearest to me – my people, be they what they may . . .

CHAPTER TWO

I have already prefixed those near to me by 'me' or 'our' for they seem more my kin in this way, and I shall continue to do so, but I will write 'my Aunt Mary' or 'my Uncle Alec' or 'my Aunt Sarah', for when I spoke of them I never used 'me' but 'my'. It was a strange differentiation, but they were outside the house. They did not belong to me in as much as I felt no responsibility for their actions; I only felt responsibility for the people in our kitchen.

In those days the New Buildings held a very mixed assortment. In some cases the contrast was striking, as with the once rich Larkins, who had owned the Barium chemical works further up the road, and who still occupied the two large houses that took up most of the first terrace, and the Kanes who lived at the top of William Black Street – not sixty feet away – and who were so destitute that the daughter not only borrowed our Kate's boots but the mother used to borrow the gully – a bread knife.

Then there were, as in any community, the social climbers. These managed to employ a daily, or send their washing out, or have somebody in to do the washing and the housework. Perhaps I am wrong in calling them social climbers. Perhaps these were just outward signs of their respectability. Then there were the strivers, those who neither drank nor smoked, and whose one aim was to keep their heads above water; water in this case being debt. Then last and by no means least came the hard cases. And there weren't so very many of these cases in the New Buildings in those days. But among them were families dominated by drink, as ours was.

And there were the Afflecks. The Afflecks lived in a little red cottage down the road near the Sawmill Bridge, in the direction of Tyne Dock. There were three daughters – the eldest kept the only shop in the New Buildings – and they were all ladies. They were ladies during my childhood, they still remained ladies when I saw them through the eyes of my late teens, and when I met May and Maude some few years ago, I had no need to change my opinion.

We did not live in number ten when we first went to the New Buildings but in an upstairs house further up the street; but we did not live there long. Number ten was a downstairs house and had three rooms. The front room, into which you stepped from a tiny hallway that allowed only for the opening of the door, held a green plush suite – two stiff-backed armchairs, four single ones and a long couch – an oval table standing on a centre leg and a double brass bed. The bed lay in an alcove and you walked down the side of it to get to the door which led into the kitchen.

How a room the size of our kitchen could hold so much I don't know, for in its centre stood a large kitchen table of the better kind, with a leather covered top. Under the window that looked into the backyard stood another table, an oblong one, which was used for cooking. The fireplace was the old fashioned open black range and on the left of it for many years stood a great ugly unused gas stove. In front of the range was a massive steel fender, four feet long, and a conglomeration of steel fire irons, none standing less than two feet high. On the floor, along the length of the fender was a clippy mat, a great heavy affair that I couldn't lift even when I was fourteen. On this mat stood a high backed wooden chair, 'the fathar's' chair, on which no one dared to sit but himself. Standing against the wall opposite the door that led out of the kitchen into the scullery was a chest of drawers. A six foot long wooden saddle – like a settee or couch – was set against the wall opposite the fireplace, but to get on to it you had to pull the table out or scramble over the head. Above it hung a picture of Lord Roberts sitting on a horse with a black man standing at his side. For years I believed the rider to be me Granda when he was in India, and when he levelled abuse at the picture, which he often did, I thought he was speaking to the black man.

What we called the scullery held two shelves and a backless chair, on which stood the tin dish used for all purposes that required water. Beyond was the pantry, a narrow slit with one long shelf. The tap was at the bottom of the yard, where also were the two lavatories. In this latter we were fortunate, there being a lavatory to each house. The back door leading to the upstairs house was on the left of our kitchen window, and opposite, running the complete length of the wall from our bedroom window to the coal house doors, were hen crees, always full of hens and ducks.

You reached the door of the bedroom by edging between the oblong table, the kitchen table and the head of the saddle, the bedroom in which I slept with my mother on a flea-ridden feather mattress, against which, with my conscripted assistance, she waged a fruitless war for years. Why didn't we get rid of the mattress? What! Get rid of a mattress that had supported countless births and a number of agonising deaths all because of a few fleas? And what would we have to lie on? There wasn't enough money for beer, let alone new mattresses.

Above us, in those early days, lived a family called Romanus. He was a trimmer in the docks, a big burly man with little to say. She was a woman of better class who was slowly drinking herself to death. Eventually she achieved this end. It was the only thing in her life at which she succeeded. I remember the day she died. There had been the usual fight the day before. The Romanus's fought in a funny way, I thought, because you could only hear thuds on our kitchen ceiling and Mrs Romanus saying, in a very refined voice, 'That's it, Jim.' There was no yelling. I think now that it was these words that drew the blows. Mr Romanus beat his wife because she drank. She was a secret drinker, and she drank because she was unhappy. She had known a different life at one time from that of Jim Romanus and William Black Street. The day she died we heard the thud but we knew that he was on day-shift. Me grandma went upstairs and found Mrs Romanus had had a stroke, and in a few hours she was dead. I remember everybody seemed to blame Mr Romanus, yet nobody had ever said anything to him or tried to stop him knocking his wife about. There were certain things that were none of your business.

At the time we moved to the New Buildings our Kate and my Aunt Sarah and Aunt Mary were in place, and strangely enough they had not been informed of the move. I first became aware of our Kate one night as I played under the lamp near the top end of the street. I had a rope tied to the lamp post and was dizzying round on the end of it singing 'When I was going to Strawberry Fair singing, singing buttercups and daisies, I met a lady taking the air for a day. Her eyes were blue, she had gold in her hair and she was going to Strawberry Fair, singing, singing buttercups and daisies, singing, singing tral-la-la-la-la' when out of the shadow beyond the rim of light emerged our Kate. I stopped my dizzying and stared at her, while the rope went limp in my hand. To me she looked beautiful – tall, dressed in a grey costume, with beautiful hair on which was perched a big hat. She took hold of my arm and shook me from my daze, saying, 'Where are they?' She had arrived at the old house in Leam Lane to find it empty and had become very distressed, for, as poor as the house was, it was a focal point. She feared the disintegration of the home then as she was to fear it until the Fathar died. I think she feared it for him more than for herself, for John McMullen had a deep secret terror, he was afraid of ever being homeless and having to end his days in the workhouse. Vaguely I remember her going upstairs into the new house, and there going for me grandma while the tears ran down her face. Me grandma said, 'Well, I just couldn't get down to writing. And besides, there was the writing paper and envelope to buy and the stamp, and I hadn't got it.'

I remember liking our Kate to come home, for she always brought parcels of food with her. At this time she was working in a baker's shop in Chester-le-Street, baking the bread and cakes, and her money, as ever, was booked weeks ahead. She took most of it in the form of groceries and what was over she tipped up on her visits home. Mary and Sarah were not called upon to do this, but then they had not committed a sin, a sin which had to be fed and clothed. When they were young girls they had had to 'stump up' their money, but as the years went on they did this less and less. Me grandma was a foolishly generous woman and a bad housekeeper and Kate used to be infuriated, she told me, when they lived in Tyne Dock – not in Leam Lane but in Nelson Street I think it was, and she would come home from her half-a-crown or three shillings a week place to find sponging neighbours being feasted with broth, and brisket, and beer, when perhaps only two days before, following a distracted appeal, she had sent home another subbed-week's wages. This never happened at the New Buildings, but there were a thousand and one other ways me grandma could squander senselessly the little money that came into the house. Yet she herself didn't drink much.

From this particular night when Kate came consciously on to my horizon she was never to leave it.

It is true to say that Kate never left the house to return to her place with anything except a return ticket in her purse. Should the Fathar or Jack be in the house, which inevitably they would be when there wasn't any money floating around, she couldn't see them doing without a drink. She was a big soft-hearted goof. It was strange, too, but she rarely touched drink then.

In these days working men, should their wives be ill, will set to and see to the house, but in those days a man went out to work and that, to his mind, was enough; the house and all in it was the woman's task, and it lowered a man's prestige if he as much as lifted a cup. The lower down the working class scale you were the more this rule applied. Even many years later I heard me granda describe a man as the nappy washer because he had seen to the house when his wife was confined to bed with her first baby. The neighbours usually did this chore with or without pay, more often without, because in those days neighbours did not expect to be paid. Both me granda and me uncle Jack would have let their clothes go rotten on their backs before they would have washed them; as for cooking a meal, even if they had known how to, they wouldn't have lowered themselves to the level of the fire, or the gas stove. Man's rightful standing in his house was a thing to be guarded, to be fought for; no weakness or emotions or kindly instincts must touch it. Our men didn't even mend the boots, Kate had to do that. With the last on her knees and a mouthful of tacks she would hammer away, soling and heeling the big ugly working boots, and after a day that would have worn out two women.

So there came a time, because me grandma became ill – this was shortly following the night Kate pulled me from the lamp post – that she had to give up her limited liberty and come home to be Jack-of-all-trades. Had there not been myself to use as a hold over her she might have refused, yet I doubt it, knowing Kate.

She worked for everybody, and anybody. Besides nursing me grandma and attending to fleeting lodgers she went out and did days washing or cleaning, paper-hanging and painting, ceilings and staircases, she even replaced window sashes and whole window frames and for never more than three shillings a day. So it is little wonder that the hopelessness of her life, looming so large before her drove her, to an antidote to enable her to go through with it. Yet her ready smile, her joking, and pleasant disposition never gave away what she felt about some of her employers. It was only years later that I knew how she had hated doing for 'those worse than yourself'.

Besides having a lovely face she was beautifully built, with a skin the equal of which I have never seen, pure milk and roses. She had two great azure blue eyes, with dark curving brows. Her hair was brown and abundant and she had a wide generous mouth full of strong teeth with which she cracked brazil nuts until she was seventy. But it was the mouth that showed her weakness, with a top lip full to slackness. She was of a dominant nature, yet this was balanced by an innate softness; she was very forgiving was Kate. She had in her a sense of humour to which she gave rein on every occasion. She was more beautiful when she was serious; there was a depth to her when she was serious, and it was the depth in her that attracted me.

I never knew her to be without swollen ankles, but this did not mar a woman in those days for the skirts came down to the top of the shoes. Her left ankle had been swollen, she told me, since she was a small child and it caused her left foot to flap slightly inwards as she walked, but her walk was stately, yet tripping – she always seemed to be on the point of a run. Constitutionally she was as strong as a horse, yet in some strange way this constitution refused to carry drink, for, from the first glass of spirit she drank, her personality changed for the worse. After three glasses she became, not our Kate, but someone of whom I was deeply ashamed, whom in my early years I came to fear, then hate; then wish dead, yet all the time loved, loved because she was the only thing that was mine; even while I disowned her in my mind I loved her. This clash of emotions presented itself to me for the first time one Saturday afternoon.

I had been to the penny matinee at the Crown in Hudson Street, Tyne Dock. I loved the pictures because at the pictures not only did I see, through my half-covered eyes, beautiful ladies being tied on to railway lines, where they lay in agony from one Saturday afternoon until the next waiting for the trains to come crashing over them, or the hero, who had already escaped death countless times, at last caught and tied to within an inch of a madly spinning saw, but I also saw gracious ladies and gentlemen in big houses, surrounded by cars, horses and servants, exactly like the pictures I conjured up on the wall when I turned my face away from life, away from all the nasty things. I never covered my eyes with my fingers and peered through the penumbra of fleshy light when I looked at pictures like this at The Crown but I would stare wide-eyed and open-mouthed into the wonder of another world, and because of this other world I didn't like Ben Turpin, or Keystone Cops or, later still, daft people like Charlie Chaplin. Charlie Chaplin always filled me with embarrassment. The poor desolate creatures he portrayed were too near to something inside myself. No, I never, even when I grew up, liked Charlie Chaplin. I just liked pictures of ... ladies and gentlemen.

At four o'clock on this particular Saturday I came out of The Crown and was walking in a happy daze down the Dock bank. I was walking backwards, which I often did when I was happy, and I turned swiftly on hearing my name called and bumped my nose right into a tram standard, to the great amusement of some of the onlookers. Then through my dazed vision I saw, coming across the road from the direction of Bede Street, our Kate, and there was something about her that startled me. Something in her walk. I thought I was seeing things funny because I had bumped my nose. She looked down at me, smiling widely, and her eyes looked smoky and she clutched my hand as we went down the Bank towards the tram terminus. When there, she began to talk and laugh. Her talk was thick and her words fuddled, and her laugh made me lower my lids. And it came to me in a sickening revelation, that our Kate was drunk. She walked up and down as we waited for the tram, and as I looked downwards I saw her left foot give a more abandoned fling to itself when it left the ground. This action of her left foot was scarcely noticeable when she hadn't taken anything, but once she touched spirit it went not only to her head but to her left foot. This was the first time I became aware that there isn't a

27

part of the body or mind that remains unaffected by spirits. And it was on this day that I first felt the sick feeling in my chest, the sick feeling that was to remain with me for long periods until as recently as twelve years ago when she died.

Kate was a good walker and rarely took the tram between Tyne Dock and East Jarrow, but this day she was for getting us both on the tram, and I became filled with panic. I didn't want to get on the tram where everybody would know us, so I must have inveigled her into walking home, because I can see myself going through the arches by her side and comforting myself with the thought that ... well she's only our Kate, she's not me ma, for I knew that the greatest disgrace in life was to have a ma who drank. It didn't matter so much if your da drank, most da's did, but to have a ma that drank made people talk about you; like they did about some women in the docks. 'They could drink it through a dirty rag', only the word used wasn't as ordinary as dirty.

There are blessed blanks which cut out many memories of my childhood; the remainder of this day is lost but I do know that the comfort I gave myself was of short duration.

I had up to that time called me grandma 'ma' and I continued to do this until she died, and me granda I called 'da', but this relationship was straightened out for me very forcibly when I was playing with some children at the top corner one day when I was seven years old. There was a chimney breast on the end of the Richardsons' house in which we used to play shops, and the ingredients in the shops were provided by broken bottles and china, which was called boody. We would break up pieces of coloured glass and divide them into heaps to represent butter, bacon and groceries, and all sorts of taffy and sweets like Cissy Affleck had in her shop; everlasting strips, sherbert dips, tiger nuts, aniseed balls, chocolate drops, scenty mixtures, lucky bags. In the business of playing shops, and buying and selling with our glass and boody merchandise, there was always a little shoplifting done. In this particular instance a prized piece of green glass from the bottom of a bottle suddenly disappeared from my shop – somebody had swiped it when she came to buy. Naturally I made a hue and cry about the robbery and accused a girl much older than myself.

'If you don't give me back me boody I'll go and tell me ma about you, so I will!' I said.

On this she shot me into the awareness of living by sticking her face close to mine and bawling at me, 'She's not your ma. If ya want to know, she's your grandma . . . your Kate's your ma and she drinks, an' . . . YOU haven't GOT NO DA, me ma says so.'

'I have so, you're barmy. Me da's in our kitchen this minute.'

'He's not your da, he's your granda. An' he's an old sod, me ma says so.'

'EE! what you said! He is me da. I'll go an' tell him. He'll sort your canister for you so he will. He is . . . he is me da. He is! He is! You're a cheeky bitch.'

'He isn't. You haven't got no da.'

'You haven't got no da! You haven't got no da!' The others took it up.

No one, unless he has been through a similar experience and has had the security of parents wrenched from him, can have any idea as to the force of this impact. How it shatters for always the whole world of childhood and reverberates through the rest of life.

When I hear of children being told they have been adopted and of their apparently strange reaction to this knowledge, I understand. I understand the feeling of fear of not belonging. The dreadful feeling of the ladder on which you climb up out of childhood being whipped away from you. The ladder gone, the hands that have been holding you on to it are gone too, and you are left without support, left to fall into depths out of which you can emerge only after years of blind groping and struggle, if at all. Such is illegitimacy.

This mad startling piece of news petrified me, yet sent my mind into a questioning dizzying strange world in which everybody's name was changed. The feeling drove me into the lavatory.

The lavatory was the only place in our environment where you could lock yourself in and be alone. That is, if there was no one next door and you weren't made hot and blushing by the sounds, to which you would add your imagination. The lavatory was a dry one – a misleading term – with a long wooden seat with a hole in the middle and, if you kept the lid on, it was a wonderful place for musing and meditation. Once having made yourself comfortable you looked out through a space between the top of the door and the framework on to the grey, sloping, slated roof that covered the wash-house and the staircase of the upstairs house, and if you were lucky you saw a grey bird hopping about – we called them grey birds because we didn't know their real names. Here you were shut in and became lost in a world apart, a secret world. That is, if the lid was on. If it wasn't and you fell into a state of musing, which often happened, you could be aroused by the back lane hatch being lifted and the scavenger rudely thrusting in his long shovel. Many a time has this catapulted me from the seat to hide my face against the door, leaving my bottom exposed.

So this day of revelation sent me flying into the lavatory, and there I sat picking the scaling whitewash off the wall and asking questions to which there were no answers. How could me ma and da not to be ma and da? How could our Kate be me ma? An utter impossibility. Our Kate couldn't be me ma because she wasn't married and you couldn't be borned without a da, could you now? It was all so simple. They were barmy. They were telling lies, all of them, lies, lies. And they were cheeky bitches, every one of them.

After picking quite a lot of plaster off the wall I decided there was only one thing for it. I would go and tell our Kate what they had said, and she would come out and skelp their cheeky faces, so she would. This last was wishful thinking indeed for Kate never took my part in any battle that I remember, perhaps because, before this particular day, I got into few scraps, and following this day, she was always too busy threatening to wallop me for what I had done to some playmate or other.

Impelled by the thought that I must straighten this thing out I slunk out of the lavatory and stood at the bottom of the little alleyway looking up towards our kitchen window, where I could see Kate darting to and fro between the table and the fireplace. I got no further for as I watched her I knew I would not tell her anything, nor ask any questions. How it came about I don't know, but as I looked at her I knew our Kate was me ma. And I turned with bent head and slunk back into the lavatory and there, sitting on the seat, my hands pressed between my two skinny knees, I tried to sort out this terrible thing. Our Kate was me ma and she drank; the shame was unbearable.

But what about me da, where was me da? You must have a da. You must. I felt the urge now to stamp into the kitchen and say, 'Our Kate, where's me da, me real da?' but I remained sitting with my hands pinched between my knees. And as I sat it came to me that I was right, everybody must have a da, you couldn't be borned without a da and you couldn't live without a da. I must have a da because me da had suddenly turned into me granda.

Now who would I pick for a da? Who did I know? My Uncle Alec, my Aunt Mary's husband? I liked my Uncle Alec. He lived in number thirty at the top end of the street. But he was my cousin Jack's da, he couldn't be me da. And anyway I wanted somebody different for a da. Mr Affleck down the road? No, Mr Affleck drank too; I knew about this. But it seemed that Mr Affleck had a right to drink because he was swanky and their Cissie kept the shop. Then what about the tall lanky minister up in Simonside Church? No, not him. My head went further down, my knees pinched harder. I was playing a game with myself for I had known from the start whom I was going to pick for me da – the doctor, Doctor McHaffie.

Doctor McHaffie had his surgery in Stanhope Road. He had brought me into the world. He had attended me grandma and granda and anybody else who was ill in the house and I don't think he ever received a penny for his visits. Nor were we, as far as I can recollect, in any doctor's club.

Doctor McHaffie was a very attractive man and he must have been young, or youngish at this time. What was more, he had a car and it was this car that had brought him into my picture on the wall. By this time the pretence game was well on its way and most of the children who were in my class in Simonside School were aware of all our wonderful possessions: the motors, horses and servants; the big house and the grandeur therein; and a number of them had dared to disbelieve me.

Doctor McHaffie was the only man I knew who possessed a motor. There was another doctor who rode up Simonside Bank in a funny cab with a hole in the top and a driver at the back. This doctor used to shout through the hole in the top of the cab. I always thought it was very funny and I knew that he wasn't a patch on our doctor because he hadn't got a motor.

It is strange about Doctor McHaffie and the car, for when

thirty years later I wrote my first novel, the hero was a doctor who had a car, and he brought an illegitimate child into the world; and he loved her and in the end he married her mother. Later still, the scene that was to take place outside the school gates gave me the opening for the first of the Mary Ann books –*A Grand Man*. So, likely, in the first place the car was the main reason for me bestowing on the doctor the questionable honour of fatherhood.

The day I made this public could have had nasty repercussions, yet I never heard of any. I was going back to school in the afternoon; Doctor McHaffie had been to the house to see me granda who had a very bad leg at the time, having had an accident in the docks. The Doctor stopped the car on the road and asked, 'Are you going to school, Katie?'

I said I was and when he told me to get in beside him I stood as if I was struck dumb. 'Don't be frightened,' he said. 'You'll enjoy it.' Oh, I enjoyed it all right; and when he drew the car up before the school gate, there, around the gate and in the road, were my school fellows. I sailed out of that car, that is the right term, sailed out, and didn't touch the ground until I was in their midst, and not even then.

'There! What did I tell ya? We have got a motor.'

They gaped at me and my head went higher. 'You wouldn't believe me, Mary Morton, would you? An' you an' all, Nellie Boyle either. An' you won't come to me party. An' now say I'm lying when I tell you that's me da.'

I pointed to the moving vehicle and I watched the eyes turn swiftly towards the disappearing chassis before turning back to me. I cannot remember anyone saying, 'Don't be daft, that's Doctor McHaffie.' I had proved we had a motor, hadn't I? Hadn't I driven up to the school gates and got out before their very eyes? If I said the Doctor was me da, then he was me da.

Indeed, this episode could, as I have said, have brought about disastrous repercussions because there were some women in the New Buildings who licked up gossip. They had just to get hold of a thread and by the time they had finished it was a hawser, iron-bound at the ends. I am sure if Kate had known what I had said she would never have looked him in the face again. She had great respect for the man, and I feel now that he must have had compassion for her from the moment he brought me into the world, and he must have pitied her as he watched what could have been, or was still then, a beautiful woman both in looks and nature disintegrating under the pressure of hard continuous work, poverty and inner shame and loneliness.

Any way, the doctor became me da. He is dead now, and I have one regret that I didn't tell him of the questionable honour I, as a child, bestowed on him.

But the teachers must have heard about the incident of the Doctor and the car, for my beloved Miss Nesbitt brought me low one day when she asked if any one in the class could get a motor horn to put on Father Christmas's sleigh. We were practising for a Christmas concert at the time. When no one answered her request she looked at me and said, 'What about you, Katie? Couldn't you lend us the horn off your motor?' If she had thrown a knife at me from where she stood, thin and young, behind her desk she couldn't have hurt or surprised me more. She had exposed me for what I was. Everybody in the class knew that the teacher knew that I was a big liar. After this I may have stopped talking about our motors and horses and servants, but in my mind I still turned to the picture on the wall, and my adopted da had a permanent place in it.

I don't know whether it was this particular Christmas concert or another when I was the Fairy Queen, but I remember Kate making a wand for me out of a broom shank. She made a star for the top and covered the whole with silver paper. She also made me a white silk dress and a crown. On the days when the dress and the accessories were being made I lived on an ascending cloud of amazement and wonder.

The actual night of the concert was a very proud one for our Kate and me grandma because I was the Fairy Queen and, as they said, my part was the biggest and the best, and I was the prettiest bairn of the lot. They talked after the concert, saying, 'Did you hear that one on about their Joan? She was in the chorus, you know the little one at the end, in the washing-day scene. She wasn't the size of two penn'orth of copper and didn't know her piece, an' her mother goin' on like that. Why, her ladyship could have knocked her into a cocked hat.' I don't know when I first came by the title of 'Her Ladyship' but between the members of the family, except during rows or when I was being called from outside when it would be, 'You Katie!' I was addressed by, and accepted the title of 'Her' or 'Your Ladyship'. I cannot remember all they said but I know I nursed their pride for long afterwards.

I can still recall some of the items of that particular concert. The washing-day scene was put over by a set of little tubs standing on three-legged stools, and busily rubbing at the clothes were four little girls, singing:

> Oh the washing day!
> The weary, weary washing day.
> Oh, the washing day!
> That comes but once a week.
> We rub, rub, rub, on each washing day;
> We scrub, scrub, scrub, scrub, all our strength away.

I also remember the scene of the duck seller. This showed a busy housewife of about eight years old, opening the cardboard door to a man of the same age selling ducks. The man was wearing long trousers, cut-me-downs, and a cap much too large for him. He carried a basket in which reposed two stuffed ducks, their elongated necks hanging almost to his feet, and the piece could not be heard for the laughter filling the school room.

Housewife: How much are your ducks a pair?
Duck Man: Five Shillings, ma'am. And very fine ducks they are.
Housewife: Five shillings! I wonder you're not afraid to ask it.
Pray put your fine ducks back into the basket, it's a thorough im-po-sition.

I was to remember the word imposition when I heard it for a second time years later. Kate had spent the best part of a very wet week washing, drying and ironing a big wash for one of the Smiths across the back lane – there were lots of Smiths in the New Buildings, but this one we called, swanky Smith – 'Ask four shillings,' Kate said to me. The usual charge was three. 'What! four shillings?' said Mrs Smith, 'it's a thorough imposition.'

Although I cannot now remember the other scenes in the concert I do remember that I used to re-enact the whole show for them at home. I can see our Kate rolling back the big mat in the kitchen and pushing me granda's chair right close to the chest-of-drawers. Then they would seat themselves round by the table, me grandma and granda, our Kate, me Uncle Jack, and once or twice my Aunt Mary and Uncle Alec, and I would dance for them, and sing, and do pieces.

These were wonderful nights, nights when there wasn't any money knocking about, when everybody was sober, when they looked to me for entertainment, and I never disappointed them. I always wanted to make them happy when they were sober.

The morning we broke up for the Christmas holidays, Miss Nesbitt announced there was a prize for the best boy and girl in the concert. I sat unthinking, unheeding. I never got prizes.

I've had only three real surprises in my life, and that day I received the first one when she called me out and presented me with a little negro's head made of china and full of chocolates. It's the only prize I ever received.

I walked down the long Simonside Bank and up the road to East Jarrow. I can feel the pressure of the day all round me yet. It was one of those dull, cold days that you get in the North when the sky seems to be lying on top of the ships' masts and the whole world is grey. The long wall from the blacksmith's shop up to the Saw Mill Bridge was grey. The water lapping against the slack bank just a few feet from the footpath was grey. The houses of the New Buildings in the distance were grey. Those people walking between East Jarrow and the Docks, they were very grey. But I was carrying a negro's head full of chocolates. I was in a palpitating daze; my world had suddenly become an amazing place where you got surprises, nice surprises. Everything was bright, dazzling, until I reached the kitchen, for there the greyness from outside had seeped in and engulfed our Kate. She was busying between the stove and the table but her movements were slow; she looked depressed and sounded in a bad temper. I can't remember what she said when I showed her the wonderful prize, but her reaction brought a funny heavy feeling into my chest.

Me grandma was lying on the couch in the front room. This was one of the days when her legs were so swollen she couldn't walk. She was pleased and said, 'Oh, you're a clever lass.' But somehow it wasn't the same. There was something up. Our Kate had the pip. But she hadn't been at it, because there was no money. Perhaps this was the reason, being so near Christmas and no money. Anyway, the greyness in the kitchen weighed on me. I looked at the negro's head. It amazed me no longer. In fact I didn't like it. I said to Kate 'Do you want any messages?' And the sadness deepened in me when she said 'No'. Things were wrong, all G.Y. when she didn't want me to go a message of some sort.

The walk up the country road of Simonside Bank holds blocks of memory. There was the day I walked up it to school with my mouth full of mustard. I had toothache and I don't know whether I was crying from the pain of the tooth or from the pain of the blisters. After three days of crying, it was decided that I had better go to the dentist, but as this would cost two shillings there was no great hurry to get me there. Oil of cloves was tried instead and this did the trick. There you are, and two shillings could have been wasted – a whole grey hen full of beer.

Often when I walked up Simonside Bank I would see Mr Sheriff. He lived in one of the big houses and he would stop me and pat my head and say, 'When are you going to give me one of those ringlets?' I liked Mr Sheriff. But one day, it was after school, I was coming home when, to my surprise, just below Mr Sheriff's big gate I saw our Kate and me grandma. They were looking into the ditch, and when I came up to them they did not turn but me grandma said, as if she knew I had been there all the time, 'Help to get your granda out.' I looked down on the long, thin, mud-covered, paralytic body. I felt no shame about me granda being drunk. There was only one person who could bring shame to me in that way, and when I said, 'Will I go and get somebody? Mr Sheriff or somebody?' our Kate answered angrily, 'Stay where you are. Get out of the road.' Then me grandma put in tartly, 'Leave her be. Let her help. He'll come for her.'

I can't remember how we got him home, but I recall thinking, our Kate didn't want Mr Sheriff to know.

It was very rarely me granda had to be brought home, his legs usually carried him to the door even if they gave way on the step. And it was after this incident also that I first registered the word mortallious. 'Aye,' they would say, 'Old John was mor-

36

tallious again the day.' And some would click their tongues and move their heads slowly. More slowly if they were saying, 'Young Jack was mortallious the day.'

And when me grandma sang it's no wonder her songs were sad and told their own tales. A favourite with her was 'Love, it is teasing':

> Love, it is teasing,
> Love, it is pleasing,
> Love is a pleasure
> When it is new;
> But as it grows older
> And days grow colder
> It fades away like the
> Morning dew.

I have heard a different version on television, but those are the words she sang as she combed my hair or nursed me on her knee. And how clearly they spoke of the disillusionment of life. In some way, too, they seemed to be connected with the times I'd be sleeping in the front room in the desk bed and where me granda and her slept in the brass bed in the alcove, and I would sit up and cry, 'Leave her be, Granda!' This would be after hearing me grandma whispering harshly, 'Leave me alone, will you?' Yet I know now I wasn't actually aware of the reason for her protest, I only knew that he was 'bothering her'.

CHAPTER THREE

Me Uncle Jack was a handsome man, in his way. More than six foot tall, broad, dark, almost swarthy like a gipsy. All his short life he worked in the docks and wore heel plates on his boots, and if they were loose they jingled like money in the pocket. And I would hang on to his arm as he went down the street saying, 'Aw, our Jack. Aw, come on, giv' us a ha'penny. Aw, man, giv' us a ha'penny.' He never spoke to girls, but would joke about them, saying, 'Aa've got a lass to meet at the Tivoli corner'. The 'Tivoli' was a picture house in Laygate, and meeting her at the 'Tivoli corner' somehow meant that that was as far as he intended to take her. It was one of those jokes without either humour or wit, but which had an underlying meaning, and invariably drew forth laughter. He looked a real he-man but was really afraid of women. Yet he wanted my mother, his half-sister, and in trying to get his way with her caused her untold agony of mind.

One night, shortly after she came home to take over the household, she was lying in the bedroom with me by her side when she was woken out of a deep sleep with his hands on her. He was whispering, 'Kate ... Kate.' She thought there was something wrong with me grandma and when she went to sit up his hands kept her down, and his voice, thick with pleading again, said, 'Kate ... Kate.' Silently she fought him, and, managing to get out of the bed, rushed through the kitchen and went down the backyard and locked herself in the lavatory until dawn. And this without any shoes on and clad only in a thin nightgown. I did not know of this until I wrote *Colour Blind*. She was paying me a visit at the time the proofs arrived, and after finishing the book she said to me, 'You've put it over amazingly well, lass.'

'The colour question?' I asked.

'No, not the colour question. That's got nothing to do with us. About the brother and sister.' When she noticed my perplexity she said, 'Well, him . . . our Jack wanting me. You must have taken it all in as a child.'

Yes, I must have taken it all in as a child.

What I had written I imagined to be a figment of my imagination. I knew that these things happened; I wanted to make a strong story. I was absolutely amazed and so sad for her when she told me the truth. And I realised then that all I had written in the previous four years – not just some of it – came from my childhood, and were things I had buried deep in my mind. Here was a page from my subconscious, a page that had written itself down as it happened.

I asked her that day why she hadn't exposed Jack, why she hadn't told her parents, for it was not only the once he tried this on but many times. Her answer was, 'Aw, lass, if I had brought this thing into the open who would have got the blame? Not Jack. Jack hadn't sinned, Jack was a good fellow. He had his one fault, he drank, but that was all. Jack didn't like women, everybody knew that. It would have been me, as usual. Jack would never have dreamed of anything like that on his own, they would have said. Not unless he was enticed. If I had showed him up life would have really been unbearable. You see I couldn't leave me mother and her with dropsy, nor the fathar at that time for he had his bad leg. And where could Jack himself have gone? He never knew when he was going to get a full week in. And anyway, he considered it his house, I was only there on sufferance. No lass. I had to keep me mouth shut and sleep light, but God, it was wearing. At times I became weary of it all . . . weary. Still it's over and I've a lot to thank God for.'

I look back to the confusion in my mind and not being able to understand why our Jack should sometimes raise his fist to our Kate when there wasn't a real row on. I can see her kneeling at the hearth taking the ashes out. It was a Good Friday and Jack was bending over her, his fist shaking in her face, then turning he dashed into the bedroom. She said to me wearily, 'Take that ginger beer bottle and go down to twenty-seven, will you?' She made it a request for it was Good Friday and I hadn't any new clothes. Everybody wore new clothes on

Good Friday and went to church and got an orange – if they were Catholics. If they were church or chapel they had the added glory of marching with a band to the market place. Good Friday was a great day, when you had coloured paste eggs. Kate used to wrap the eggs in wallpaper and boil them and all the children that came to the house would get one, as on Carlin Sunday, the Sunday prior to Palm Sunday, when she had a great dish of soaked carlins – little brown peas. These too she would dish out to all comers. But this particular Easter was different, there weren't even any paste eggs; but I was more sorry for Kate than I was for myself, so I took the sixpence, all she had, and the ginger beer bottle and went down to twenty-seven.

It says something for the attitude of me grandma and granda towards Kate that on this particular day they had taken a trip to Birtley to my Aunt Sarah's and they couldn't have done that without money. Yet all Kate had was sixpence. Me grandma never gave her a penny, but all she earned had to go towards the house. No wonder she became crafty with the years, withholding sixpence here, a shilling there in order to get a drop of hard.

I was about six, I think, when our Jack first brought a few fellows from off a boat up to the house to have a meal, and a drink. Jack, like his father, worked mostly on the iron-ore boats, but this week they were unloading a long voyage boat. The men on it had just finished a two-year trip; they were from Maryport. One of them was called Jack Stoddard and another David McDermott. David McDermott was married to Jack Stoddard's sister. He was a pleasant-faced, thick-set man with a quiet manner, and he used to bounce me on his knee. They were clean spoken, jolly men, and always remained so. Yet as the years went on the thought of them was like a nightmare always hovering in the background. And when they docked the nightmare would spring on me, for they had money and they spent it freely. There was a big eat-up, and a big drink-up, not usually followed by a big bust-up, except once. For the strange thing was that these men never quarrelled; they sang and they drank but they never quarrelled. After these visits the dray cart always came for the empties. This was something to brag about. 'Twelve dozen bottles besides draught!' they would say. 'And whisky and rum bottles actually counted by the dozen an' all. And all got through in four days. By! those were the days! And not a wrong word mind, not a wrong word.'

Jack Stoddard took a fancy to our Kate, but as she told me years later she could never go out with him, so what was there to do but just sit in the house and drink. The fathar would have raised hell and her life would have been made more unbearable than it was if she had gone out for an evening with a man. I don't think she was out of an evening, in fact I know she wasn't, for ten years, with the exception of going down to twenty-seven or up to the Alkali to get the drink.

Sometimes she would say to me, 'Come on; put your coat on and come down the road.' If it was dark I didn't mind because nobody would see me standing outside the bar waiting for her, but I hated going with her in the daylight. When she was just going for beer it didn't matter so much. Beer was nothing, the beer hadn't been brewed that could make her drunk, it was spirits I was afraid of, petrified of, because spirits turned her into a different being. But there's one night I remember. We had been down to twenty-seven and there were only two bottles of draught in the bass bag. The moon was riding high over the Saw Mill and the Afflecks' house. It was showing up the corn-field and the first of the two seats that were placed outside the cornfield railings for those who were tired by the long walk between Tyne Dock and East Jarrow. It was reflecting off the slate roofs of the houses in the New Buildings. It was shining on the high tide that was licking the slack bank showing the frothy edge broken with cabbages, pieces of wood, boxes, and all the interesting jetsam from the boats in the river. The wind was whirling the ends of my hair and threatening to take Kate's hat off. She looked down at me and laughed, and clutching not so far back to the spirit of her childhood she grabbed my hand, crying, 'Come on, let's race the moon.' And together we ran along the slack bank, the bottles rattling in the bag, her hat hanging on by one pin, my long ringlets bobbing, and my thin sticks of legs taking gazelle leaps over the cement slabs of the path. Just before we reached the New Buildings we stopped and I leant against her thigh and she put her arm about me and we stood panting and laughing. 'Ee! aren't we daft?' she said. 'If Morgan' – the policeman – 'saw us we'd get locked up.' We laughed again until we nearly choked. Then all of a sudden she stopped and straightened her hat and we walked on sedately. And as I walked I realised that if she had entered the New Buildings 'carrying on' they would say she had had some. But the fact was that Kate could 'carry on' more without drink than she could with it, but I don't think that she herself ever fully realised this. On a moonlight night when the wind is high I can bring back the feeling of that night when, like two children, we joyed together.

As I can recall the gipsies when I smell water on hot ash. The gipsies came at least once a year and camped in the field behind Lancaster Street, the field that was part of the open space belonging to the Barium Chemical Works. The field adjoined the grounds of Morgan's Hall, a large grey stone hall which had originally been built to serve as a workman's club for the men who worked in the Barium, but for some reason or another it had never been put to this use. It was named Morgan's Hall because of the policeman who lived there in the caretaker's rooms.

The gipsies placed their camp in part of this waste land near the railings of Morgan's Hall, and a thrill of excitement ran through the buildings when they arrived. I think that they were the real old type of gipsy, and all of one family. I do know that they were ruled by an old man; he was a tall fine looking man and I remember him and his wife clearly, because they too brought fear into my life.

I must have been seven at this time and I can see myself sitting outside their tent and opposite the fire on which a pot was boiling. It spilled over and there was the pungent smell that rises from hot wet ash. Next I can see myself sitting in the tent between the old couple; the old man had hold of my hand and he was saying, 'How would you like to live with us?' It was then the cold fear attacked me. I had a compelling urge to get into our kitchen, to see me granda, and grandma and our Kate. I would be safe once I got into the kitchen.

When I was in the kitchen Kate said to me, 'Why aren't you over with the gipsies, they're going the morrow?' For answer I gave my usual evasive reply, I was tired.

The next morning, coming back on an errand from Tyne Dock, I saw the old man walking down past the saw mill, and

42

I ran across the road and turned my face to the wall and walked sideways until I was past him, and I knew he was standing still watching me. It is strange but the gipsies never returned to the New Buildings. I wonder if I had anything to do with this, or was it because one of the younger families left owing Cissie Affleck a tidy bill? They had left before owing bills but had always paid up on their return. But they never came back to the New Buildings.

I remember me grandma saying, 'The gipsies don't come any more, I wonder why. The old couple were very fond of you.' She touched my face.

I must have started going for the beer when I was seven. I had gone round the back lane to twenty-seven, with two empty bottles in a bag, and as I opened the backyard door a great beast sprang at me and caught me by the arm. I screamed and screamed, and was lying by the rain barrel with the dog still hanging on to me when the barman rushed out. The next thing I remember I was walking back home by the slack bank carrying two full bottles of beer in the bag and hugging my left arm to me. When I got in and showed them my arm there was great concern. Me grandma was lying on the couch in the front room again, and Kate said, 'I'll have to get her to the chemist.' So she took me all the way to Stanhope Road, where there was a herbalist who had a shop on the corner, and I recall him saying to me, 'Oh, you're not going to cry, you're a big girl,' while he cauterised the arm just as I sat there. Then he put it in a sling.

Back home again, I sat near the head of the couch cradled in me grandma's arm, and I can see Kate bending over me and hissing in a warning tone, 'Now let him get his tea afore you say anything.'

Me granda came in at half past five and his tea, a heavy cooked meal, was always waiting ready for him. Someone had to stand on the cracket to enable them to see above the cornfield railing and some distance down the main road, and as soon as he came in sight the meal was dished up so that it could be on the table when he entered the house.

It seemed a long time this night before he finished and I so wanted to tell him about my arm, and when I did there were ructions. What had happened to the dog? he wanted to know.

43

Oh, that had been put down.

It was a big Dalmatian dog, and the barman had promised to have it destroyed, but it was strangely resurrected some time later. I have its teeth marks on the inside of my left arm yet.

So this day registers the age when I first went for the beer as being about seven, for me grandma was still alive and she died when I was eight. This day registers other things too. It recalls to my mind that our Kate looked after her mother with great care, and also on this day I became aware of me granda's love for me.

Me granda's tea might consist of a big plate of finny-haddy and mashed potatoes, or a piece of steak and eggs and chips, but whatever he had he nearly always started with a boiled egg, and I had to have the top off his egg. The top of his egg usually went two-thirds of the way down the egg and he had to turn it quickly to stop the yoke running out. I would stand by his side with a slice of bread and marge and he would ladle out the egg, spoon by spoon, on to the bread until I'd had it nearly all. I often wondered why they couldn't give me an egg to myself. But no, I had to have the top of his egg. I remember this went on for a long time, right until during the War, the first War when eggs could be sold for sixpence each. Then we had very few on the table. He kept hens in the backyard for years, hens, ducks, and rabbits, but he kept the hen crees cleaner than some people kept their houses. But to get back to going for the beer.

From when I was about eight there was scarcely a day of the week that I didn't go down to Hudson Street or even as far as Brinkburn Street in Stanhope Road for the beer. During the War it was scarce and of an evening I would have to stand in queues. By this time I was carrying the grey hen. The grey hen was a large narrow necked stone jar; it was heavy when empty, much heavier full. I carried it on my left hip. True I was given my tram fare back, but I would often walk the whole distance from Tyne Dock to East Jarrow carrying that great jar to save the ha'pennies.

There was a great deal of comment in the New Buildings about my being sent for the beer. It was looked on in some quarters as a disgrace; in the less refined quarters it was termed

44

openly 'A bloody shame, sendin' that bairn for the beer with that great jar.' I think I was the only child in the New Buildings who was sent on such an errand.

As the years went on I became filled with shame at having to carry the grey hen. Yet for a time it had it's monetary compensation. There was an outdoor beer shop in Hudson Street and the woman who kept it was getting on and her arithmetic wasn't as good as mine. Pound notes and ten shilling notes were in then and it sometimes happened she gave me the change of a pound note when I'd only given her a ten shilling note. Once I told her about this and gave her the money back and she gave me some sweets. But when it happened again I kept the surplus, but was terrified to go back into the shop in case she remembered. But when I was forced to, and she didn't remember, the woman's poor arithmetic became a source of revenue to me, until the fine point of stealing by finding, or stealing by being given too much change, was forced home to me as I prepared for confession one night. After this it was a battle between my conscience and my need as to whether I kept or tipped up the money to the woman.

Although as I've said I didn't like going for beer I recognised also that it had its good side, for when I was sent for the beer funds were low in the house. If funds were high Kate would have gone herself, and when Kate went out it usually meant that she would bring back a drop. The drop would perhaps be in a medicine bottle or a flat quarter whisky bottle and would be hidden here or there behind utensils in the cupboard. I remember finding one one day and pouring some out and filling it up with water. I only did this once, for the fear of her finding out what I had done was, in a way, worse than the fear of her drinking the stuff.

It is impossible for me to describe the sick terror that filled me when Kate took whisky. If she had been able to carry it like my Aunt Sarah then I suppose I wouldn't have been so affected. But she became another being, the colour of her eyes seemed to change, her mouth did actually take on a different shape and she developed a little sniff. This last seemed to me in some way to be a form of cover-up, and yet it gave away the very thing she was trying to hide. When she had had just one or two glasses of whisky she always wanted to placate me in some way, and

45

when I wouldn't be placated she would get angry. In drink she also wanted company and gaiety. In this state she would talk to people whom she would have ignored when sober, considering them beneath her. There were quite a number of people even in our station of life who were considered beneath us. I could always tell by the look on Kate's face whether she'd had just beer, or was on the hard stuff, and I could tell whether she'd had two, three, or four glasses.

One day when she had a load on I stood in the corner of the kitchen and stared at her, and she rounded on me, seeming to sober up completely, as she said, 'Don't stand there looking at me with his eyes. Don't look at me like that, I'm telling you. Haven't I enough to put up with?' I must have known to whom she was referring, for it was from then that I treasured the fact that I was like my father. It is the only time I can remember her alluding to him, until a few years before she died.

It seems strange looking back but quite often they'd have a party. These parties too filled me with a sick dread for they nearly always ended up in a fight. If my Uncle Alec was at the party he would sing 'The Spaniard who blighted my life'. Standing with his eyes half closed and his head back he would sing verse after verse. I liked to hear my Uncle Alec sing. If Jimmy Hines was at the party – he was my great Aunt Maggie's son – he would sing 'I am but a poor blind boy'. This used to make me want to laugh and I knew I mustn't. Then Kate would be called upon to sing and I would bow my head and the shame would descend upon me. Our Kate had a nice voice, a good voice, but she rarely used it unless she'd had a drop: then she'd sing 'Thora' or 'I dreamt I dwelt in marble halls', and she'd strain at the high notes and move her head from side to side. Sometimes me granda would interrupt with a laugh and say something nasty, and then a row would start.

It was after such a night that I stood with my back hard against the old box sewing machine that we had under the window in the bedroom. She was bending down to me and the hateful smell of whisky wafted from her as she said, 'Give us a kiss.' My stomach turned over. I wished she was dead. I pushed her face away with the flat of my hand and hissed at her, 'I hate you. I do. I do. I hate you, our Kate.' Never have I seen such a look on anyone's face before or since. It held a mixture of anger, humiliation, bitterness and sadness, such sadness. And I felt the sadness most of all and couldn't understand why when I hated her I could be so sad for her.

But most of the time I felt protective towards her, going out of my way to defend her, just as mothers do when defending the black sheep of the family.

The painful times would seem to dominate the memories of my childhood. But there were other times. Nearly every night after tea, and when I had been for the beer, I went out to play for a while. Winter or summer we would play round the street lamps, or outside Cissie Affleck's shop. There were certain parts of the New Buildings we selected for play at certain times of the year, as also we did our games. In the winter, towards Christmas, it was usual to gather around the shop, for then Cissie would be putting the Christmas decorations in her window, and if you were in the Christmas Club you could stand for hours pointing out what you were going to get. A shop with real scales, and bottles, and a counter; a doll . . . a black doll perhaps, or boxes of chocolates, or a long gauze stocking filled with an assortment of useless things. And in between gazing and planning we would skip or play tiggy, or Jack, Jack, shine your light.

In the summer, we would usually gather on the open space before the terrace, or on the slack bank and the timbers. The big timbers were tied together with sleepers to which ropes were attached allowing each timber some leeway. When the tide was high and the timbers were floating you ran over each one, pressing it down into the water and jumping on to the next before your feet got wet. This was called playing the piano. Or we'd make tents and play houses, or gather round Richardson's top corner and into the chimneypiece and play shops, or bays on the pavement, what others call hopscotch. And then there was diabolo, and scooters, and rounders, and hot rice, and . . . knocky-door-neighbour. Some nights we would get dressed up and go singing in procession round the five streets.

We were only following our elders in this, for like a spring fever, there would come at certain times of the year among certain women of the buildings, among whom were Kate and Mary, a madness, a jolly madness, that would force them to dress up in any old clothes, and singing and beating tin cans, parade around the five streets. I've seen Mary leave her washing and Kate her baking and, getting into the men's clothes, go dancing round the doors, and she solid and sober. There was a primitive weirdness about this which I recall whenever I hear the Kerry Piper's song.

Sundays were a sort of respite to me, but boring to everybody else in the house, because, not having best clothes, they couldn't go out. I connected Sundays with big dinners, everybody going to bed in the afternoon – and Cissie Affleck, because nearly always I watched Cissie and her young man taking their weekly walk after Church on a Sunday afternoon.

You could almost tell the time from Cissie and Mr Maitcham passing along the slack bank opposite the end of our street on a Sunday afternoon after chapel Sunday school. I can see them now. He was a tall well-dressed, superior looking man. You couldn't put the prefix lad or boy to Mr Maitcham. I think he must have been about thirty at that time and Cissie in her early twenties. There they would walk, keeping a specified distance apart; sedately, even regally they would pass by the New Buildings. I cannot ever remember Cissie casting her eyes across the road to where, at the corner of Philipson Street, was her shop. No, this was Sunday. A day for Church and courting, a prim kind of courting. You didn't wear your heart on your sleeve in those days. Couples didn't fling their arms about each other in public, even go as far as kissing in public, that was left to the darkness of a back lane, or better still some place up the country, and courting in the front room was only sanctioned by the, morally speaking, broad parents, and this, as was well known, led to a quick wedding and evoked the remark 'Well, what d'ya expect. It was askin' for it.'

But I could never connect the front room or a quiet spot up the country with Cissie and Mr Maitcham, and as for the back lane, never.

I next see Kate standing on the steps of Simonside School talking to the Headmistress. I was standing against the grey granite wall, my hands on my buttocks. I was pressing them tightly against the roughness because of something Kate was saying. She was saying, 'She's a Catholic and has to go to the

Catholic School.' And then comes a memory of disjointed words all about names. 'McMullen isn't her name,' Kate said. 'It's Fawcett.'

It was this name sticking in my mind that caused me such distress in later years. Fawcett was Kate's maiden name but I didn't know it wasn't the name on my birth certificate, it should have been, but my birth certificate held my father's name, at least the name he had given her. The certificate also gave him a fictitious occupation. She had forged both his name and occupation, for at the registry office she had been too ashamed to write the truth. Also on that birth certificate it didn't say the 20th June, 1906, but the 27th June, 1906. She had left my registration until the last minute, and then she was too ill to go down to Shields and she didn't want anyone else to do the registering because she wanted to fix it for me. When she did get to the office she stated I was born on the 27th in case she would get wrong for not having registered me earlier.

It seems strange now but in that generation poor people had an inordinate fear of the law, yet would go to outrageous lengths, such as forgery, to cover up some simple misdemeanour. But if only she had told me about the name on the certificate I wouldn't have had to say so often 'I haven't got a birth certificate,' or, 'I cannot get my birth certificate.' The truth being I didn't want to get it because of what it would show. When at last I did get it, it showed me the name of a supposedly legitimate father and his occupation.

It was me granda who was the instigator of me changing schools. He was the dominating factor in all the happenings of the house. He was a Catholic who never stepped inside a church door, but who would strike a blow for the Pope, yet at the same time scorning and decrying the Richardsons and the McArthurs, close neighbours, who were strong practising Catholics. Pulling them to shreds almost daily, he would hold them up as a sample of everything that was bad. He despised them as he despised all churchgoers, yet it was he who insisted that I was to go to a Catholic School. And with this change of school God came into my life, and with him came the Devil, and Miss Corfield, the schoolmistress of St Peter & Paul's, Tyne Dock, and with her came mental and physical torture. The physical she accomplished with the help of the cane, the mental by sarcasm. And with God came priests, and the confessional, and nightmares, purgatory and repentance – and fear.

From this time the fight started within me and it had to have expression outwardly. I bossed, bullied and slapped out. In any game in which I played I had to lead or I wouldn't be in it. It was I who had to do the counting for 'deady one', shouting as I stabbed a finger into each small chest:

Eeny, meeny, miny mo,
Set a baby on a po.
When it's done
Wipe it's bum,
Eeny, meeny, miny mo.

It was I who would run after Willie Weir, one of a large Scots family who lived above my great-Aunt Maggie, me grandma's sister, in number twenty-six. I must tell you about my Aunt Maggie, as I called her, later. But there I would be, shouting, bawling after one of this tribe:

Scotty MaLotty,
The King of the Jews,
Sold his wife for a pair of shoes.
When the shoes began to wear,
Scotty MaLotty
Began to swear.

And this particular Scotty MaLotty did swear, and chase me in return.

Although always afraid of being chased, or attacked, I would stand my ground. And this resulted in many a good pummelling. But it did not deter me. I was bent on showing them; showing the lot of them.

Number two William Black Street was a complete house and I always considered the people who lived there a cut above the rest in the street, for to have an upstairs and down, seven rooms altogether, was really something in those days. So thought my Aunt Mary, for later she occupied this house for many years. But at the time of speaking there was a family called Christopher living there, a highly respectable Chapel-going family. He was something in the docks; he worked in the offices I think which automatically pushed him up the ladder.

Lottie Christopher was the only daughter; there were sons but I didn't know much about them – they were older than me and always kept themselves to themselves. One day I was waiting for our Kate coming off the tram; she had been to Birtley for a week to look after Sarah, who was having another baby. Me grandma was managing to get about at this time. Well, the tram was a long time in coming, but down the slope flanking the terraces came Lottie Christopher. She was skipping with a new skipping rope with handles on, not knots in the end. 'Can I have a skip of your rope?' I said.

'No,' she said. 'You can't.'

'Aw,' I said. 'Just once.'

'You're not going to,' she said. 'I don't play with you . . . I'm not kind with you.'

I don't know how long this conversation went on but I dragged the rope from her, and because she protested I brayed her with it, not being particular which part I aimed at. She was screaming blue murder when the tram came into sight and I threw the skipping rope at her and hopped and skipped to the tram, like a nice little lass who had been patiently waiting for her ma.

Kate alighted from the tram. She looked nice, lovely; she was wearing a three-quarter length coat. She had got it second-hand, and as me grandma said, it looked class. She was very pleased to see me and touched my face as she looked down on me, but the next minute she said 'Pull your stockings up and get Charlie off your back.' My stockings were always coming down, because my legs were like thin shanks, and Charlie was my round shoulders. But what did anything matter, our Kate looked bonny. I went proudly up the street carrying a brown paper parcel while she carried the straw hamper.

The straw hamper was of very little interest to me because I knew it would hold nothing more than vegetables and black pudding. My Aunt Sarah always sent vegetables from their allotment and black pudding, which she made herself. Looking back on the family she had to work for – my Uncle Mick stopped work through deafness only a few years after they were married – I wonder that she spared all the vegetables and black pudding that she did. Anyway, Kate was no sooner in the house and had taken her hat and coat off when there came a knock on the front door. And there stood Mrs Christopher.

51

Mrs Christopher was a quiet spoken, very polite woman . . . a refined woman. Did Kate know what Katie had done to Lottie?

No, Kate didn't know.

Well she had thrashed her with the skipping rope, her own skipping rope, and there were weals all over her.

OH? OH? Kate was most contrite. She would deal with Katie, she would that. By, she would.

As the door closed I made my escape and locked myself in the lavatory. After some long time, when I emerged and went tentatively up into the kitchen Kate took no notice of me. She was talking to me grandma, saying, 'Well, I just wouldn't. I wouldn't scrub his back, and I told her so. And she started to cry and said, "Oh, she wished she was up; he wouldn't be able to get himself clean if his back wasn't scrubbed." "Well," I said, "he can remain mucky because I'm not scrubbing your Mick's back, so there." ' I watched her fling round and attack a pan on the stove, grinding it into the embers, saying as she did so, 'I'm not scrubbing any man's back, least of all Mick Lavelle's.'

My Uncle Mick at that time was a pit-man; he was a very small man and had a very white body, of which he took great care, and like all pit-men in those days he washed himself in a tin tub on a mat before the fire. This too seemed to annoy our Kate, for she said, 'As bad as ours are they go in the scullery and close the door.'

It was odd the things I clutched at to make our family superior and I remember this as one of them: our men washed in the scullery and closed the door.

Then breaking off in the middle of a sentence she turned and, looking at me, said, 'Get into that bedroom there and you wait!'

If she had slapped my backside straightaway it wouldn't have been so bad but often when she sent me into the bedroom for punishment I might have to wait for an hour or two, and this was real torture to me for my imagination would be working overtime, and an hour could take on the endlessness of a child-year. But I never looked upon this torture as the outcome of my determination to show them.

My Aunt Sarah hated the fathar and justifiably. If in his later years his welfare had depended on either her or Mary he would, as he knew only too well, have ended his days in the workhouse. Once, when Sarah was about twenty, she was working in Newcastle. She had an aunt living near there and she went to visit her on the evening prior to her day off. The family were apparently going to a play and they took her with them. It was her first play, and she stayed the night at their house. The next morning when she came home – the family were living in Nelson Street, Tyne Dock, at the time – the fathar whipped her round the backyard with a horse whip. She never forgave him for it and I don't blame her. In those early days he must have been frightful. Narrow, bigoted, unable to read or write, he was a torment to himself and took it out on those around him. He had to master somebody. Although many times he threatened me with the buckle end of his belt his hands never got any further then unloosening it. Never once did he lay a hand on me. If he was really capable of loving any one, it was me.

This softness he had for me was certainly put to use, for many and many were the nights I have been woken out of a deep sleep by our Kate and me grandma standing over me and Kate whispering, 'Katie, come on, get up, do you hear? Get up and go and get your granda to bed.'

Half-blind with sleep I would stumble into the kitchen whinging. 'Aw! Granda. Come on man . . . come on, get yourself to bed. Aw! man, come on. I'm tired, man.'

He'd be sitting sprawled in his chair, alternately singing and swearing. The song that he sang most often was 'The Seagull'. 'Seagull, seagull, fly away over the sea.' Another was 'My Bonnie Blue-Bell'. But he had to be in a very good mood to sing 'My Bonnie Blue-Bell'. Very often he would be holding Dennis in his hand. Dennis was a three foot long steel poker about an inch thick. He had had it specially made, and sometimes he poked the fire with it and sometimes he knocked the pictures off the wall or the legs off the chairs with it, and very often he whirled it on high, threatening to bring it down on the head of either me grandma or our Kate. But not very often against Jack, because as Jack grew older his father left him alone.

Eventually I would get him to his feet and into the front room and would help him off with his trousers and put him to bed. He always slept in his long linings – disgusting, nauseating sight and smell. But the main thing was he was in bed, and after a while me grandma would have to take her place by his side. And then the house would settle down to one more night of uneasy rest. Had either me grandma or our Kate attempted to get him to bed when he was mortallious he would have surely gone for them with Dennis.

But there were times when even I daren't go near him, for instance, when he sang the Irish Comallya. This would come on him suddenly. Following a strange silence he would jump up from his high-backed chair with Dennis in his hand, and, his voice raising the roof he would sing the Irish Comallya. At these times Kate would hold me fast in the bedroom and from there we would watch him through the partly open door. There he would stand, swaying on his feet brandishing Dennis over his head as he sang:

> Sing us an Irish Comallya,
> Sing us an Irish tune;
> For Patsy Burke has buggered his work
> All by the light of the moon.
> Sing us an Irish Comallya as we dance around so gay
> And bring back the days when we were lads
> In old Ireland far away.

Following this there would be dead silence for a few seconds, when we would wait for the next part. It always came.

In heartrending tones he would now say: 'Old Ireland far away . . . And begod! it's far away, it is at this minute.'

Then he would proceed to tell us how old Ireland had been moved far away across . . . the watter. From a small child I was under the impression that Ireland had once been the capital of England until it had been moved across the 'watter.' And by whom? – the dirty Protestants!

At this stage Dennis would be brought into action, and he would attack the dirty Protestants who had moved old Ireland far away by hitting at the pictures on the wall and as he did so naming the tryants who had bespoiled Ireland – they all happened to be neighbours.

The funny part about it was that from the time he left Ireland when he was twelve he had never returned to his native land. He was like many another Irishman before him and since, yelling about his homeland, patriotic to the point of murder, yet making no effort to return . . . across the 'watter'.

It was the same with his religion, for it was said he had been in church only twice in his life. There was even a doubt about the first time since nobody could prove that he had been christened in church, only me grandma could prove that he had been married in the church – she wouldn't have had him else. But he was a staunch Catholic, he was a fighting defender of the faith, and I was a sort of liaison officer running between him and God, for every Sunday of my young life when I went to mass and Sunday School and in later years to Benediction also I thought I was going to church to save me granda's soul. Every Sunday I prayed for his soul and that he would die a happy death; and he did die a happy death, if you can go by externals. He passed away peacefully, Kate attending him to the last and breaking her heart when he went, whereas no one could have blamed her if she had celebrated with a brass band, for she'd had her bellyful of the fathar and no mistake.

I still at times wake up at nights hearing a voice saying: 'Away with ya to Mass now and pray for me soul, pray that I might die a happy death.' Oh, me granda.

But it was this ignorant man who first told me I was a writer. He didn't exactly say I was a writer, not in so many words, what he actually said was, 'It's a stinking liar you are, Katie McMullen, a stinking liar.'

I remember the day he said that to me. I was very small, and I can see myself running up the backyard and into the kitchen and going straight for him where he sat in his chair, crying, 'Granda! you know that little man you tell me about, the one that sits on the wall in Ireland no bigger than your hand, you know him? With the green jacket and the red trousers and the buckles on his shoes, and the high hat and a shillelagh as big as himself, you remember, Granda?'

'Aye, what about him?'

'Well, I've seen him, Granda.'

'Ya have?'

'Aye, Granda. He was round the top corner.'

'He was, was he? And I suppose he spoke to you?'

'Aye, Granda, he did.'

'And what did he say?'

'Well, he said "Hello, Katie." '

'He said "Hello, Katie", did he? And what did you say?'

'. . . . I said "Hello, Mister, me granda knows you." '

He wiped his tash with his hand while raising his white eyebrows, then he said, 'You know what you are, Katie McMullen, don't ya? You're a stinking liar. But go on, go on, don't stop, for begod! it will get you some place . . . Either into clink or into the money.'

I was the only one who ever dared to argue with him, but one day I had to run for it. I was about thirteen at this time and I was quite concerned because of the fate of my Protestant friends, for I had a lot of nice Protestant friends and the fact that they were all going to end up in hell worried me. It had been hammered into me that there was no hope for the Protestants, simply because they were Protestants. If they were sensible and changed their coats then they could be assured of an eternity in heaven; if not, it was the devil and hell for them. From an early age I developed the faculty of seeing two sides to everything and one night, after listening to a particularly bitter haranguing against the Protestants, my imagination running wild, I saw most of the neighbours in a state of undress being forced to sit on hot grid-irons – because that is what happened to you in hell – and my mind protested and said it wasn't right. The following day was Sunday and on my return from the first session of praying for me granda's soul I passed the Salvation Army standing outside the line of bars opposite the Dock gates, openly proclaiming their allegiance to God. I saw them as a courageous group of people and I knew that I wouldn't have the pluck to stand in the open and acknowledge my God. This filled my mind all the way home and when I got indoors I answered the unintentional brain-washing of years by saying, without any preliminary lead-up, 'I like the Salvation Army, they've got pluck.'

I can see his face now. It seemed to stretch at all angles until it covered the whole fireplace and was as red as the blazing coals that were cooking the gigantic Sunday roast.

'What did you say?' His voice seemed to come up through the floor boards. I ignored the wild signalling of Kate from the scullery. She, I know, thought I had gone clean doo-lally-tap, but nothing could stop me.

'The Halleluyahs aren't afraid to praise God in the open.' I went on, 'And another thing, they don't go to Church and then come out and get drunk.' Of course the last bit didn't apply to him because he got drunk without going to church.

'GET OUT!'

'You'll not frighten me like you have everybody else, so you needn't think . . . '

Kate saved me by dragging me by the scruff of the neck into the scullery, and from there pushing me into the backyard, the while hissing at me, 'Have you gone stark starin' mad? What's come over you? Stay out for a minute.'

As I stood at the bottom of the backyard I heard him yelling, 'Salvation Army now, is it? Did you hear her? Begod! we'll have her comin' down the street next knockin' bloody hell out of the big drum, or sitting at the harmonium at the street corner leading the lot. You'll see.'

And you know, I think he was a bit afraid of what I might do if driven too far, so for a while, at any rate, there was no tirade against the Protestants.

He had the power to put the fear of God into most people, even when he was sober. The women of the New Buildings, gossiping at their back doors, would disperse when they saw him coming, for he rarely passed them but in an aside would make some blush-raising remark while keeping his gaze directed ahead. I remember an angry husband coming to the door one night because me granda had told his wife to get indoors and into the family way. Me granda looked at the man and said, 'If they don't want to hear such remarks tell them to get inside their houses and keep them clean instead of gossiping in the back lane. As for me mucky remarks, your wife and her pals raise the scalp from me head when they get goin'. Get yersel away, man. Get away, and don't be so bloody soft.'

He was right about the quality of the stories that some of the women indulged in. But only some; there were others who considered it beneath them to stand at their back doors and were never heard to even say Damn.

Although our Kate had a great sense of humour and liked telling a story, even one that was slightly risky, she would have no smut or midden-chatter, as she called it. And I can hear her remark to me grandma, 'I can't get out into the back lane to hang the clothes. There's that lot around so and so's back-yard door, and by the laughin' and squealin' they've all got their beds with them.'

Often at this stage she would lead off about the respectable married women. And once I can remember her ending, 'And they look down on me because I take a glass of beer.'

CHAPTER FOUR

One night I went into the kitchen and said to our Kate, 'What's a bax . . . tard, Kate?' She looked at me. 'A bax . . . tard? What do you mean? A bax . . . tard?'

'Somebody called me a bax . . . tard.' I saw her eyelids droop and she cast a quick glance towards me granda. She was working at the side table cutting up the meat for a pie for the morrow when she would be out working, and I saw her drop the knife and I noticed that the blade touched the wood of the table. It is odd the things you notice which have no reference to the matter in hand, but I'd heard her say you could tell a good knife by the balance, the blade should never weigh heavier than the handle, and at that moment I thought, that isn't a good knife. I watched her leaning over the board looking down on her floured hands. Me granda turned in his chair and said roughly, 'Where did you hear that?'

'It was Mrs Waller,' I said, 'We was playing knocky-door-neighbour. I was tyin' a can to her front door knocker, and had the string across the road into the cornfield, through the railing, you know, and she came round the bottom corner and caught me and that's what she said, "You're a bax'tard. Inside and out you're a bax'tard," she said.'

On this me granda, scraping his chair back with his foot, made swiftly for the door, but Kate, thrusting out her hand, caught at his arm, saying quietly, 'Don't, we want no rows. And she'll hear more than that afore she's finished anyway.'

'Aye, she might, but she's never heard it in this house.'

No, I had never heard the word bastard spoken in the house, not even when me granda and me Uncle Jack had been roaring drunk. I had heard many different kinds of swear words but none you could label under the heading of bad or vile language.

I never learned what a bastard was that night nor did it in any way link up in my mind with having no da, but it seemed to me that from that night a sort of unspoken understanding grew up between Kate and the fathar. They still had rows but strangely they would more often than not defend each other against a third person.

Shortly after we came to the New Buildings my Aunt Mary and Uncle Alec married and went to live in number thirty, the end house at the top of the street, and they had it furnished properly straightaway, with a bedroom suite which had a dressing table with swing mirrors. These mirrors were always a delight to me, and if I could get a chance to stand in front of them I was in my element. The front room was set out with a modern suite, and even in the kitchen there was a lovely sideboard which today would still be classed as valuable. Mary had bought it second-hand, and inset in the front of it was a painting of Christ releasing chained men from prison. Mary was very proud of her house and she kept it beautifully clean; but there was no harmony in her home for she had a shocking temper; and she made enemies all round her. She was possessed of a gnawing desire to be better than her neighbours, even the best of them. I don't think she ever knew a day's real happiness in her life.

As the years went on I used to baby-sit for my Aunt Mary, minding Jack and Alex. I used to like this job because I could open all the drawers and cupboards and see what she'd got.

Mary could be generous in her way. Often I got a big slab of new bread when she was baking, or a cake. I liked to go up there when she was baking. Her cakes were different from those our Kate made. When Kate baked it was to fill the men's bellies; when Mary baked it was to set out a nice tea. At least that is how I looked at it.

Kate was very fond of Mary's two boys, and there grew up a love between young Alec and her. It started in a monetary way. He had a paper round in the evenings and when she was very hard up for a copper she would say: 'How's it the night, Alec?'

'I've got sixpence,' he might say.

So he'd lend her the sixpence on the unwritten understanding that he would get eightpence in return. He very often got more when she was in funds.

Up to the time she left the North, Alec called on her every week and she looked forward to his visits because she thought of him almost as a son.

I look back to periods of calmness, like short rests between battles, and these rests held flashes of happiness; quiet evenings in the kitchen when I would sit curled up on the corner of the big steel fender before the roaring fire reading a comic, or my 'conscience-pricking book' as I came to look upon the annual that the caretaker's daughter of Simonside School, by the name of Taylor, had lent me. It was the first real book I'd ever been able to peruse, and I couldn't bear the thought of giving it back to her. And when Kate took me away from the School it was an easy thing to pretend to myself that I had forgotten all about the book. But for years after I couldn't pass that girl and look at her because I remembered that book.

Very often when I sat reading the saliva would be running free in my mouth because finney-haddie might be cooking in the oven, or there might be panhacklety sizzling in the big black frying pan on the hob. The wind would be whirling down the chimney, and the gas mantle making little plop-plopping noises. Me granda would be sitting at the centre table as usual, cheating himself at patience, and, of course, to his hand would be a pint mug of beer, into which he would thrust Dennis every now and again, after having heated it in the heart of the fire.

I cannot see me grandma on these nights, only our Kate and me Uncle Jack. Sometimes Jack would be sitting opposite me reading the paper while Kate stood at the other table near the window ironing or baking.

And later, during the War and after, I have a picture of Kate sitting at the corner of the table reading the newspaper aloud, me granda nodding occasionally or stopping her to question some point. Every night during the War she read the paper to him; always first going to Philip Gibbs' despatch from France. This was all brought back clearly when I heard recently that Sir Philip Gibbs had died. How his every word had been awaited in that kitchen in ten William Black Street, for Jack was in France most of the War. Sometimes the kitchen would ring with laughter when Kate read aloud such books as, *Handy Andy*, or *Wee McGregor*, or *Tales of an Irish County Court*.

And there were nights when I'd be bathed before the fire.

A mixed joy this because I couldn't stand anybody looking at me. So a towel had to be rigged up to protect my modesty, and when later, clothed in my nightie, I would stand between me granda's knees having sips of beer from his pint pot, I would experience a happiness bred by a fleeting sense of security.

But the feeling of security would be wiped away when, perhaps the very next day, I would be sent to borrow. I hated to ask any one for the loan of money. And most of all I would hate going up to my Aunt Mary's. I would knock on her shiny front door because very often she kept the back door locked, and after one look at her face I would lower my lids and deliver my begging message.

There were periods when the two sisters did not speak for months on end and I would gain a blessed respite.

It was during one of these periods that Theresa, Mary's only daughter, was born and in consequence, I did not see her until she was nearly six months old.

Often my Aunt Sarah would pay a visit from Birtley. My Aunt Sarah was like neither Kate nor Mary in looks or temperament. She was big-boned and downright in manner. The sisters had little in common, except perhaps that all three could get through a colossal amount of work, and they all had a dominating streak in them.

Sarah liked her beer and her whisky and she would have what she could afford. But she had one advantage over Kate, she was able to carry it. She could take three or four glasses of whisky and you wouldn't notice it, yet should Kate take two she was well away.

Lately, at a small dinner party I sat looking at a woman who was drinking her second large brandy with her coffee. She'd had two sherries before dinner and her glass filled four times with wine during dinner and was now becoming very merry and the night was young. Why wasn't I nauseated with her? Why, because she wasn't our Kate.

I did not like my Aunt Sarah, at least not in my youth. I was afraid of her. But in spite of this she always held a certain attraction for me, and I never knew what it was until many years later; it was her voice. It could be raucous and loud as she yelled at the children, but it was a different voice, there was something about it.

Mary did not drink – at least, when anyone was looking, as Kate said, but I really don't think she had any desire for it. And Kate's drinking afforded her a superiority she would not impair by self indulgence; never once did she discuss Kate without showing her disdain. Whether this was aggravated by the knowledge that my Uncle Alec liked Kate, and never tried to hide the fact, I have been made to wonder. I loved my Uncle Alec. To me he was a clever man because he did competitions and later crosswords when they were in their infancy. I liked him until the day he died – strangely enough in Kate's arms – because, in spite of Mary and her tongue, he always defended our Kate.

I did not immediately go to a Catholic School, but for some days went to the Meeses School just up the road near Bogey Hill – this was the name given to a group of houses which, with the exception of a few, were very slummy. Most of the children from the New Buildings who weren't Catholics went to this school. I can only remember my sojourn there as a very depressing experience. But it was while there that I realised I had loved being at Simonside School, and that I would never again dance round the maypole.

My next memory of being at school was going to the Catholic School in the heart of Jarrow. It was about two miles from East Jarrow. I took my dinner with me and the days were long. It was about this period of my life when I first remember feeling tired. If I told Kate I was feeling tired she would say, 'Serves you right. You got a ha'penny each way for the tram and you likely walked and spent it. So serves you right if you're tired.'

This was often true. I would get the money for the tram but walk at least one way so that I could buy bullets, as we called sweets. But I did not always buy bullets, often I would save my ha'pennies.

I did not like the Jarrow School, and I did not learn there as I did at Simonside. All the lessons to my mind seemed to be about God. We started the day with one and we ended the morning session with a lesson on the same subject. And this was repeated in the afternoon. Then there was confession.

I must have taken instruction although I cannot remember doing so, but I do remember the night I made my first confession. It was on a Friday evening. We were marched straight from school to the church. As I knelt in the pew with the other penitents I went over in my mind what I had to do. I had to tell the priest how wicked I was, and when my turn came I did just that. But instead of going into the penitent side of the box I pushed the curtain aside and groped at the priests's knees. A strong hand on my collar hauled me away from my personal contact with God, Heaven and the Angels and thrust me into a black box in which I could see nothing but a glimmer of light high above my head. And in it an outline of a profile which had no resemblance to a priest or his Master but gave me every evidence of their opponent.

From the time of my first confession I had nightmares. The first one I remember clearly. I dropped down through layers of blackness and as I dropped, struggling and groping at this tangible lack of light, I knew I was going straight into Hell, and just as I was arriving at my destination I screamed, scream on top of scream, to wake up tangled in the bedclothes. Kate was standing above me saying, 'Wake up and stop that noise. No more late suppers for you. That's the taties.'

These dreams kept to the same pattern for a long time, for a matter of years I would say, until one night I woke up to find myself at the front door with the draught from the big key hole blowing on to my face. At the time I was sleeping in the front room in the desk-bed – a bed that folded up into a cupboard. It had a wooden base on which was a biscuit-thin flock mattress, which I preferred to the feather bed The draught on my face woke me up and I was terrified at finding myself at the front door. Afterwards I always told myself before going to sleep that I mustn't get up in the night, and I didn't.

There was another dream that used to accompany the nightmare and went on for a long time after the nightmare stopped. It would take place almost as soon as I fell asleep. I could feel it happening as my lids drooped. I would walk up a long staircase towards where a man and a woman were waiting for me at the top. The woman I recognised as our Kate, the man I did not know. I could not see his face; the only impression I got was he was of a great height. Kate would take me under the arms and the man would grasp my feet and after swinging me back and forwards a number of times they would hurl me down the stairs.

I always woke up before I reached the bottom. I did not yell with this dream just gasped and grabbed at the air to save myself. I remember me grandma saying, 'As long as you wake up afore you hit the bottom, hinny, you'll be all right. If you ever hit the bottom you'll be dead.' I never told her it was our Kate and a strange man who threw me down the stairs. I just said I had a dream of falling downstairs.

I used to walk up to the tram sheds near Bogey Hill to take the tram to school. There was a lane by the side of the tram shed leading to Cleveland Place which consisted of a couple of rows of houses near a railway line, and a signal box. The signalman had a garden near the railway line and in the spring Kate used to send me up to his cottage for two pennorth of shallots for pickling. This morning something happened to the signals and the early train to Newcastle crashed. When I reached the tram sheds they were bringing the dead and dying down on stretchers. They lined them up on the main road waiting for the ambulances, and as I stood, not horrified, or appalled, but just interested, for I couldn't take it in that the people were dead, a priest waiting by one of the stretchers patted my head and asked my name, and when I told him and also that I was going to Jarrow School he told me to call in at the vestry that night and he would give me something in commemoration of the event. Later that day I did as he bade me and he presented me with a rosary. I still ask myself why he gave a child something to commemorate such a scene: the only answer I can think of is that he intended I should pray for the souls of the dead.

Why I was moved to Tyne Dock School I don't know. Perhaps the trek to Jarrow was too much for me. I used to cry because I didn't want to go to school, and when Kate enforced this there would be a row between her and me Uncle Jack, for nearly always, with the craftiness of the young, I made my protest in front of our Jack, or me granda.

I would feign sickness and would actually retch and vomit to order; at least make such a realistic attempt at the latter that it was taken for the real thing. The result of these little rehearsals would be Jack's voice raised to Kate, crying, 'You're not going to send that bairn to school in that condition!' and she, knowing her daughter, would say, 'She's going, sick or no sick.' When she said this in a certain way and I knew she wasn't

65

to be softened, I would depart to the lavatory and lock myself in, and no coaxing would get me out until I knew it was too late to go to school.

But my feeling of tiredness was not put on. I must have been anaemic from the day I was born. I was very small for my age, and although I was quite used to being told that I was a bonny lass I had weak eyes, which in my early teens were so covered with sties that I lost all my eyelashes. Moreover, the nose that my mother told me had been so beautiful when I was a baby, had been split at one side when I fell on a broken-neck beer bottle.

One thing of beauty I really did possess and that was my hair. It was a bright reddy chestnut and naturally wavy. Every night me grandma or our Kate put it in rags – a painful business. I lay on these rag corkscrews for many years. And it was this hair that caused a tug-of-war between Miss Corfield, the Headmistress of St Peter and St Paul's, and Kate. And I was the rope so to speak.

I feared Miss Corfield, as every pupil in Tyne Dock School did, and from the first sight of me she must have taken a strong dislike to me for she never left me alone. I can see her standing in front of the ranks in the school yard and pointing at me, saying, 'Put your hair into plaits.' I moved out of the ranks and tried to comb the curls out with my fingers and do as she said – a difficult job for I had never plaited my hair before. This was the beginning of the tug-of-war. For weeks and weeks Kate and me grandma together would send me out arrayed in my curls, and Miss Corfield would see that I came back with plaits. Miss Corfield I suppose was right in this one instance: you were less likely to get dickies in your hair if it was tied back. But me grandma saw that I didn't get dickies in my hair because every dinner time when I returned home, I had to sit on her lap or stand protestingly between her knees while she 'looked' my head, and then went over it with a small tooth comb.

Nevertheless, at last Miss Corfield got her way and I went to school in plaits; but it was too late, I had become a target.

Church again took up a great part of the school life. On a Thursday night the children went to confession, and on Friday morning you got up, very often on a bleak snowy morning, and without bite or sup you went to Communion. You took your breakfast with you, usually bread and marge, in your school bag.

Right from my very first Communion I carried with me a feeling of sin, for the simple reason that I didn't like Communion; I thought nothing about the spiritual side of it at that age except that I was taking God into me – and I didn't like the way He came. The feeling of that round cake sticking to my palate, turning to a gluey tasteless substance filled me with nothing but nausea and guilt. I hated the taste of that bread and was almost vomiting by the time I swallowed it. I was always laden with a fearful dread when I went up to the altar rails, because then, at least for the time when the host would be in my mouth I would be disliking God, and this was a sin, a terrible sin.

But nevertheless I rarely missed Communion, because you could go to Communion in your school clothes. But Mass on a Sunday was a different thing. Not all the children went to Mass in Sunday clothes, by no means, but Kate wouldn't let me go if I hadn't something different to put on. Perhaps I possessed a decent coat at the time and it would be reposing in the pawn, and if funds were short it would be the last thing thought necessary to be taken out at the end of the week; more often I 'missed Mass on Sundays' because of the condition of my shoes.

Following all Sundays came Mondays. Mondays were awful days. They were as bad in a way as Friday night when the men got paid. On a Monday Miss Corfield came round the class to find out, not who had been to Mass and praise them, but the few who hadn't to flay them. So fearful was I of being cornered by her that I would ask one of the Richardsons what the sermon at the Children's Mass had been about. She usually made me stand on my seat and she took a delight in taunting me. She called me . . . 'Grandma', and it caused the whole school to titter and laugh.

Undoubtedly I was old-fashioned; in some ways I was much older than my years, but in others I was so young, so gullible, it would appear I had just been born.

'Well, Grandma, and were you at Mass, yesterday?'

'Yes, Miss Corfield . . . no, Miss Corfield.'

'Come on make up your mind, Grandma, and tell us who took the Mass.'

'Father Bradley, Miss Corfield.'

'Father Bradley was it? And what did he talk about?'

'About going to Hell and a man called Las-a-vis.'

'Las-a-vis?'

'Yes, Miss Corfield.' My legs would at this point have a great desire to cross themselves because my bladder was answering my nerves. I would move from one foot to the other and rub my knees together. As she said again 'Las-a-vis? Does anybody know who this Las-a-vis is?' she would look round at the swarm of faces, which by now would be rising and falling before my eyes. Then her jocularity would disappear, and she would say, 'You have made another mistake, Grandma. Father Bradley did not speak of Lazarus. You weren't at Mass, were you?'

N . . . No, Miss Corfield.'

'Why do you lie? Were you at Confession on Thursday?'

'Yes, Miss Corfield.'

'And Communion?'

'Y-e-s, Miss Corfield.'

'But not at Mass yesterday?'

'No, Miss Corfield.'

'Hold your hand out.'

She had a cane four feet long with an end that was split, not intentionally but from usage. Even the first swish of the cane splaying its agony across my hand was enough to knock me backward. Usually I got three, sometimes more.

Then there was the business of being late. It was quite a walk from East Jarrow to Tyne Dock School. And I was almost as bad at getting up in the morning as me Uncle Jack. Often I was running the last few yards past the church, taking the short cut up the wall where the children's feet had carved out steps over the years, and into the playground, just too late. The bell had gone, and the last of the crocodiles had disappeared into their classrooms. And there we would be, the late-comers. I had just . . . just missed getting in by a matter of seconds. I would tell them so, and keep saying it to anyone who would listen. Then in the middle of its protest my voice would be silenced by the overpowering feeling of dread descending on me. Sometimes we had to stand fifteen minutes waiting for her coming. And those fifteen minutes were like years full of agony. Down the waiting line the boys would be spitting on their hands and rubbing them on their breeches, which was supposed to toughen the skin. I, like most of the other girls, would be standing by now with my legs crossed doing a kind of minor St Vitus Dance. Very often the dance became reality, for when your hands were frozen and that cane swished through the air and split them in two you left the ground and jangled out animal sounds.

I became so terrified of this woman that I began a snivelling, placating campaign. I would go to Mrs Dixon's at Simonside, mostly on a Monday morning, and there with a penny I had kept hidden for the purpose I would get a penn'orth of flowers, and a big bunch at that. These were for Miss Corfield. Very often because I would stand talking to Mrs Dixon I would be late and Miss Corfield would take the flowers from my hand, lay them aside, then say, 'Hold your hand out.'

I remember hugging a great old book to school. It was about two feet high and four inches thick and bound in warm leather. Kate had seen this book lying on a side table in a butcher's shop in Leygate. The butcher was going to tear it up for wrapping. It was full of old illustrations of London and she asked him for it and brought it home. A great value was put on this book in the kitchen, the pictures were so old, so I asked if I could take it to school to show Miss Corfield.

I remember going to her with it, but what happened I don't know. I next see myself waiting at dinnertime outside the gate and walking with her towards her house above the station, trying to open this huge tome as I went along to show her the pictures. All to no avail.

I came home from school one day and said, 'Miss Corfield says we've all got to take three yards of flannelette to make a nightie.' Kate made no reply. They were all out of work at the time. A month later: 'Our Kate, Miss Corfield says if I don't bring the flannelette I'll get wrong. I've kept on tellin' you for weeks I've got to take the flannelette.'

It was on a Friday night when I started again and I kept on all day on the Saturday for I was petrified of going to school on the Monday morning without the material.

Around tea time she suddenly burst out, 'All right, I'll get you the blasted flannelette. Come on.'

She took me into Jarrow. We walked all the way in the dark. I don't remember to which shop we went, but I do remember that my eyes nearly sprang from their sockets when I saw her pick up part of a bale of flannelette that was standing on display in the shop doorway and walk away with it. I scrambled after her into the back lane where she pushed it up under her coat, and then we both ran. I remember coming round by the lonely Quay corner and her having to stop because I was sick. I retched and retched, and when she got indoors she retched too.

I took a piece of the flannelette to school on the Monday. It was cut out into a nightdress, and when I left three years later it was still there, unfinished.

There were three Corfield sisters in the school. The one next in age to the Headmistress took Standard Six and I was afraid of ever reaching her class because she had the name of being a devil too. But the younger Miss Corfield into whose class I went when I moved from Jarrow School became almost a friend. When I entered her class for the first time she recognised me. Apparently she had taught in Jarrow School while I was there. I remembered her just vaguely but was so pleased and grateful for her recognition. Tuition under the youngest Miss Corfield had moments of happiness, such as on a Friday when we had poetry and plays.

I used to say that I learned nothing at Tyne Dock School but religion, but this was not true. I learnt poetry. When I hear certain pieces of Wordsworth, Tennyson and Shakespeare now I say to myself 'I know that part,' and also remember where I first heard it, in Tyne Dock School. But for the rest, I learned very little and my days were filled with fear. Yet I was fortunate in my particular teachers. Miss Barrington, in Standard Four, I remember with love; she was a very big woman and she liked me. It was Miss Barrington who would give a penny for the first one who could recite a piece of poetry she had written on the board. I nearly always got the penny.

'Had I but served my God with half the zeal I served my King, he would not in mine age have left me naked to mine enemies' . . . and on and on. The day I first said Wolsey's 'Farewell to Cromwell' Miss Barrington said, 'Can you remember who wrote that?'

'A fellow called Shakespeare.'

I can only name two of the girls I used to play with – Maggie Kelly and Mary Knowles. The playground was divided by a railing, cutting off the priests' yard and presbytery and I seem to remember seeing a parrot in a cage in the yard. It belonged to the priest, and I also have an idea that this parrot could swear. Undoubtedly if the boys had had anything to do with it it would have achieved this.

When not petrified by Miss Corfield or weighed under the guilt of not liking God, who after all was only a piece of bread, or sick with apprehension about our Kate I managed to give time to falling for a lad. There were, I remember, Willie Birket and Tot Lawson, but I made headway with neither. Tot had dreamy eyes but they didn't look at me and in an endeavour to turn them in my direction I gave bullets to his sister Ruby to pass on to him. They had no effect on his eyes. But when I was nineteen he sought me out and he became my lad, for a while.

In my school days I cannot remember any lad ever giving me a bullet, I was the one who proffered taffie or bruised fruit. On one classic occasion I spent my little hoard on a deceiving male. His name was Eddie Youlden. He sat behind me in Standard Four, and I thought he had made a song up about me that he kept singing down my neck. It went:

> K-K-K-Katie,
> Beautiful K-Katie,
> You're the only g-g-girl
> that I adore.
> When the m-moon shines on the cow shed,
> I'll be waiting at the k-k-k-kitchen door.

I'd passed him bags of bullets before I realised I was being deceived. Never trust a ginger headed man.

There were two priests at Tyne Dock, Father Bradley and Father O'Keefe. I loved Father O'Keefe. He was a gentle, kind man. But I was as much afraid of Father Bradley as I was of Miss Corfield. He was a stern man, and his sermons were dull and punctuated by long drawn out 'and ers'. Me granda spoke scathingly of this priest. 'What was he anyway? His old fathar was nowt but a workman.' The scorn of the poor for the poor.

It was often to be heard when me granda got talking about someone who had got on and moved to higher planes. Perhaps he had heard that someone he knew was living in Westoe – the select end of Shields. Or they had gone to Jesmond, in New-castle – the pinnacle of ambition where it was said there were 'dress suits and nee hot dinners'. But one day me granda came in from work and sat down to his meal, without uttering a word to anyone. This was his usual procedure, except of course when he was drunk, but there was something about him on this particular day. After he had finished his meal he pushed his chair back, sharpened the end of a dead match with his knife and while cleaning his teeth remarked,

'Know who Aa saw the day?'

Me grandma returned his uplifted glance but did not answer.

'Arne Fuller.'

'Arne Fuller?' Me grandma's eyes were screwed up with enquiry.

Me granda lost his composure and his pale blue eyes did a revolving stunt while he sucked his lips in between his teeth.

'Don't be so bloody gormless, woman: Arne Fuller . . . the papers an' the huxter shop.'

'O . . . h.' Me grandma nodded her head at him. 'Fuller's the newsagent?'

'Aye. Fuller's the newsagent.' His tone stung her to reply quickly.

'Well, what about Arne Fuller? He's been left the docks for years.'

'Aye. Aa know that woman. We aall know that. Everybody knows he's got a chain of shops as long as the slacks.'

He stopped and continued to probe his teeth until me grandma in exasperation said, 'Well, what about him?'

'He asked me in for a drink.'

'Arne-Fuller-asked-you-in-for-a-drink?' Me grandma's eyes were screwed up again, and me granda's head was cocked up towards her.

'That's what Aa said, he asked me in for a drink. Aa was comin' out of the North-Eastern—' this was one of the many public houses that lined the street opposite the dock gates – 'An' Aa dunched into him. "John McMullen!" he said. "It's years since Aa clapped eyes on ya." And then we got crackin' and he said to me, "Come in and have a wet, John." '

'An' what did you say?'

'Aa said—' Me granda's voice was now slow and held a

72

note that I couldn't understand – 'Aa said Aa'd had me nuff for the time being an' Aa was on me way home.'

It was many years later before I was able to translate this scene and to appreciate the effort it had taken for me granda to refuse that drink from Arne Fuller. Because Arne Fuller had got on he was a bloody upstart and me granda was not going to be seen drinking with a bloody upstart, yet from that day he ceased to apply this name to Mr Fuller. Arne Fuller had remembered him, had even spoken to him. Later conversations would begin with 'It was on that day that Arne Fuller asked me to go in for a drink, remember?'

My playmates in the New Buildings varied; sometimes it was one of the Weirs, sometimes it was Florrie Harding or Janie Robson or Olive Swinburn or Joan Woodcock, or her sister Lottie. I didn't care for Lottie Woodcock very much for she was too like my Cousin Mary, my Aunt Sarah's eldest daughter, pale, thin and claiming people's attention. Everybody was very careful of Lottie Woodcock as they were of my Cousin Mary. They both died in their early teens of consumption. I often wished that I could be bad so that people could make a lot of me.

I was very jealous of my Cousin Mary. She was a year younger than me and used to come down for the holidays, when she would cry most of the time, saying, 'I want to go ho-er,' meaning home. I was jealous of her because my people were nice to her. I hated the attention she got in the kitchen. I also hated her because of her nice clothes. Yet we used to lie in the desk-bed in the mornings playing happily.

There was one morning when Mary couldn't find one of her petticoats: the house was searched and nobody could find the petticoat. I too searched for the petticoat. 'Well,' said Kate, 'it couldn't have walked and nobody's eaten it.' So Mary was taken back to Birtley that day with one petticoat missing. I think she was wearing four at the time, besides vest, stays and knickers, a dress, a pinny, and a coat. When later that night I undressed for bed I couldn't hide the petticoat, and Kate said, 'My God! What are we going to do with you? You'll end up in a home, see if you don't.' Being sent to a home was a constant threat, but on this occasion she was laughing as she said it.

I was about eighteen when my cousin Mary died and after

this I lost sight of my seven Birtley cousins for over twenty years. The four boys all worked in the pits. I never cared much for pitmen. Me granda, when slating them among others, said, all pitmen heaved more coal at the corner end, or at their games of quoits, and pitch and toss, than they ever did down the mine. Added to this impression was my own experience of miners, but this I derived more from the way they treated their wives and families, the females thereof, than from the men themselves.

It wasn't until about 1952 that my opinion of miners turned a complete somersault. I was meeting my cousins for the first time after the long separation, and I angered them with my remarks about the high price of coal in the South. The result of our verbal battle was that they challenged me to go down the mine. The thought petrified me, but what could I do with those four indignant men facing me. I went down with Peter – he was a deputy at the Betty Pit in Birtley – and was down about three hours. I almost embraced the daylight when I stepped back out of the cage, and from that moment wanted, sincerely and genuinely wanted to pin medals on every pitman. The outcome of my nerve racking experience was my fourth novel, *Maggie Rowan*.

I can't ever remember going to bed before nine o'clock, and as I grew older there were certain duties to be done in the evening. One was to help me granda try the hens. He would take the big cree and I would take the small ones. The trying of the hens, to find out how many eggs were forthcoming on the morrow, was accomplished by inserting the index finger into the back passage of the hen. You could then tell whether the hen would lay in the morning or not until the afternoon. Me granda could tell the exact hour.

Trying the hens was repulsive, but not as repulsive as having to hold them while he slit their gullets. There came the night when I rebelled against this barbaric chore. I must have been about eleven, and I was standing holding a duck, a favourite duck, tight under my arm. Its head was swinging protestingly from side to side. The dish that stood on the broken chair in the scullery was waiting for the blood. I opened the poor beast's bill and then it was done. Me granda threw the duck on the floor where it regained a second's resurrection of life and stood on its legs before finally toppling over. It was too much; I ran into the kitchen, and standing with my back to the table I shouted at him, 'I'm not doing it! I'm not doing it any more! Do you hear me?' I was crying loudly, and our Kate was saying, 'Now, now. There's nothing to make a fuss about. All right, all right.'

I'm sure me granda had got me to hold the fowls for execution because he liked having me near him; he liked the idea of us working together. Our Kate could have caught a hen, killed it, dressed it and had it in the oven before the bird's flesh was cold. She had a stomach for those things.

The kitchen was the hub of my life; it was the centre of the universe from which all pain and pleasure sprang. In it would be enacted battles both physical and mental. One particular battle happened at least once a week between Kate and myself. It would begin with her saying 'I don't want you to go to school this mornin'.' This should have filled me with joy but it didn't. For it meant only one thing, she wanted me to go to the pawn. I would stand nearly always at the kitchen door leading into the scullery, from which you went by another door into the backyard. I would take up this position as if ready for flight. She would not look at me as she told me why she would have to send me to the pawn but would go about her business of clearing a table, or preparing food, or lifting up the mats, or throwing a great bucket of slack to the back of the fireplace in preparation for the tea leaves that would be put on it to clag it together. And she would be saying, 'It's the rent, I've just got to have it. This is the second week and they could put us in Court.' Being taken to Court had the same horror for her as the workhouse had for me granda. She would not have been 'put in Court' for two weeks rent, but there were outstanding arrears of something between four and five pounds, and as the rent was only about four and six a week they represented many unpaid weeks. Her debts hung over her head like an avalanche about to plunge down and bury her. Yet the irony was that if they had all kept off the drink for a few weeks the debts would have been cleared and she would have been without that particular worry. But people with Kate's weakness don't reason. They can only satisfy the craving in their stomachs, and answer censure with, 'Well, what else have I got?'

From my position by the door I would say, 'I'm not going, our Kate.'

She would remain silent, moving swiftly from one place in the room to another. My eyes would follow her and when she didn't answer I would go on, 'I hate going. It's awful. Everybody looks at me. I'm not going, do you hear?'

Sometimes she would suddenly stop in her darting and sit down and rest her head in her hands. This would be too much for me. I would bow my own head and step into the room and wait. But at other times she would turn on me, crying, 'You'll do what you're damn well told. Now get your hat and jacket on and get away.' Sometimes I would stand and watch her as she parcelled up the things. Very often they were just bits of underwear still damp from the wash. Sometimes it might be a suit, me Uncle Jack's suit, never me granda's. I never knew him to have a suit or anything worth pawning, until I was fourteen or so. Sometimes she would go to the drawer and take out her blouse, her only decent blouse, and there I would stand watching her parcelling the things up while she said, 'Ask him to stretch a point and make it five shillings,' knowing as she said this that I'd be lucky if I returned with three.

I would go out of the front door with the parcel and nearly always there'd be somebody in the street doing their step or their windows, and they'd know where I was going. But this was nothing; the real agony started when I reached the bottom of the dock bank, for the dock bank was always lined with men, waiting to be signed on for work. They would all be standing against the dock offices and the railings that led up to the little photographic shop where the road divided, the right hand section leading up to Stanhope Road, the left going to the station and The Crown.

But opposite to where the men stood the streets went off at right angles, Dock Street, Bede Street, Hudson Street. Gompertz the pawnshop, known as Bob's, was situated in Bede Street. To get to it I had to pass the gauntlet of men. They all knew who I was. I wasn't known as Kate's daughter, but old John's grand-bairn. Nearly always opposite Bede Street, among the men, would be standing Black Charlie. He was a negro and, I understand, an interpreter. Yet he lived in Bede Street with his black wife and black children. They were a happy and good family and the children went to Tyne Dock School.

How do you assess the agonies of childhood? How do you go about putting them over? There is no way to measure these agonies. As an adult you can translate pain into description; you can describe the effects of some particular hurt whether mental or physical. But as a child you have as yet acquired no words to fit the pain. Even if you had you wouldn't be capable of applying them to your particular torments. All you can do as a child is feel and protest through tears. Should you struggle to translate your feelings all you can convey is that you are frightened, or that you've got a pain, or that you don't like this or that, and you can cry as you say this, or bash out, but nothing you can do at that age has the power to convey the feeling of being buried under a tremendous weight of fear, of humiliation and shame.

But I was going up Hudson Street to the pawn. To avoid the eyes of the waiting men I would often hang on to a ha'penny in order to take the tram from the Dock Gates to the station, just two stops up. This was the Shields tram. I wasn't known to anyone on this tram. I imagined when the men saw me getting on to the tram they wouldn't think I was going to the pawn. I would get off at the station, go up the slope and down the steps and past The Crown, to which I joyfully escaped on a Saturday afternoon, and make my way down Bede Street back lane. I would go in the back yard of Bob's shop, then through the passage where the pawning cubicles were. But I never went in these, that would have been the last straw. No, I went out now into the front street, turning my back on the men standing facing the bottom of it. Then I would look in Bob's shop windows. In one side he had an assortment of watches and jewellery. In the other was a show of clothes, mostly moleskin trousers, blue-striped shirts, so stiff they would stand up by themselves, and great sailors' boots. When I had let myself be observed long enough to prove to all concerned that I was going in to buy something, I would open the door and step down into the dark well of Bob's shop. Sometimes, even when in the shop, I carried the pretence still further. To the right hand side was a bench on which was a conglomeration of garments from unredeemed pledges. Among these I would sort as if looking for something to buy. The pretence would be rent apart when Bob would say, 'Well, what is it, hinny?'

With my voice very humble I would answer, 'Kate says can she have five shillings on these?'

He would open the parcel and sort out the things, making comments perhaps on a garment, saying, 'Well, this has seen its last days, hinny, hasn't it . . . and that's not worth tuppence. I'm sorry, lass, but the most I can give you is half-a-crown.'

I would just stare at him and he would repeat 'I'm sorry.' Then he would walk away into the back shop and there would follow a period of waiting, for I was well under age and according to law a person under fourteen could not put in a pledge.

Sometimes I hadn't to wait long and a woman would come into a cubicle and he would say to her 'I've got a bairn here, will you put it in for her?'

He was a kind man was Bob, an understanding man. I look back upon him with affection, for he must have realised how I felt about this business. He knew all my tricks but never alluded to them, and he always did the asking for me. If the woman was in the shop when he asked her I wouldn't look at her. Yet if I got over five shillings I would hand her tuppence for signing the ticket. If I got under five shillings I would give her a penny.

All the times I went to Bob's I never saw a child of my age there, nor yet a man, other than Bob himself.

I had been going to the pawn for some years and was about eleven I think when I asked myself, 'Why can't our Kate go herself?' and it came to me that she was as ashamed as I was to be seen going to the pawn. She didn't want to run the gauntlet of eyes either. And this was the reason why, when I couldn't be kept off school to go to Bobs – perhaps the board man had paid one of his frequent visits only a day or so before – I was sent on almost equally painful borrowing excursions. Anything to save her having to run the gauntlet.

But these weren't the only bad mornings. There were mornings when I had to go across to Mrs Flanagan's in Philipson Street and ask for the loan of a suit.

Mrs Flanagan was a good friend to Kate and Kate in her turn repaid her with hard work, but she did things for Kate that others would not have done, like lending her Mr Flanagan's suit to pawn. Mrs Flanagan was a nice small timid looking little woman, always ailing, and I felt sorry for her, except when

78

I had to go and ask her if she would lend Kate Mr Flanagan's suit to take to the pawn. In these moments I hated her, I hated her for existing, I hated her for having a man who had a suit that was pawnable. But Mr Flanagan had not only one suit, he had a number of suits. He was a man who saw to number one. The Flanagans had a nice house and a lodger, and were comfortable. Sometimes on a Saturday I would go over and scrub the scullery out and the long bare back stairs and she would give me sixpence. I would return from my labours feeling very tired and Kate would say, 'What is it?'

Sitting limp in a chair I would answer, 'I feel tired.'

'Well, you only scrubbed the stairs down, didn't you?'

'Yes, that's all, but I'm tired, funny tired.'

She would look at me and shake her head. I think it troubled her at times that I should feel funny tired. She was afraid I would get consumption. She would say rather hopelessly, 'Well, you should eat your cabbage at dinner time. Cabbage is good for you.' It might be, but I didn't like cabbage.

There was one thing from which I never suffered in my childhood, and that was boredom. There was never time to do all the things I wanted to do, because most of the time was taken up with the things Kate wanted me to do, like going to Jarrow for the washing.

Kate washed for a woman who lived somewhere near Croft Terrace and I was the means of transport. I brought the washing in a clothes basket so wide that when I stooped over it I had to stretch my arms to their fullest extent in order to reach the handles, and when I lifted it up I would wedge the rim above the line of my stomach and propel the whole forward with a minor knees-up-Mother-Brown movement. I would take the tram from the bottom of our street to Dee Street then walk to this particular house. This was a very quiet part of Jarrow, a swanky part, because there were no public houses at all to be seen. It was a section of the town which at that time was restricted from having even an outdoor beer shop within a certain radius.

I used to put the basket of washing under the stairs at the back of the tram and sit next to the door to make sure that people wouldn't knock it as they went in and out. Then from Dee Street, my arms spread to breaking point, I would carry the basket for ten steps before stopping and dropping it with a flop on the pavement. Ten steps were the most I could do at one time. I cannot remember anybody offering to take the other handle for me.

I arrived at the house with the washing one day just as the lady was coming out with a friend. She gave me three shillings and then walked down the street with me. I remember the two women coming to a stop and laughing down at me, for I was showing how tough I was, how I could bash and fight anybody in the New Buildings, slap their faces, box their ears, the lot. The friend put her fingers under my chin and said, 'You're too pretty to do any of those things, you're just making game, aren't you?' I wanted to say I wasn't making game, but she had said I was pretty. So for the remainder of the journey I tried to act pretty.

About this time Kate's temper was very short, and can you wonder at it? Cooking and cleaning and washing in that house besides looking after an invalid mother, and me granda, our Jack and lodgers. The lodgers at this time slept on the feather bed in the bedroom with me Uncle Jack. Me granda slept in the brass bed in the front room. Me grannie remained on her couch opposite him. Kate and I slept on the saddle in the kitchen. This was convenient for she had to get up before six o'clock. Her first chores were raking out the two fires and setting them. If possible she would clean the fireplace – no small job with all the fire-irons and the steel fender. And if she was due to go out to do a half-day's or a day's work she would have to get the kitchen cleaned up before she went and the dinner left ready on the hob. Very often she had to dash from where she was at dinner-time and see to the meal. If it was a full day's work, and she didn't return until tea-time, there was me grandma to be seen to again, all the dishes to wash, the bedroom and the front room to put to rights and the meals prepared for the following day.

When she did washing at home it was even harder for her. Sometimes I would turn the mangle, and the big old-fashioned rollers screeching on contact with a button would set my teeth on edge and shudders would discover all the veins in my body. Or I would try to do the possing. I was never much good at possing, I couldn't lift the poss stick very high. The wash-house was next to the upstairs staircase, the end wall of it being opposite the lavatory door and forming a little alleyway. The boiler was in the corner, the table for scrubbing ran from this to the wall, there was space for the mangle and the poss tub, and the floor was always running with water. You put the lines out in the back lane and you would be very lucky if you hadn't to take the clothes down to let a coal cart up the lane.

For days on end the kitchen would be hung with damp washing. Week in, week out, year in, year out, it was the same. Even to this day I hate the sight of lines full of washing.

With such a life can you wonder that Kate was bad tempered; and I am merely relating the work she had to do. Intersperse this with the tyranny of me granda towards her. And also give place to the unwanted affections of her half-brother, and the ever present knowledge that her life was 'running out fast through a dark alleyway', as she said. Yet she could laugh and be jolly; she had a great sense of fun and was kind to those less fortunate than herself, such as the Kanes. Mary Ellen would come to the back door stammering K...K...Kate. Would you l...l... lend me y...your boots to po...pop into Jarrow?' Kate lent her the boots so often that at last she told her to keep them. I can remember her being vexed at times by Mary Ellen's constant borrowing. Sometimes a coat, sometimes coal, sometimes bread, but most times the boots. I can also remember her saying, 'God help her, what a life!'

Referring to the phrase life running out through a dark alleyway, reminds me that Kate had a feeling for words too. She wanted to talk properly and in her endeavour she made many bloomers.

In her later years she read a great deal, as many as half-a-dozen books in a week, but she still used the form of pronounciation she had used when I was a child. When she got going, Mrs Malaprop had nothing on her.

She would often use the statement: 'They would blind you with science.' What did this mean? It sounded silly, and I would think...Oh, our Kate, she's just trying to be clever. I didn't like Kate trying to be clever. I suppose it was because it was mostly when she had had a drop that she went out of her way to show her superiority with words and sayings.

Many years later when the fight was over and her days were

indeed running out, she said, 'Aw, lass, if I'd only had half a chance I would have made something of meself. But there, I've harmed nobody in me life but meself and you. But what I longed for and lost, you've got. All I want, all I've really ever wanted deep down is for you to be happy . . . Can you believe that?'

I could . . . Poor Kate.

But our life wasn't all work and misery. Sometimes I did have nice clothes like the lovely white silk dress I had when I walked in my first procession at Tyne Dock Church. It was Our Lady's Procession on the first Sunday in May, and besides my beautiful dress I wore white shoes and socks and a long veil with a wreath of blue forget-me-nots on the top. I did look bonny. There was nobody belonging to me at Benediction to tell me but I felt I looked bonny. I walked behind the bier supporting the statue of Our Lady which was carried by four boys. All shapes and sizes of white-robed, veiled and crowned children walked round the church singing, 'Hail Queen of Heaven', then we filed into pews, where we knelt in heavenly bliss. I felt so good, so holy. I asked Our Lady to stop our Kate drinking and she said she would. I felt more good, more holy . . more bonny, and this must have shown because I was escorted home by two boys from my class, who had never before looked at me.

Still in my white dress, white shoes, and socks, but carrying my wreath and veil in a paper bag I came through the arches with my escort. Then we arrived at the slacks. I forgot I was dressed in white and I had been walking behind Our Lady in the procession. I forgot I was good and holy and might one day be a saint, so I invited my companions to come and play the piano on the timbers. I led the way, and to show them how clever I was I did not use one foot at a time but jumped with two feet on to each timber. This was more difficult because you had to jump off quickly again if you didn't want to be caught in the water that was flooding over the partly submerged timbers. There must have been a gap covered with refuse that did not show the gleam of the water, for using my two feet I jumped on it and went straight to the bottom. The tide was high and as it was hemmed in by the saw mill wall, the side gut, and the steepness of the slack bank there was always a swirl of water at this point and it took me under the timbers where I must have remained until the tide turned had not two great arms dragged me clear.

When I was brought out gasping and choking and covered from head to foot in the residue of the river my companions had fled. And had not this man – whose name I can't remember – been passing at the time then I would surely have gone out with the tide.

The road and the New Buildings were always quiet on a Sunday night and the man and I met no one until we came to our front door. I can see our Kate's face as she looked down on me in bitter amazement and can hear the man talking. Next I was in the kitchen as she whipped the clothes off me. Besides bits of cabbage, seaweed and sticks, I was covered with a veneer of scum, and she didn't open her mouth until after I was stripped and put in the tin dish and scrubbed red, then she said, 'Get into that room there and you wait!'

That was the only time I walked in a May procession.

I was ten years old when I first accompanied Kate on a brake trip. Her intention was to give me a holiday. A brake trip was often the only holiday that two-thirds of the population of the New Buildings ever had, and in my case I would willingly have foregone it.

Somebody would get up 'a trip', usually one of the Powers. Old Mrs Power who lived across the road in Philipson Street ran most of the trips and money clubs. You paid a shilling to join a club, and I was sent to draw the lots. Sometimes Kate had two lots, hoping to get an early number so she could pay off this or that debt. Old Mrs Power kept hens and the backyard gave evidence of this. And their kitchen wasn't like our kitchen, but dark and gloomy. I only went in on club days and was always glad to get out. When the lots were drawn you handed over your shilling or two shillings as the case may be, and then, when subsequently you drew your pound club you were always expected to give a little backhander in return for the privilege of someone keeping your money for you.

Every week when you paid your club you put a sixpence or so towards the brake trip, then one day in the summer – with the sun shining if you were lucky – you clambered in with your neighbours and sat on the hard seats that lined the wagon-like structure. Then the man climbed up behind the horses, cracked his whip and amid a throng of running and yelling children you were off for the holiday of the year.

'Hoy a ha'penny oot!' The children would be screaming and yelling as they ran after the brake, and there were ha'pennies and pennies thrown at them, and some of the gay spirits in the brake would sing out:

> We'll not be back till mornin',
> We'll not be back till mornin',
> We'll not be back till mornin',
> A hip, a hip-hooray.

More and more as the years went on I looked towards brake trip time with apprehension and that awful sickly fear, for the trip was always an opportunity for Kate to get bottled up.

Once, our destination was deep in the heart of the country and after a meal everybody walked through a wood which skirted the side of a stream. I can see the pattern of the sunlight flickering over the grass and the sunlight as always emphasised my sadness, and on this particular day my shame. For our Kate was acting the goat. She'd got a load on early in the trip and now she was having fun, laughing and singing and being boisterous, and drawing to herself looks of disdain; especially from my Aunt Mary. I felt this disdain; it pierced me in every part of my body. I hated our Kate for being the cause of it and I hated those who dared to look down on her, for I knew inside myself that when our Kate was all right there wasn't one of them fit to wipe her boots.

The brake would come rattling back at eight or nine o'clock at night, it all depended on the time of the year and the light, and the children would be waiting for it with their cry again of 'Hoy a ha'penny oot!' But now most of the pockets were empty and the cries went unheeded, although everybody would be singing:

> We're back to canny awd Jarrar,
> We're back to canny awd Jarrar,
> We're back to canny awd J-ar-rar,
> A hip, a hip hooray.

Following such a trip Kate would be quiet. The next day would find her perhaps in a bad temper; perhaps she wouldn't move out of the house for two or three days unless she had to.

The shame that had been in me would be in her now, torment-
ing her, and drawing from me a pity that would bring me to her
side to say, 'Do you want any messages, our Kate, or anything?' Sometimes she would look at me and say quietly, 'You
wouldn't go to Bob's for me, would you?'

Oh, the payment of pity!

Nearly every night in the summer after I had come from
school, after I had run the messages, after I carried the grey
hen to Tyne Dock and back, I would go on the slacks, not to
play, but to gather wood. Coal had to be bought. We had no one
in the pits and could not often come by a pit-load, so mostly
we had to buy the coal from Jackie Halliday. But if you had
plenty of wood you could do a baking of bread on that alone;
it was quick heating, and if it had tar on it it blazed nicely.
There was hardly a day passed but I took my sack on to the
timbers.

The slacks was an open space starting from the saw mill wall,
and finishing at the wall of the Barium Chemical Works. Altogether I think about one thousand feet of open frontage. I'm
not very good at measuring distances. I imagine that Howdon,
across the river, was about three-quarters of a mile away. But
much nearer to us, say four hundred feet from the actual road,
lay the gut. And the space between the gut and the slack bank
which bordered the road was used as the timber storing pond.
The whole of the slacks emptied when the tide went down.

In the centre of this area, on a permanent floating raft, was a
substantial hut. This was the headquarters of Mr Tulip, the
man in charge of the timbers. Son followed father in this job
and they lived in a nice house on the terrace right opposite the
slacks. One of old Mr Tulip's unofficial duties was to keep the
children clear of the timbers. He never chased me, but always
said, 'Be careful, hinny, don't go over to the gut.'

Meeting him one day in my teens he looked at me and shook
his head as he said, 'You know, hinny, you shouldn't be alive,
you should have been drowned seven times a week. Somebody
must have been looking after you or you wouldn't be here the
day.'

I wondered too how I had escaped drowning.

I have always been afraid of water, yet I used to walk along
a single rotten plank very much like a man on a tightrope, my feet

splayed to get a grip. The pond was cut into a cross and this cross was formed by single timbers tied to posts at regular intervals. I would cling on to one post, take a breath, then make a steady dive for the next post. Most of the timbers that were beyond Mr Tulip's hut were rotten, green and slimy, and those bordering the actual gut were death traps. I very rarely got as far as the gut for I was terrified of the black creeping mud in it. It was in this gut, some years later, that one of our neighbours was drowned. He was a nice lad, Matty Kilbride. He had just recently married and had taken a boat along the gut to look at a ship lying in the main river over on the Howdon side. The tide turned and caught him in a whirlpool. His wife, if she had been looking, could, from her window, have seen him drown.

The gut was a treacherous place. Yet with my sack on my back I went within yards of it to retrieve some piece of wood. Sometimes I would find myself clinging on to a post terrified to return the way I had come, then having reached Mr Tulip's cabin at last I would tell myself I would never go past it again, but I did.

Great Aunt Maggie lived up the street next door to my Aunt Mary in number twenty-six, downstairs. She was near sighted, yet she read avidly until she was eighty, and often by the light of the street lamp that shone outside her window. It was years later when I really came to know her and like her, even love her. She had a wonderful sense of fun. But this day she was on the slacks gathering sticks.

Among the floating pieces of debris I noticed a sleeper. Sleepers were pieces of wood about three feet long and six inches wide that were used to hold the timbers together. This one had a staple in the middle which held a length of rope. I pulled it out of the water and laid it on one side with the intention of coming back after I had got my bag full of little bits. But when I returned my Aunt Maggie was humping the sleeper up the bank. 'That's mine,' I said.

'What's yours?'

'That sleeper.'

'The whole slack's yours!' She looked down on me with her round piercing eyes.

I didn't dispute this but said, 'It is mine. I pulled it out an' just left it, I was comin' back for it.'

There followed a verbal battle which I must have won, for with the sack over my shoulder and pulling the sleeper by the piece of rope I went home, and me granda, seeing it was a nice piece of wood, used it to renew a post of the hen cree, without bothering to take the staple out.

Morgan, the policeman who lived in the Hall, wasn't exactly loved by the people in the New Buildings and he was hated by me granda. One day we had a visit from him. He was looking for sleepers; a number of them had been cut away from the timbers, and this was serious as the timbers drifted apart and took some getting together again. And there facing him, with the staple for proof, was a sleeper.

Eventually there was a summons and me granda had to appear in Court. It was a dreadful state of affairs. It was the first time me granda had been in Court in his life, which was surely a miscarriage of justice, and on this occasion, being innocent and indignant, he absolutely refused to plead guilty and they were for sending the case to the Assizes, for as the Magistrate said, 'How could a child of eight years carry such a piece of wood as this?' – the sleeper was no longer in the hen cree but now reposed on the bench before him.

To this me granda had replied, 'You don't know me granddaughter, Sir.'

The Magistrate, apparently seeing that me granda was determined to go to the Assizes, decided to disappoint him, he fined him; me granda said flatly he wouldn't pay, he was an innocent man, but Kate paid and got them out of the Court, as she said, at a run.

The report of the case duly appeared in the papers and I felt very important for a while. Me granda was an honest man. Everybody knew that me granda was an honest man.

I still continued to gather wood from the slacks; and there was the joy at night of watching it, piled high in the grate, making blue and orange flames. Sometimes I would catch me granda's eye as he too turned from the mesmerism of the fire, and he would say to me with a deep sigh, 'Aye, hinny, that's all a man wants, food and flame.' If this had been true it would have been a wonderful life.

CHAPTER FIVE

It was just before I was eight that me granda got the compensation for the hurt to his leg. The dock company, The North-Eastern, as it was called, gave him one hundred pounds for the injury, but also stated that he would never be allowed to work in the docks again. As he was around sixty at this time that didn't matter much.

The hundred pounds was considered a fortune. Me grandma took charge of it. She locked it in the drawer of the box sewing machine. I was going to get a bike. Me granda was going to be rigged out, as was me grandma. Me Uncle Jack was going to have his share, and we were going to have new furniture in the house.

But what was our Kate going to get?

Nothing.

Me grandma would dole out the money for beer or spirits and Kate would go for them. But they never gave her a farthing in actual money. What she received for a lifetime of service was a second-hand pair of rinking boots. She was understandably bitter over this.

I didn't get my bike. I can't remember either that me granda got any new clothes nor yet me grandma. What was bought was a lot of timber to rail round a piece of land we were leasing from a man who had a smallholding. Me Uncle Jack and me granda were actually putting the railings up, with great excitement because it was a wonderful thing to have a piece of land, when the man came and said he had been told he wasn't allowed to sub-let.

This was a great blow, and to the blow was added anger when, just a few months later my Aunt Mary and Uncle Alec took over this very plot. It caused a rift between the two houses for many a long day.

88

But what we did get out of the hundred pounds was some pieces of furniture. There was a family called Regan who lived up in Bogey Hill. The wife died and the husband sold the furniture, and the children were distributed amongst neighbours. But from this sale me grandma bought a huge Scotch chest-of-drawers about seven feet tall and five wide – a big ugly piece of furniture but well veneered. For years it stood in the front room and I was very proud of it; it wasn't everybody who had a big chest-of-drawers. But it was very rarely full of anything but useless oddments, such as a Maltese cross, a padded monstrosity with a love poem worked in the middle – Jack Stoddard had brought it home for Kate after a voyage. The little chest in the kitchen held all the linen we had and the clothes were hung on some pegs behind the front room door and also in the cupboard that ran off the bedroom and under the stairs of the house above. We also bought a picture of all the Popes from Peter, everyone of them was there, packed tightly in rows. If because of the little you could see you doubted this, their names were at the bottom to prove you wrong. Everybody in the house knew this picture was of great value. It was even suggested it might have supernatural powers. Nobody knew that I didn't like it except Father O'Keefe, because it was a grave sin to think Popes looked awful. My penance was three Hail Mary's.

The main part of the money was dribbled and drabbled away, as was all money that came into the house. But almost the last five pounds was stolen from me granda, and our Kate's reaction to this was 'Devil's cure to it', the meaning of which I cannot interpret except that it meant, 'Serve him right.'

We had staying with us at that time the elder brother of the bereaved Mr Regan. He was a dour, taciturn man. He worked in the Chemical Works and was a firm Catholic, and it was he who hinted he would like his nephew with him. There was a great deal of sympathy for the poor homeless children. I think there were six of them, so Kate decided to take one of the boys. His name was David and he stayed three weeks with us and nearly drove Kate mad. He was six years old but looked nine or ten. He slept on a make-shift bed in the bedroom and every night without fail he not only wet his bed but did his business in it too.

Kate could not stand this. She had enough in life without

89

this, so David had to go – up to my Aunt Maggie's. Poor Aunt Maggie. She tried to train him, and because he was always stealing stuff from the pantry – he could eat like two horses – she would lock him outside, and she tried to have her meal before letting him in. David, knowing this, would hang on to the sill of the front window, and pressing his nose against the pane would keep up a flow of running abuse, 'Ya greedy old bugger, ya! I hope it chokes ya. Luk-ara. Luk-ara stuffin' her kite.'

David was eventually taken away. Just in time, my Aunt Maggie said, to stop her being sent to Sedgefield.

The advent of new lodgers invariably meant that the beds would be turned round, me granda and me grandma sometimes having the feather bed in the bedroom, and four lodgers sharing the two beds in the front room. For one short period I re-member Kate and I slept at Mary's, while the saddle in the kitchen was taken up by Jack. At another period there were five men sleeping in the front room, one on a shake down. But these particular lodgers were different. They came from away, to install a new kind of boiler in the works opposite the saw mill, and they were ever remembered by Kate as nice men.

I remember them too as nice men. I remember Kate was happy during their sojourn with us. I can see one of them scooping a handful of froth from the poss tub and throwing it at her and I can see her coming out of the wash-house and turning the hose on him and the laughter filling the yard.

They were jolly men, and strangely enough they didn't drink, or so little that it made no difference. This must have been an enlightening period for me Uncle Jack too for he went out with them a number of times of a Saturday night to a show and returned solid and sober and happy. During this period his suit never went to the pawn.

Over the years the lodgers came and went, and not a few of them wanted to marry our Kate. One of these was a docker called Billy Potts. He was a rough, coarse man, and very ignorant, but nevertheless had a kindly disposition, and he was very much in love with Kate. He would go to great lengths to get into her good books. When he was unloading the grain boats he would tie his yorks tight – yorks are strings which are tied around the trousers below the knees – then pour the grain down the top of his trousers. This form of transportation must have been very uncomfortable, as was to be seen from his laboured walk, and I don't suppose it hoodwinked the dock police one jot.

From time to time he would pester her with, 'What aboot it, Kate lass, eh? What aboot you and me hooking up, eh?' And although she never took him seriously, she felt bound at last to tell him to go, and try as he might she never allowed him back in the house. Billy was always kind to me, but even at an early age I shuddered at the thought of him being me da. Years later when I was working in the Institution I would pass him often standing on the dock bank, and when he was out of work I would slip him a sixpence, or a shilling, to get 'set on' in the pub, which meant having just enough to buy a drink and who knew but someone would stand you another once you were inside. He took to waiting for me on pay day. 'How ya keepin', Katie? By, ya'a bonny lass.' Another tanner gone.

There was also the lodger who had a row of books standing on the chest in the bedroom, they were all by that fellow Shakespeare. Kate said to me, 'Leave them alone. They're not for you. You wouldn't understand them, they are like a foreign language.' I read the end of one where it said *Sonnets* and in a way I did understand them enough to think 'Ee, fancy saying things like that in a book'.

Then there was a man from Hexham, Dick Cartner. He was young, athletic, and good-looking. He lodged with us during one of the many slump periods. I can see him standing in the kitchen with his back to the fire leading off to me granda and Jack while Kate busied herself with the chores, and I can hear him saying, 'I will find work! I will demand work, it is my right! And who is there to stop me if I am in the right?' He had a nice voice and spoke differently from us.

She wouldn't marry Dick or give him a promise that when he got the job he desired she would be his wife, and so he went away. The only thing I remember about him afterwards is that he sent us a great box of mushrooms and with the mushrooms a bottle of black stuff. When I had the house to myself I always made for the cupboard, it was the only place of interest for there would be cocoa and condensed milk, and a spoonful of each mixed together made stuff that tasted like chocolate. The black bottle intrigued me. I smelt it then took a long drink. When Kate returned home it was to find me terribly sick; concentrated essence of mushroom is not to be swallowed in mouthfuls.

Then there was the sea captain from Shields – I've forgotten his name but I've never forgotten him. Was it the height of him? or the breadth of him? or his beard? or his blue eyes? or his teeth, strong and aggressive in their overlapping? was it the smell of the shore suit, a mixture of moth balls and brine? or the way he filled every crevice of it? Was it the way he rolled in his walk when he was sober? or the way he rolled when he was drunk? Was it his laugh deep and easy flowing, born of the sea bed? Or was it his stopping whenever he saw me and exclaiming in a very good imitation of awe, 'Yes, you are! You are bonnier than you were a month ago.'

I think it was this, this telling me I was bonnie, that has made me remember him.

The captain was not a good husband, and I've heard he was an indifferent father; but what could you expect, he loved so many women that any one person could only have a portion of his affection.

Once, walking with him along his zig-zagging course, he said to me, 'Have one aim in life ... happiness! If you are happy, you'll make at least half the people you know happy. Don't believe in Heaven or Hell, it's only imagination. Everything's imagination ... even the sea and the sky.'

I remember him stopping at this and exclaiming, 'My God! am I imagining I'm drunk?' His head went up and his laugh rang out, in which I joined.

He went down with his little ship in 1917. I was eleven at the time, and I cried when I heard of it; and I remember thinking, He'll know now if there's a Heaven or Hell.

Incidents in my childhood keep moving in a circle round and round. When I focus on one and hold it I think it might have happened when I was seven and then I find it could only have happened when I was nine. But somewhere in the circle between seven and nine the following incident took place which terrified me, and bred in me a deep distrust and, for a long time, almost a hatred of Irishmen.

Although me granda was Irish he did not speak the brogue; he mostly showed his Irish trait in his bigotry, superstition and intolerance. But the man who came to lodge next door was a brogue slurring Irishman. He was tall, very tall and handsome;

he had a great smiling face and a thick laughing voice. But he did not come to my notice any more than did the other men of the New Buildings until I learned that our Kate was going to marry him. How long she had known him I did not know and so delicate was the situation ever afterwards that I never asked outright.

It was on a Saturday night when it happened. The house was empty but for this man, Kate and myself. I imagine that me Uncle Jack had by this time joined up for he does not appear on the screen of my memory. However, we were in the kitchen and I can see Kate hurriedly putting on her coat. She took her purse from the mantelpiece, pushed it into the basket with the empty bottles, said she wouldn't be long, and was gone. I can see this great man lifting me on to his knee – I was quite used to being on a man's knee. I sat a lot on me granda's knee, or me Uncle Jack's knee. When I yelled at him he lifted me in his arms and carried me to the old leather chair where he set about kissing me in a terrible fashion. I was stiff and petrified with fear, which seemed to rise from me like steam for I was wet with sweat, and I can still hear myself screaming, 'No! No! Don't do bad things. Let me go. I'll tell me da – I'll tell our Kate.'

How long it was after this that I opened the door to Kate I don't know, but I do know that I told myself that I mustn't tell her anything. Nor must I ever let me granda know because he would kill him. I knew with an absolute certainty that should I even hint at what this man had tried to do me granda would surely kill him. Yet what was it that caused the terrible row later, the worst row that had happened in the house? Did I in some way imply what had happened? In my own mind I feel sure that I said nothing, but in my memory there is another blank between the time Kate entered the house and the fight that took place when me granda and me grandma returned. Memory plunges me back to where I was kneeling on the floor in the midst of stamping, of screaming, bashing and yelling. I was crying and was trying to get me grandma to her feet. She had been knocked clean under the table.

Whether this man was still in the house at the time I don't know. Then in the silence of the next day – and the house was always strangely silent after one of these rows – I knew that our Kate was not going to marry this man.

Somewhere in these years there was another incident along these lines. Like the seasons bringing forth the set games for children to play there would at certain times of the year spring up in the New Buildings house-shops. There was always this urge to do business, to make money. People started drapery shops, or sweet shops, or they made cakes and sold them, as we did years later. But at the time I am thinking about there was a sweet shop in Lancaster Street. It was in the front room, and had a real counter, and they sold Woodbines. When Cissie's shop was closed at nine o'clock, sometimes ten on a Saturday, you could always get Woodbines at this particular house-shop. The man and woman who lived there rarely served in the shop. This job was taken over by the father of one of them, an old man, and I became terrified of this man. I used to dread our Jack saying at the last minute, 'Go and get me a packet of tabs, Katie, before you go to bed, that's a good lass.' If I had the right money and could put it on the counter and grab up the Woodbines and run, it was all right. But if I had to wait for change this man would hold it in his hand and come round the counter, and would not give me the change until I had kissed him. Again I knew that I must not tell anybody in the house about this, because there would be murder done.

My nightmares were frequent about this period and Kate said, 'Something will have to be done about this, you read too much.' And the reading too much brings me to our new neighbour upstairs.

After the first Mrs Romanus died Mr Romanus was not long in taking another wife. She was in her thirties and as opposite to his first wife as could be imagined. She dressed in the brightest of colours, which was very unusual among the women in those days, and, what was really shocking, she painted her face. She was always full of surprising new enterprises, such as starting a fish and chip shop in the upstairs kitchen, or a sweet shop – I got a lot of sweets for nothing – or a baker's shop with bought cakes. She wasted more money in this way than would have kept three large families going. Mr Romanus was a trimmer and made very good money, and unlike me granda, who was a casual dock worker, he was always in work.

Mrs Romanus was not cut out to be a housewife. She was laughed at by many and talked about by all, while those who laughed took from her. She caused a lot of speculation did Mrs Romanus, and a great deal of scornful amusement from behind our lace curtains as Kate and me granda would watch her attempts at washing in the open yard. For some reason she would always wash in the yard in a small tub on a chair, and with a rubbing board.

In those days you were considered lazy if you didn't use a scrubbing brush and a poss-stick, and you were quite beyond the pale if you didn't bake your own bread. Eva, as she was called, did none of these things. She attempted to eliminate hard work and, because of it, brought derision on herself. But if only Kate had had the sense to resort to the rubbing board her arms would not have ached so much. Many a night she was forced to get out of bed and burn them into numbness with raw liniment.

But I am for ever and eternally grateful to Eva Romanus for it was she who bought me my first book. It must have been my birthday and she said, 'What would you like, Katie?'

'A book,' I said.

I can see her now smiling at me and saying, 'You shall have a book, any one you like.' And she took me into Shields and I picked Grimm's Fairy Tales, the complete works. I think I loved her for buying me that book. I sometimes got an annual at Christmas but this was a real book.

As the years went on and her family grew she was at times very harsh with the children and it was understandable. They were all boys and always round her feet. And perhaps like the first Mrs Romanus she longed for another way of life. But she was always kind to me, more than kind. I remember that when she got her pay she would often go out and have a spend-up – drink wasn't her failing, just extravagance – and she never, or rarely came back from Shields without bringing me something, some fruit, or a cake; something.

With Grimm's Fairy Tales the wonder of a new world was unrolled before me. I read them dozens and dozens and dozens of times, and more and more frequently the saying could be heard in the house, 'Will you get your nose out of that book and go this errand this minute! I know what I'll do with that afore very long. It'll end up in the fire, you see if it doesn't.'

In the community of the New Buildings, which consisted of

about fifty houses all told, there were some families who managed to keep their lives surrounded by a close privacy, you knew very little about them, other than that they were comfortably off and went to Chapel. But in the main the private lives were public property. Yet, except for one or two exceptional occasions most families were left to work out their own problems. It would have been better if this had not always happened.

There was the woman who split her child's thumb with a flat-iron. The child must have been sitting on the floor crying, its little hand in the hole of a cracket – this is a small stool – when a knock came on the door, which meant the tally-man had called for his money. The woman didn't mean to answer the door and when the child would not stop crying she hit it on the hand with the flat-iron.

I can remember Kate saying, 'I'll go to the Cruelty Inspector,' but she didn't. Nor was anything done when this woman struck at a puppy as it ran round her legs when she was cutting the meat. The puppy's tail was sliced almost off and ever after when it sat on it it would cry.

Again Kate said, 'I'll write to the Inspector,' but me granda said, 'Mind your own business; you'll have enough to do if you mind your own business.'

There were other incidents of cruelty but they were never reported. People in general closed a blind eye. They might get angry, they might stop speaking to the woman, they might talk about her to the neighbours, but they rarely did anything. Except once and then it wasn't for cruelty. It was because a woman was trying to take another woman's husband. The moralists who, strangely enough, numbered the smut-talking women among their ranks almost ran this woman out of the New Buildings. I recall Kate remarking on this in the kitchen, saying, 'It's a good job for some folks that everything isn't known else there'd be a number of them leaving the buildings at a gallop at this minute. It's a good cover-up to be a chaser, there's less likelihood of being chased then.'

CHAPTER SIX

I longed, as every child longs, for Christmas. Yet as it came near my feelings were always tinged with apprehension. In spite of this, however, I can still feel the excitement of rising in the middle of the night and going into the kitchen and just being able to make out in the dim light of the turned-down gas jet the sailor's bag which was my stocking, hanging from the brass rod supported on brackets from beneath the mantelpiece. I always hung up a sailor's bag and this bag was always full to the top. But half-way down the parcels would turn out to be turnips, or cabbages, or vegetables of some kind done up in paper.

Although aeons of time had passed since the previous Christmas when I had undone the packages of vegetables in my stocking I always immediately recalled having done this before, and I would become both sad and irritated when I reached this stage in the proceedings; but I went on unwrapping, right to the bottom of the bag just in case I might be missing something nice.

There was one Christmas when the vegetables started almost at the top of the bag and I stared wide-eyed at the cabbage, I had just unwrapped. I couldn't believe it. When I reached the bottom of the bag I was overcome by a colossal sense of disappointment and disgust. I recognised the feeling as disgust. Disgust that our Kate could have been so silly as to wrap up all these vegetables, the potstuff that I had been sent for yesterday, which would be used for the dinner the day and the morrow.

I sat at the table surrounded by paper and pot stuff, and there in the middle of them the little shop that was my sole present. I had looked forward to having books. I knew for certain I would get an annual, but there wasn't an annual in my stocking that year. Funds must have been very low, perhaps no work. It often happened that the men could be out for weeks and at such times there was only the money Kate earned to keep things going, or the money from a lodger – if he was in work.

There were other years when I did get annuals and lots of toys. Mary was usually kind to me at Christmas, always supplying something towards my stocking. But the Christmas of the 'pot stuff' as I think of it, she must have been hard up too, or she wasn't on speaking terms, I can't remember.

But if I dreaded Christmas, New Year was a waking nightmare. Christmas was for the bairns, New Year was for the grown-ups, and everybody, no matter what their station, gave a party. To our party would come Mary and Alec, reluctantly I fear. As the bearer of our invitation, I can see Mary now, standing in her kitchen, her thin face tilted sideways, her eyes closed, and her head shaking just the slightest as she said, 'A party! and they'll be rotten with drink.'

New Year's Eve was a day of work and preparation. It is more true to say that New Year's Eve was the end of the work and preparation, for you had likely been scrubbing and cleaning and baking for two or three days previously. Everything must be ready for twelve o'clock on New Year's Eve, and after that you did not work for the next twelve hours, except what entailed eating and drinking.

I am back in the kitchen now. The stove is newly black-leaded, the fire is roaring away. The tables, the saddle, the chest-of-drawers and the chairs have all been scrubbed or polished. We have a new clippie mat down, kept for this special occasion. It has taken Kate a year to finish it, doing it at odd moments of an evening, and the pattern is clear and bright. On the white scrubbed table there is a cloth and on it the bottles of beer and glasses – the whisky is kept out of sight until after twelve. On a big square centre table covered with another white cloth is a lump of cold brisket, ham, and a tongue, mince pies, sausage rolls, bacon and egg tarts, a rice loaf, and a Christmas cake.

The jollification gets into swing at about ten or eleven o'clock when the bars have closed, but things never get really going until the first-footing starts. Whoever is going to be the first foot, usually a dark man, goes out of the back door with a bottle of whisky and a piece of coal. And he waits with all the other first-foots at the bottom corner near the main road until twelve o'clock, when the ships and the churches herald in the New Year. We are all in the front room looking towards the front door, and when the noise starts . . . ships' hooters and sirens blowing, blowing, blowing, and the church bells ringing, you look at the faces around you and you know that a New Year is actually being born. You can see it in their eyes, the birth giving them renewed hope; even with them sometimes well gone in drink something of great momentum is happening to them. The old year and all it contained is dead and buried. The ships' whistles are welcoming in this New Year, and that means work, and money, and prosperity; more food, more clothes, and of course more to drink. And then there comes the rat-tat-tat on the knocker and Kate, who was nearly always near the door – she couldn't wait to have good luck touch her – lets in the first foot.

Happy New Year! Happy New Year! Everybody shaking hands with everybody, everybody kissing everybody, everybody in the kitchen now all drinking, holding their glasses up to each other, and if they are very drunk crying, crying for somebody who had died and for whom they didn't really care a damn. Then everybody eating and then the sing-song starts. One after the other, they stand up and sing.

When our Kate sang I would put my hands between my knees and bow my head and lend my concentrated gaze towards the floor.

The parties did not always end up with a row but they had one never failing result . . . they broke the bank.

But there is one memory I hold dear, the one time when Kate sang with a difference. It was when there seemed to have been a lull in the anxiety that was ever gnawing at the centre of my breast. It was a dark winter afternoon and we were sitting with the mat frame stretched right across the two tables. Kate was sitting on one side and I on the other, both progging away. My back was towards the fire. She always let me sit at this side because I felt the cold so. The firelight was playing on her bent head, and as I looked at her I thought, our Kate's bonny. And at this point she looked up at me and smiled, and as she did so my thought developed and said, She's more than bonny, she's

99

beautiful is our Kate. She bent her head again and began to hum, then shortly she was singing. She sang quietly and without strain, her favourite Thora.

I stand in a land of roses,
But I dream of a land of snow,
Where you and I were happy
In the years of long ago.
Nightingales in the branches,
Stars in the magic skies,
But I only hear you singing,
I only see your eyes.

Come! come! come to me, Thora,
Come once again and be
Child of my dream, light of my life,
Angel of love to me!

I stand again in the North land,
But in silence and in shame;
Your grave is my only landmark,
And men have forgotten my name.
'Tis a tale that is truer and older
Than any the sagas tell,
I loved you in life too little,
I love you in death too well!

Speak! speak! speak to me, Thora
Speak from your Heaven to me;
Child of my dreams, love of my life,
Hope of my world to be!

Child of my dreams, love of my life. Hope of my world to be ... Her face, the firelight, and her singing was too much. I choked and began to cry. She stopped in surprise, and putting her hand across the mat and stroking my head said, 'Aw! lass, don't, don't. Come on. What is it? Don't.' Then she added in a conspiratorial way, 'Let's have a cup of tea and a bit of cake afore they come in, eh?'

On that day in the kitchen with the help of the firelight and her voice we became close, we became one. At rare moments in our lives we touched like this. One other such moment was two days before she died when she held me in her arms and said, 'Lass, I've been a wicked woman,' and my tears washing away every hurt she had dealt me and the love that I had tried to bring back and supplement for the hate that I had borne her, gave me the power to say, 'You have never done a bad thing in your life.' And when I came to think about it she really hadn't. It was my nature that revolted against her weakness. It was my nervous, sensitive temperament that couldn't stand up against the rough background into which she bore me. Yet at birth she gave me some part of herself, without which I would never have survived. She passed on to me her sense of humour and, I like to think, a little of her humanity and kindness of heart, these last two virtues which were large in herself and of which she received sparingly from others.

She wanted no praying at the end, she wanted no priest. Although I knew that in her own way she would have made her peace with God. As she said, 'Let him judge me. He knows all the whys and the wherefores.' And I knew she was right in this. If she was going to meet God, if there was one to meet, why send frantic prayers ahead? Wouldn't it be better to speak face to face? Wiped away for her too were all the intermediaries of my childhood. Our Lady, the Holy Family, the innumerable saints that one had to pass before one could speak with Christ. At least that is how I saw it. And then of course there was purgatory. But on that day I knew that my mother would not go to purgatory. She would not have to answer the examiners as to whether she had conformed to the doctrine of the Holy Catholic Church. If there was a God, and on that day the 'if' was loud in my head, if there was a God then she would have access to Him straightaway – Together with all the thousands who were dying at that particular moment? This last came as a question to me, not aggressively, but quietly.

Talking of praying, reminds me that I used to walk through the arches with my hands joined as if in prayer. I usually did this on a Friday because the men were paid on a Friday, and I used to pray to Our Lady that I would go home and find them all right. I would think in the plural, but it was Kate that I meant.

People used to stop me and say, 'What are you walking like that for? Are you cold?'

101

And I would say 'Yes. Me hands are freezin'.'

Years later a woman reminded me of this. When she had noticed me walking with my joined hands under my chin on a warm day she had realised I was praying. She ended by saying, 'But aye, hinny, you had something to pray for with old John and that lot, they were enough to make anybody old fashioned.'

CHAPTER SEVEN

I remember very distinctly the day in nineteen hundred and fourteen when the First World War broke out. I sat a long long while on the slack bank looking across the timbers over the gut to where the ships were passing up and down the river. I was waiting for the battle to begin – I couldn't understand why they were so long about it.

I walked up Philipson Street. There seemed to be no children about, but Mrs McArthur was cleaning her front step, and as I had to talk to someone about this war I went up to her and said, 'Mrs McArthur, do you know there's a war on?'

'Yes, Katie, I do,' she said.

'I've been sitting on the slack bank waiting for ages for it to start. They take their time, don't they?'

She smiled at me and said, 'You're a funny lass, Katie. Ee, you are a funny lass.'

In the very early stages of the War me Uncle Jack and his pal got blind drunk one Friday night and woke up on the Saturday morning to find themselves soldiers. We were all very proud of this unconscious voluntary act of Jack's, me granda particularly.

I was only eight years old when the War broke out but the feeling of change that came over the country was felt in the kitchen, as it was in every house, and I can recall the atmosphere that pervaded the world ... my particular world at that time. It was full of bustle and urgency. I seemed to spend my days standing in queues. Sometimes at Allen's, the butchers, I would stand for hours, because meat was scarce. And then again in the evening, hours and hours in the beer queue. I have only isolated pictures of the War, such as returning from The Crown and meeting me Uncle Jack on the road. He was solid and sober and it was a Saturday afternoon. I recollect the happy feeling of this day; he was in his khaki uniform and he gave me a penny. He was stationed at the time in Mortimer Road School in Shields and he used to bring me back little infant exercise books. There was one in particular. In it was a picture of a little girl sitting before a fire and to her side was a small table on which stood a cup and saucer and at her feet sat a kitten. For years and years that picture spelt security to me. I was the little girl sitting snug and warm. Nothing could touch me. Jack always remembered to bring me something from the school even if it was pinched. When he went to France I wrote to him every week, but my writing was so bad that Kate always had to do the envelope. In return he sent me cards with silk patterns woven on them. I have one still. It has a mandolin on it.

Then there was the time when Jack came on his one and only leave. He was a changed individual. No longer was he shy; he was fighting for his country, he was a big-shot. To my amazement, he took me by the hand and went visiting round the New Buildings. We went to Mrs Bolton's in the terrace. I had never been in Mrs Bolton's backyard before, and I can see him now chatting and shaking hands with everybody. Of course he had a little load on but he wasn't drunk. Yet before he joined up whatever his condition he wouldn't speak to the neighbours, let alone visit them. No, Jack was a changed individual.

He also had, I remember, a row with my Uncle Alec. Why wasn't my Uncle Alec in the War doing his bit? The row took place in my Aunt Mary's backyard. For medical reasons my Uncle Alec had been turned down. But this did not satisfy me Uncle Jack. It would appear that he was the only man in the War, the only man doing his bit, but things weren't going too well and he wanted help. How could he win the War if he didn't have help?

The night he went away we went hand in hand to the docks, and on the way to the station we called in at Walker's, the chemists, in Hudson Street, and old Mr Walker gave him a box of powder that would kill lice. I was very proud of our Jack that night and sad because he was going away, but when we reached Newcastle Station I longed for him to get himself off so that I could get our Kate and me granda back. Our Kate was 'bubbling like anything', she always bubbled loudly at a certain point in her whisky intake. The shame was heavy on me that night.

Then came the day when the letter arrived from Jack saying that he had been offered promotion. This was wonderful news, fantastic news. Jack was a sniper and because of his prowess in this direction he had been offered a stripe.

'No,' said me granda, 'you write back this minute and tell him not to take it.' Me granda had been in the Army and to him anybody rising from the ranks was suspect.

But Jack did take the stripe and when this news came me granda said, 'It's the beginning of the end, it won't be long now.' And in a very short time we had a letter to say that Jack had been wounded, and then a letter from the priest to say he was on his way home.

It was on a Saturday morning that Kate went up to Jarrow store. She had got three big clubs out and was buying new bed linen and all the things necessary for a wounded hero. And before she came back a telegram arrived. I took it into the kitchen where me granda was feeding the canary. He had a way with canaries. I read out the wire to him and he sat down. It was one of the three times in my life that I saw him cry. The other two times were when the canary died, and when I kissed him goodbye the day I came south.

When Kate came in she, too, cried. But shortly after this, holding me in her arms, she spoke, as if to me but more to herself, saying, 'It's God's will. And the best thing that could have happened, for there'd be no place for me or you here if he'd come back. One of us would've had to go and it wouldn't have been him.'

Another good thing that came out of me Uncle Jack's death was that me granda got a pension. He got this because it was put over that he had relied on his son's money before he enlisted. If me granda had relied on me Uncle Jack's money in order to live he would have been dead many years earlier.

The pension was a godsend and every Tuesday morning me granda would wash himself with a great deal of spluttering in the tin dish, part his hair while he looked in the mirror above the mantelpiece, then don his overcoat – he had one by now, Kate had seen to that – and he would then walk up to Bogey Hill where the Post Office was. The Post Office was kept by the Misses McFarlane, and the elder one, the postmistress, a lady of terrifying refinement and austerity, at least to me, would sign his name where he put his cross.

I first became aware of indulgences after me Uncle Jack died. Among his possessions the priest sent home was an illuminated watch of no particular value, so I was allowed to keep it, and I would take it to bed with me at night and hold it while I prayed for the release of his soul from purgatory. Certain prayers had attached to them certain indulgences. You said so many prayers for so many days and you got so many indulgences. What were indulgences? The dictionary says that indulgence in the Roman Catholic Church means 'remission of punishment still due to sin after sacramental absolution'. All I knew at that time was that the more prayers I said for him the quicker I would get him out of purgatory, for Jack I knew was sure to be in purgatory. So night after night I would drag him a little further out of the black depth. Sometimes I would grab deep down and get hold of his outstretched hand, and holding him tight pull him up towards me. At other times I would peer through vast iron gates to see him ascending out of a great hollow. After months of praying I got him to the actual gates, I could see his face and it was saying to me, 'Hello, Katie, I knew you would get me out of this.'

But where was I to take him? what was I to do with him? By all accounts he should now go to Heaven, up to God. I had never thought of going to Heaven, my thoughts never ascended that far. I was either saying prayers to prevent me being thrust into Hell, or saying prayers to get somebody out of Hell and purgatory. Heaven was a closed shop I knew nothing about it, so regretfully I left me Uncle Jack on the other side of the iron gates and I can't remember praying for him any more.

Me grandma too was dead by this time. I do not remember the date on which she died but I remember the night very well. I was lying in the desk-bed and she was now lying in the brass bed in the corner of the front room. The room, too, was full of people. My Aunt Mary, my Uncle Alec, my Aunt Maggie, me granda, and Kate, and some others. Somebody said to me, 'Go to sleep, hinny.' But I couldn't sleep, and then I heard me grandma make a funny noise and she was sick, and I thought to myself, She'll be better now she's got it up.

It was the death rattle and she died within a few minutes. And no one took me out of that bed. I woke up the next morning and she was laid out. And she lay like that for two days.

'You must see your grannie before she is screwed down,' somebody said, and they took me into the front room and the sight of this blue-black terrible looking face frightened me to death. One glimpse was enough and I ran out of the room, out of the house, to the slacks.

Me grandma lay in her coffin on trestles in the centre of the front room. She lay there for three days, and every now and again Kate would put a bucket under the coffin to catch the blood and water. I was sick a lot during these days and people said, 'The bairn's missing the old girl.'

There was no wake or sitting up at night – Kate put her foot down on this – but there was drinking in the kitchen.

It snowed on the day me grandma was buried in Jarrow Cemetery and Kate's crying at the graveside was like the howling of a dog, and I was stiff with cold and loneliness and shame and I wished I was dead too. I missed me grandma. She had always been a haven to me. Perhaps she had stood between me and Kate, but her going did not draw us together. Why hadn't our Kate died instead of me grandma, I asked the unseen power that made people die. If she had I could have looked after the house and everybody and saved money and paid off the rent.

Immediately after me grandma's going things changed, and not for the better. Me granda was determined to have dominance over Kate, as he had had over me grandma, and for a time he drank more heavily and brought less money home. There were no lodgers and Kate used to go out half days here and whole days there. She did try to get taken on at the Barium Works but the female ganger was a loud-mouthed woman from Bogey Hill who had her favourites, and Kate didn't happen to be one of them. All during the War she rarely earned more than three-and-sixpence a day.

During this period in her life Kate must have felt very

lonely indeed. She had promised to marry Jack Stoddard, one of the Maryport men. His sister was married to David McDermott, the man who later became my step-father. But at this time it was Jack Stoddard whom Kate was going to marry, but early on in the War he was taken prisoner. I remember writing letters to him. Then one night as we lay in the desk-bed Kate whispered to me, 'Don't write to Jack Stoddard any more.' I turned towards her, hissing, 'I am going to write to him . . . I like him.'

I knew why she didn't want me to write to him now, she was finished with Jack Stoddard and had taken up with the man called Davie, whose wife had just died. I thought it was dreadful of her to throw over poor Jack Stoddard and him a prisoner in Germany, and I didn't forget to let her feel this.

For a time there came upon the house a feeling of comparative tranquillity and respectability. This was the result of a show-down between me granda and our Kate. One Friday night after having blued nearly all his wages he came in drunk – he was now working in a shipyard in Jarrow – and when she remonstrated with him in no quiet voice he threatened to beat her up. She had never raised her hand to him before and when she raised it this time it was holding the big black frying pan. She did not hit him with it but it was a deterrent. Then she walked out of the house up to my Aunt Mary's, taking me with her. We slept there that night and I likened it to heaven.

I thought life would be full of peace if we could live in my Aunt Mary's house. I was shutting my eyes to the fact that my Aunt Mary had a name for raising hell – and this without drink. And her own family suffered almost daily from her temper and tantrums.

That Saturday evening was one of the few times I remember not being sent down to Thornton Avenue, to the public house that stood on the corner, there to pay me granda's Union dues. Even if there wasn't money for beer there must be money for the Union – no Union, no work. I would climb the brass bound stairs and stand in a line and wait my turn, and when I came to the little table with the round faced man behind it, he would smile and say, 'Ah! old John.' He would then stamp the card, hand it to me, and end 'Ya'ra bonny lass.'

But Kate was not easy in Mary's house. Two days there were more than enough and she knew in her heart that she could not leave the fathar, an aging man, a frightened man behind all his bombast. So we went back, but under her conditions, and peace reigned. From this time a companionship sprang up between them; and this is strange for she had to fight him too, not quite in the same way she had fought me Uncle Jack but along similar lines, for he would now bring her a cup of tea in the mornings and to wake her he would grip her in the loin and bring her sitting up out of a deep sleep, spluttering, 'All right! All right! I'm awake. I'm awake. That's enough!' Nearly always before she drank the tea she would let out a long drawn breath.

Poor Kate.

Every Saturday afternoon, I went to The Crown. But I had to work for this privilege. My chores usually started on a Friday night after coming home from school. I would clean the ginger beer bottles – we were then selling ginger and herb beer – we did a roaring trade during the War. The bottles were washed in a sawn-off poss tub and my job was to make sure that all the old yeast was cleared away from the necks. I hated this job, it was never ending, and to make the time pass I would push a bottle down into the water, saying with it, 'Guggle! guggle! guggle! guggle!' Then shoving the wire brush into the neck of the bottle I would make a similar sound.

By the time I had finished washing the bottles my miming would almost result in lockjaw. Then all the necks had to be restrung in order to hold the corks. This chore was usually interrupted when I had to go for the beer, and sometimes I didn't finish until the following morning.

On the Saturday morning I nearly always had to go to the Jarrow store for the corn for the hens. The store was in Hope Street and I would lug a stone of wheat and boxings home. I would take the tram of course, but even with the tram it was an arm-breaking load, and all this because of the checks and the dividend. But of course this latter was no small thing, for at one time a Jarrow store was paying as much as half-a-crown in the pound.

Then I might have to clean the big steel fender, or do the kitchen window, or do the brasses, and if money wasn't plentiful I would have to go for the beer on a Saturday dinner time. If it was plentiful, Kate would just slip out, as she put it. But always after my dinner she would give me some coppers and I would away to The Crown. She knew how I valued this trip to The Crown and often during the week if I refused to do something or other she would threaten me with no Crown on Saturday.

'There'll be no Crown on Saturday mind you. I'm tellin' you, it'll be no use you askin'. There'll be no Crown on Saturday for you. And remember that, me lady.'

But always on Saturday I went to The Crown. Until this particular Saturday when I said to her, 'Can I have me clean pinny on, me Sunday pinny?'

She looked down on me, 'Don't you want to go to The Crown?'

She was actually asking me if I wanted to go to The Crown. This had never happened before.

I said, 'No, I want me clean pinny on.' And still looking down at me, she said quietly, 'You'd better go to The Crown, hinny.'

'I want me clean pinny on,' I insisted.

She said no more but gave me a clean pinny and a clean hair ribbon. I got a bucket of rain water – I always washed in rain water – gave myself a great wash, meticulously cleaned my nails, put on my clean pinny and my hair ribbon, and then made to go out of the kitchen door. But before I went over the step Kate's voice stopped me and I turned towards her. She was standing on the middle of the mat and there was a funny look on her face. She spoke to me quietly, words that I didn't really understand, enigmatic words. 'It's no use, you know, hinny. It's no use,' she said.

What was no use I didn't enquire but I went down the yard and I stood at the backyard door. And there I waited. I waited a long time, and presently my patience was rewarded. They came out of their backyard doors, around the top corner and around the bottom corner, all the girls who were going to the party.

One of the girls in Philipson Street was having a birthday

party. I hadn't been invited but I knew I would be. I knew I was going to that party because hadn't all my playmates been invited? There they were now, all going towards this particular backyard door. But the funny thing about it was that they all passed me without even looking the side I was on. I might have been a brick in the wall for all the notice they took of me. They had their best dresses on; some had pinnies over the dresses. They all wore nice hair ribbons, and each carried a little parcel.

When the last one had gone in I still hadn't moved, but when I thought I heard Kate's voice calling me I went swiftly down the back lane, keeping close to the wall, past the low lavatory hatches, past the higher coal hatches, until I came opposite this back door. And there I stood looking towards the upstairs window. And as I stared there came into my body a riot of feelings, anxiety, disappointment, urgency, all churning round a sort of breathless desire. I stood with my mouth open panting. I had to get into that party, it was imperative that I got into that party, because I had never been to a party except once when I was five when I went to a birthday party in Mrs Lodge's in Leam Lane. But I only remember that occasion because my Aunt Mary had put some pearl beads on me, her own beads and I had snapped them, and I got a spanking for my pains. We had parties, I have described them, but this party was different. It had been talked about for days, even weeks. There were going to be lovely cakes on the table, all kinds of lovely cakes, and then games and carry-on. I had to get into that party.

I knew what had happened. Mrs X had forgotten to ask me ... I knew it wasn't girls who picked who were coming to their parties, it was their ma's who said, 'You can have that one, and that one, and that one.' I knew I had only to attract Mrs X's attention and I would be in at that party.

I could see the outline of figures moving backwards and forwards behind the lace curtains so I set about attracting the attention of one of them. I jumped up and down, I did a lot of Ooh, ooh, oohing! because I knew that if any one saw me they would tell Mrs X and she would come to the window and say 'Aw, there's little Katie McMullen. Why, come on up, Katie. Fancy me forgetting about you. Come up, hinny.'

But my antics attracted no one to the window. The back

lane was empty. There was no one in the whole wide world for me to speak to. There descended on me a feeling of desolation, of aloneness, it wasn't to be borne. I ran across the back lane, pushed open the yard door, went up the stone steps to the staircase door and knocked.

At this point memory dims. I seem to see one figure after another coming to the top of the stairhead and looking down. Then the hostess herself came towards me. I can see her face now, round, flat-looking, full of self-importance. But she deigned to bend towards me as she whispered, 'You can't come up. Me ma says you can't.'

Perhaps I was foolish enough to ask 'Why?' I don't know but I do remember her next words.

'Well, me ma says you haven't got no da.'

Children need no preliminary lead-up to vital statements, they simply make them. I turned from her, closed the door quietly, went down the stone steps, out of the backyard, across the back lane and up our backyard. I was no longer alone in my aloneness, for with me now was a concrete thing, it was hard and painful and its name was rejection and it was to gather to itself as time went on, shame, anxiety, remorse, and bitterness.

I had been aware for some time that I had no da, but with the protective mechanism of childhood I had imagined that there was only me and our Kate and the girls who had first enlightened me on this point in the secret. But in this moment I was aware that everybody knew, the whole world knew. The back lane was no longer empty and desolate, it was full of people; the New Buildings were full of people, and they all knew about me having no da.

When I stepped into the kitchen I remember being surprised at seeing Kate still standing in the middle of the mat. It seemed she hadn't moved from that spot and yet I had been out of the kitchen for a long, long time, so much had happened since she had last spoken to me. Her face looked tight, her lips were pressed together and her chin looked knobbly and was moving in little jerks. Once again she spoke to me enigmatically, and now bitterly. 'Never you mind, lass,' she said, 'you'll see your day with them. By God, you will . . .'

It was after this incident that my aggressive tactics came more into evidence. I had bossed before, following the choosing of a da, but this was different. If I was with my playmates and any one of them dared object to a suggestion I had made I would stare them out, creating a silence. I became very good at creating this silence. And should it not work and bring my opponent to my way of thinking, then I would say what became famous words in the New Buildings, at least for a period, 'Aa feel like a fight.' This often had the desired effect and I got my own way. But at times I miscalculated my opponent and a fight would ensue. This was usually followed by a rat-tat-tat on the back door and some woman saying, 'Kate, ya'll hev ta do somethin' with her. Ya know what she's been an' gone and done? She's gone an' nearly wiped the lugs off wor Mary. Kate ya'll hev to do somethin' with her. Aa'm tellin' ya.'

And Kate did something with me, if she could catch me. 'Get into that bedroom there and wait!'

I remember the only man who came to the door, and he started by apologising. He said 'Noo, Kate, ya knaa me, Aa divn't like trouble, an' God knows Aa don't want to bring ya any more than ya've got, for ya've got plenty on your plate. But Kate ya knaa what she's gone and done? She's nearly drooned wor Billy. Why, lass, she not only pushed him in the slacks but the little bugger held him under. Kate, lass, Aa'm tellin' ya if it hadn't been for a bloke sittin' on top of the Jarrow tram where it was waitin' at the crossin' near Morgan's Hall an' he sees the whole thing and dashes doon the stairs. Why, Kate, wor Billy, would be up the gut at this minute . . . Ya'll hev to do somethin' with her, Kate, ya just will.'

On this occasion Kate certainly would have done something with me but I locked myself in the lavatory and all the hammering on the door would not make me unbolt it.

Apart from wanting me out of the lavatory to give me the skelping of my life, Kate also wanted me out because I was causing a great deal of inconvenience. We had a number of lodgers at the time and it happened to be dinner-time. At last me granda came down the yard, and there came a bang! bang! bang! on the door.

'Do 'ye hear me in there?'

I heard him all right. He could have been heard in Howdon. When I didn't reply he too became silent and nothing could be heard but his heavy breathing, until his voice, dropping into a coaxing wheedle, said, 'Katie, d'ya hear me? Come on out, come on out and take your medicine, there's a good lass. It'll soon be over, like salt on a sore.'

I came out and took my medicine and it was like salt on a sore.

With regards to me granda's reference to salt, whenever he had a cut, and sometimes he had very deep cuts on his hands, he packed them with salt. The agony must have been terrible but the cure was effective.

The end of my aggressive period came one day when I was playing at the bottom of the back lane with a number of the bigger girls. I must have been about twelve. I had proposed some game; I remember it was to do with a ball, and one of the girls didn't see eye to eye with me. Her name was Olive Swinburne. I stared at Olive but without effect. Then I said the famous words, 'Aa feel like a fight.'

And she came back with equally famous words. 'So do I. And take that! you've been asking for that for a long time.' Whereupon she gave me a terrific wallop on the ear and I landed on my back.

I can't recollect whether I was hurt or I cried but I do recollect the feeling of surprise. Olive Swinburne had done the trick. I know that I never afterwards lifted my hand to anybody.

But it was after I stopped fighting, at least outwardly, that I became more aware of the feeling of aloneness. And over the years this feeling grew, and created a section of life entirely its own and at times I would be sucked into this life, much against my will, for when there I would be confronted by another being, to whom I would talk and reason, for this being had a kind of cold aloofness I couldn't get at. It would not co-operate, it would not be comforted, it would not be drawn into the warmth of my real character for it was developing fast a life of it's own, an all-knowing desolate life, a negative life that told me there was nothing of any value, nothing worth striving for. As the years went on it began to answer back, saying, 'Why try to justify yourself? Where will education get you? Where will all your striving get you? In the end you'll be alone, as you were in the beginning, only more so.'

In my teens when these moods would overtake me Kate would ask, 'What's the matter, hinny?'

114

'Oh!' I'd say, 'I've got the blues.'

'Aw, lass, I know what that feeling's like, I've had me share. Come on, cheer up.'

Kate did not know what my particular feeling was like. Whatever she had had her share of, it wasn't the shame of having no da.

CHAPTER EIGHT

Towards the end of the War beer and spirits were very scarce, but I could get a certain amount of beer if I queued, especially at the outdoor beer shop in Brinkburn Street, near Stanhope Road. But with spirits it was a different thing, you nearly always had to know somebody if you wanted to get any.

Kate was at this time working for a publican in Jarrow, somewhere near Palmer's shipyard, and as women who were willing to work for three and sixpence a day were all too scarce, the publican and his wife were grateful and Kate would get her drop when she was there, and when she wasn't and had enough money she would send me up to this particular public house. The sickly dread of these journeys remains with me to this moment. And I used to pray over and over again as I sat in the Jarrow tram, 'Oh, Holy Mother, let them be run out. Dear Sacred Heart of Jesus, I implore the grace to love thee more and more ... an' will you not let there be any stuff for her. Lamb of God, who takest away the sins of the world, hear my prayer.' On and on it would go, and when I reached the public house I would stand in the passage and make one final plea to the Holy family. 'Blessed Mary, ever virgin, Saint Joseph and the Infant Child. Please, please let them be run out.'

On this particular day I was carrying a letter for the publican's wife, and when I handed it over there was a bit of confab between her and her husband, then what must have been a half bottle of whisky was wrapped up. As I watched this I felt all the blood draining from my body, I wanted to be sick. I don't know what followed next but I remember hearing myself imploring them not to give it to me, to say they were sold out. And I remember the man and woman sitting side by side in front of me, looking at me with the most strange expression on their faces, and the man taking my hand and saying, 'Don't worry any more. Your ma'll never get another drop of whisky in this house. We promise you, God's honour.'

The woman stroked my hair and kept saying, 'Dear God, Dear God.' Then she wrote a note and gave it me and I went back home filled with a mixture of relief and fear. Would our Kate find out what I had done? I didn't know, but I didn't think so because I trusted that man and woman.

Kate couldn't have found anything out for she didn't go for me, not even the next week when I learned she had lost her job at this particular public house.

I knew that I was pitied and Kate must have felt this also and her protest took the form of a mad extravagance. She bought a piano. We were in debt with rent, we were in debt to the shop, we pawned every week, but she bought a piano – one hundred pound piano!

At this time you could get a second-hand piano for as little as a pound or two, but she was having no second-hand piano, she was having the best, and the best of the best at that. She was going to give me a chance that she had never had. She did not think that this mad gesture was merely to show the neighbours, and her sister in particular, that she was as good as any of them, better than most.

How she got the reference to get a hundred pounds worth of credit remains a mystery to me to this day. As also does the source of the five pounds she had to put down. I just don't know where the five pounds could have come from. The only thing I am positive of is that it wasn't through selling her virtue. So there we were, in Sunderland buying of all the things on God's earth a hundred pound piano.

It was a thing of beauty in rosewood, and it stood in the front room where the great big chest-of-drawers had been. These were now wedged in the corner. There a stool with the piano and I could just squeeze on to this, for it was pressed, of necessity, against the back of the couch. The lino on the floor at this side of the room was worn away with scrubbing but you couldn't see it very much because of the closely packed furniture, and yet mind, every piece of this furniture was moved once a week so that the floor could be scrubbed; that is, all except the piano.

It was Bob of the pawnshop of all people, whose daughter went to Mrs Dalton's in Hudson Street for piano lessons, who recommended me also to go to her. What Bob must have thought of me taking piano lessons and still paying him my weekly, even twice weekly visits I don't know. Perhaps Bob saw so much of the odd side of life that he wasn't surprised at anything. I do indeed remember that man with affection.

As with everything else, except talking, I was slow at the piano, but when I look back I can see it was fear and fear alone that paralysed my learning. With the piano as in school, it was fear: fear of our Kate not being able to keep up the payments, and greater fear of her not being able to pay the twelve and sixpence a quarter for my music lessons to Mrs Dalton.

The first quarter was paid in two payments, the second quarter was paid in dribbles and drabs, the third quarter could not be met. I was in the fourth quarter and practising for my first examination when Mrs Dalton pressed home the need for payment. She was a big boned woman was Mrs Dalton and also slightly terrifying to me at that time, but she was a fine teacher and harassed by the education of three sons. I was very conscious of the eldest son, and he was sometimes sent in to supervise lessons. To me he was a being apart for he went to college and was swanky. But even weighed down with awe of him I didn't like him, and it was the thought of him knowing that my lessons weren't paid for which further paralysed my fingers.

Then the shame was transferred into a burning, head bowing misery, for our Kate decided to pay off the lessons in pies and peas, which we were selling at the time.

The Dalton boys came up the long road to East Jarrow with cans and took away with them the equivalent of a lesson. Sometimes they would pass me carrying the grey hen. The irony of it.

Under such conditions how could I practise? How could I learn? I exasperated Mrs Dalton beyond measure. The examination was looming up and one night she pushed me off my seat, out of the door, and threw my music at me.

She was in bed ill the day the examiner came and she kept me until the last and she talked to me until it was my turn. There were twelve of us, the others were all going in for the second year examination. I was the only one taking the preliminary.

It was my turn. I went in, looked at the man and liked him

right away, and he liked me, for he patted me on the head and said, 'You're very small, the smallest of them all . . . begin.'

When he walked to the window I turned my head and asked, 'Aren't you coming to watch me?'

He looked at me over his shoulder and smiled as he said, 'I'll be watching you. Go on.'

I went on. The last bar of my main piece I played backwards. I knew I had done so and he knew I had done so. After I had finished he didn't send me out of the room but talked to me; at least I talked to him. I found talking to people I liked very easy and I liked this man. I stayed in the room so long that when at last I went into Mrs Dalton's bedroom she gasped out, 'What on earth happened?'

I looked at her quietly, 'I played the last bar backwards, Mrs Dalton.'

She closed her eyes and said, 'That's finished you.'

Some time later, on a Monday morning, there came a long envelope that aroused not the slightest interest in me although inside was a certificate to say I had passed the examination with honours. I had achieved a hundred and thirty one marks.

I was in the front room standing opposite the fireplace, the sun was shining through the window, streaming on to the rosewood piano, showing up its beauty and in stark comparison the drabness of the room and all it held. I didn't care. I didn't care about anything, I was taking no more lessons. The piano was going back.

It went back on the Wednesday afternoon. Kate had passed the word round that she was selling it. This I am sure deceived nobody. When I heard the van come I hurried down the yard and into the lavatory, and there I sat with my head bowed and my hands as usual pressed tightly between my knees, telling myself over and over again it didn't matter, it didn't matter. Because now there would be no more worry about the payments, or Mrs Dalton's twelve and sixpence a quarter, and Kate had said we would get a hornless gramophone, there was one going in Bob's.

There was still nearly a pound owing to Mrs Dalton; this included the examination fee. And it was twenty-seven years later when, the breakdown spewing up the torments of the past,

I remembered that debt and I settled the bill. It must have been one of the surprises of Mrs Dalton's life.

I think it was after the loss of the piano I went in for words. I would get an idea from a word and this would lead to a story, and I would tell it to myself on my trips down to the docks with the grey hen, and making it up helped to pass the time away.

When did I start following the coal carts? I don't know but I do know I was still following them when I was twelve or more. The carts used to come from the gas works in Jarrow. They were high carts driven by horses and filled to the top with large lumps of coke.

Near Morgan's Hall was a double stretch of tram lines and the down tram had always to wait there until the up tram passed. Then they both went their separate ways on the single lines, one into Jarrow and one into Tyne Dock. It was at places such as these where the cart wheels wobbled over the points that the loose pieces of coke rolled on to the road. And it was at the crossing at Morgan's Hall that I first started picking up the coke in my pinny, and when I ran into the kitchen with it Kate, not knowing whether to be vexed at the condition of my pinny or pleased with the addition of some fuel, would say, 'Oh, dear me! is it worth it?'

But when I started to take a sack to gather the coke she did consider it worth it. But never once did she send me out to pick up coke. At first it was no disgrace just picking the coke from the road between the bottom of the street and Morgan's Hall. It was the beachcomber instinct again working, and perhaps the feeling for the elemental need of life, warmth, that drove me to go further afield and follow the coke carts. The journeys behind the carts became longer with the years. I would meet them at Bogey Hill and follow them to Tyne Dock, but only once did I go past the Docks, for I became filled with as much shame as if I had been to the pawn.

I did not look at people when I was out gathering coke, I would be walking behind the carts and when they suddenly came into view I would pretend not to see them. It was the old illusion that if I couldn't see them they couldn't see me.

Some of the coarser types expressed their thoughts verbally by saying, 'It's a bloody shame the things that bairn's got to do.'

120

And it was a bloody shame that I had to go for the beer every day and go to the pawn. I thought so too; but not that I had to go on the slacks, or gather coke, because these were of my own choosing. But I remember the day I decided I would no longer follow the coke carts; it was on the day that I also decided that I would drink no more beer.

I had followed the coke cart from the tram sheds to Tyne Dock and kept my head turned away from a number of people and must have come to a decision, because that night in the kitchen when me granda, pointing to the glowing coke, said, 'Best sight in the world, isn't it, lass? Here, have a drink of that,' I shook my head, and rising from the old leather chair in the corner where I had been sitting reading by the light of the naked gas mantle, I looked from him to Kate and said, 'I'm goin' for no more coke an' I want no more drinks of beer.'

What it was caused me to make this double decision I don't know; perhaps the pitying glances of the neighbours. Perhaps this was really the beginning of telling myself that I was different, that I was cut out for something other than the life that I saw about me. Whatever caused me to come to this decision I had no sooner made up my mind than I told them, and doubtless flabbergasted them.

It must have been before this time too that I went picking cinders. But I remember that it was during the time that Kate was making cakes to sell.

I was all for our Kate making cakes to sell because it gave us a kind of prestige, it was like having a business. She remembered all she had learnt in the baker's shop in Chester-le-Street, so she made one basic mixture out of which she could bake half-a-dozen different kinds of cake. There were two or three people selling cakes in the New Buildings at the time, and wanting to outdo them she resorted to a little trick of the trade that needed very careful handling. This was the addition of ammonia to a batch of mixture. It swelled the cakes to twice their normal size. I remember arguing with her and telling her there was a funny taste about the cakes and that people would detect the odd smell. But she wouldn't believe me – she never ate any of her own cakes. The end of the ammonia trick came one day when she overstepped the dose and the batch nearly knocked her out when she opened the oven door. When she got over the shock we laughed as we hadn't laughed together before; we laughed until the tears rained down our faces.

But it was at this period that I went on the tip. There was a coal strike on and you couldn't get fuel for love or money. So, always resourceful, I said I would go on to the tip behind the tram sheds and pick some cinders.

Now nobody from the New Buildings had ever been known to go picking behind the tram sheds where only the very poor and the rabble went. But I would get up early in the morning and take a sack and a rake with me and scrape among the refuse for cinders, because I would have done anything to make Kate happy and keep her happy as long as she wasn't on the bottle. And this was one of the times when she was going very steady. Having the daily beer of course – that didn't count with me – and only a glass of hard at the week-ends, which was really nothing to worry about.

She didn't want me to go picking, it was very lowering, yet at the same time she was pleased with me for doing it because it enabled her to bake when the others couldn't, and she was kind to me and I was happy.

Me granda would come and help me down with the sacks but he wouldn't demean himself to pick on the tip. He had never sunk that low in his life and he wasn't going to do that now. He didn't express this in words but I knew how he felt about cinder picking.

It was Kate's cooking that attracted so many relations to the house at the week-ends I'm sure. We used to have more visitors than any other house in the street. All the Hogan children at different times – these were the family of me grandma's elder sister Lizzie, there were thirteen of them – then there were the various offshoots of me granda's side from Jarrow. Young people were always hungry and they were sure of a shive of stotty-cake – my name for oven-bottom bread. This was a large flat piece of dough baked on the iron shelf in the oven, and what could be better, especially on a winter's day than a shive of oven-bottom cake split in two and laden with dripping. No one ever went out of that kitchen empty-handed, which, as I look back, seems remarkable.

Later in my early teens, perhaps it was I that drew them, especially the lads. Hardly a week-end passed but Jackie Potts –

the stepson of me granda's nephew – and his pals would come in on a Saturday night. And me granda liked this; he enjoyed heartily the back-chat and talk. He was at this time a different John McMullen, tolerant, mellow, and behind his gruff front very proud of me.

I was to have many lads in my teens, and I made a point of bringing them home, always making sure that our Kate was all right. Of course I hadn't any power over people dropping in and Jackie saw her lively at times. Some years later when, resplendent in his Merchant Navy Officer's uniform and in company with a friend so dressed, he pretended he did not see her in the tram, she was very cut up about it for she had been kind to him from when he was a boy. Although I too, when I heard this, was vexed for her, I understood Jackie's side of it, for how many, many times had I wanted to disown her.

The house was always clean, and although not as well furnished as some in our community it was better than the homes from which my beaux came, for they were all of big families, and with one exception none of them looked down his nose at me granda or our Kate. The exception was the one I really fell for. As I had ideas about gentlemen, he also had ideas about ladies, and after having my company for two years he decided I hadn't sufficient background or education to fit into his picture on the wall, so he threw me over for someone he thought more qualified for the glorified position of his wife.

Part Two

THE SHORT TEENS

CHAPTER NINE

I was thirteen at the time I had the accident. I was playing with a girl who had a deformed arm which had more strength in it than any ordinary arm. She was another Katie. Over one section of the school yard there was either concrete or tarmacadam that had a rough edge, and Katie, catching up with me, gave me a dig and I fell on my left side on this edge, and that was the beginning of the trouble. This happened on a Friday afternoon at playtime; on the Saturday morning I said to Kate, 'I've got a pain in me leg,' to which she answered, 'You've always got a pain somewhere.'

The tiredness that I was always complaining about, and the pains in my arms and legs, were put down to growing pains, for now I was sprouting up. For days I would feel no pain in my hip at all, at others I was limping badly with the pain. Now in relating what follows Kate might appear to have acted with utter callousness, but I've got to stress the fact here that she had had years of my acting and doing anything in order to get off school to keep clear of Miss Corfield, also getting up to various ruses to get out of carrying the grey hen. And so when I would say my leg was paining and would limp to illustrate it, she would say, 'I know all about it, hoppy-on the-Don.' This was a name that had been given to some cripple who had spent a lot of his time sitting on the Don bridge where the murky river flowed round the foot of St Paul's church in Jarrow.

Sometimes when I would ask if I could go out to play she would look at me and say, 'Isn't your leg bad?' And when I would answer, 'No', she would come back with, 'There, what did I tell you? You'll have something one of these days that'll stop you making game.'

My trips with the grey hen to the docks became excruciating excursions, and I remember one Saturday dinner-time very clearly. I took the tram from the bottom of the street and got off at the dock gates but I couldn't carry the grey hen up the bank to the outdoor beer shop in Hudson Street, so I asked a paper boy if he would go and get me the beer and I gave him the jar and a pound note and then stood leaning against the iron railings sweating with fear in case he didn't come back. A pound note was a lot of money. But he did come back and I gave him a penny.

On the Sunday it began to snow, and when Kate got me up for school on the Monday morning I started to cry. The kitchen was cold, I was cold all over. 'I'm sick, our Kate,' I said, 'I've got a pain in me leg.'

'You're going to school, legs or no legs,' she said.

It took me a long time to get to school and when I entered the warmth of the class room, an hour late, I collapsed. Miss Harrington sent for Kate and I was taken to the Doctor's across the road from the school, and the Doctor said I mustn't use the leg, I must rest.

Mr Weir, the Scot from up the street, was passing at the time and he gave me a piggy-back from the tram into the kitchen and laid me on the saddle, and this started my long acquaintance with the wooden couch. I felt better that afternoon after lying down, and towards tea-time I sat up and had a game of cards with the lodger. I have forgotten his name but I remember he always let me win, and as we played a ha'penny a game my bank account was rising steadily. Kate used to chastise him about this but he would say 'I'm not letting her, she's a clever lass, she's beatin' me as she'll beat everything that hits her.'

Then an odd thing happened. The man and the cards disappeared. The kitchen disappeared and I began to see funny things. Funny things like the ladies and the gentlemen in my picture on the wall, but now they were moving about and the horses were galloping and I saw a pony and trap coming right through the kitchen. I remembered this pony and trap – I had seen it before outside the house where I was born and our Kate was in it – her master and mistress had given her a ride home one Sunday – but there it was, this horse and trap in the kitchen. And there also in the kitchen was the man who stood at the top of the stairs and helped to throw me down; and there was the Devil, and Miss Corfield, and the Irishman who had been going to marry our Kate; these three were together and they were talking, talking, talking.

Their talking woke me up and I heard a voice saying, 'What time is it?' and another replying, 'Just on two.' And then the voice of me granda breaking as he said, 'If she lasts over three she'll pull through.' And it came as a surprise to me that it was in the middle of the night and everybody was up and that my Aunt Mary and Uncle Alec were in the kitchen. I remember Kate bending over me, and the waft of whisky from her breath brought me into full consciousness. I can feel my lids lifting heavily as I looked at her, and then I turned my face away.

When I next awoke it was still dark and the pain in my leg was dreadful, so bad that I cried out with it. There was no light on in the kitchen and I was shivering. Then Kate came out of the bedroom, her eyes bleary with sleep, and ordered me to stop making that row.

Now it was this particular memory of her going for me in the early morning that stuck in my mind for years and caused a festering resentment. I had not taken into account that they all had likely been up until after three o'clock and my cries had dragged her from a much needed rest. Also Kate was not at her best in the mornings, especially after she had taken spirits. But such is the human mind that years later I couldn't recollect one of the many kindnesses she had shown me, but only how she had used me, and in particular, the dark painful morning when she had gone for me.

Later on that day when I woke up to see a black moon hanging above my face I thought it was one of the funny things I had been seeing on the previous evening, but it spoke, a black hand came up and touched my cheek, and a nice voice said, 'We're going to put you right.' And it was this black doctor that time – he put me on to boards and there I lay in the back bedroom for a long time. How long I can't recollect, and with one clear exception I can only recall isolated instances of my sojourn in the bedroom, such as seeing a patch of sky between the rain barrel and the hen cree. The big rain barrel almost blocked out all the light from the lower half of the bedroom window.

I have the feeling of a Saturday afternoon when I heard the fruit man calling in the back lane, and then Kate bringing me a large bunch of white grapes, and my thinking, oh, they're fresh from the tree because the sawdust's still on them. And another Saturday night when there were visitors in the kitchen and I heard Kate saying quietly, 'The sinews were almost gone, she could have lost it. A boy in the docks had the same thing and they took his leg off in the Royal at Newcastle.' And the day when the gas man came and emptied the meter, and Kate came into the bedroom, her joined palms full of coppers, 'Look,' she said, 'discount. I hadn't a penny. I didn't know where to turn. God's good, by He is that. If the fishman comes would you like a kipper?'

The clear exception concerns Miss Corfield. All during my stay in the bedroom I prayed daily that she would die. I prayed very earnestly for this after the fashion of, 'Make her die, sweet Mother Mary. Or if you can't see your way clear to do that, then keep me leg bad so's I won't have to go back to school. Name of the Father an' of the Son an' of the Holy Ghost. Amen.' I used the phraseology of the kitchen when praying, and once again I was shown the efficacy of prayer, for Kate came into the bedroom one day and said, 'Miss Corfield's dead.'

I was sick, no pretence this time, and now I prayed frantically to get well so that I could go to confession.

Would this be the time when the mission was on and I went to confession and the missioner said, 'It's a wonder you're not in Hell's flames burning', and sent me staggering out of the box in terror? It could have been. I became a very good Catholic after that mission. But I had nightmares again about Hell.

Miss Corfield died of cancer but I didn't find this out for some years.

Sometimes I imagine me grandma was alive at the time I was lying in the bedroom for I seem to recollect her helping to lift me. But she couldn't have been alive. It must have been my need of her and her presence still strong in the house that made me imagine this.

Then came the day I stood on my two feet alone; I can see myself limping out of the bedroom and leaning for support on the white scrubbed kitchen table and looking through the window down the length of the yard. The yard door was open and I could see into the back lane, and there passing was Florrie Harding and Janie Robson and as I watched them I said to myself, 'I'll never play with them again.' I did not know childhood had left me, but I remember saying to myself 'What are you going to do?' and that this question was accompanied by an odd feeling in my chest. It was a mixture of many feelings, the feeling that I had when I went to the pawn, and when I carried the grey hen; the feeling I had when I humped the coke sack on my back; the feeling I had when I passed some of the other girls on the road with their nice clothes on while I was wearing an old costume coat of Kate's that reached to my knees and bulged out like a balloon from my hips – the feeling I had of being different. But on this day, to the mixture of emotions was added a very definite feeling of worry and anxiety about my future, and I answered the question, saying, 'Well, I can only do two things, I can write and I can do housework.' But even at that age I knew I couldn't earn my living by writing. There was no lack of ideas or even complete stories, the impediment was the mere matter of grammar and spelling. I should do something about it.

Perhaps it was with the idea of doing something about it that I picked up a knife from the table and began to sharpen a pencil, only to hear Kate yell at me, 'Do you know what day it is? Sharpening a pencil on a Friday!'

I lived with superstitions from my earliest recollection so they became natural to me for never a day passed without hearing Kate saying, 'Uncross those knives, there's enough trouble in the house.' If later in the day there would be a row she would say, 'I knew it was coming, those knives.' And should she, perhaps the very next day, see the knives crossed again when I was washing up she would cry, 'What have I told you? You know what happened yesterday.'

As for cutting your nails on a Friday she would have sooner

thought of jumping off the dock wall into the river. I remember being so bemused by the beauty of my nails that unthinking I took the scissors to them one Friday; I had just cut into the thumb nail when the scissors went flying across the kitchen. Was I mad cutting my nails on a Friday! What was I asking for? And when I came to think about this I knew I must be stark staring mad to tempt fate with scissors on a Friday.

The word pig was another superstition. When Kate referred to a pig she said grunter, or made a dramatic gesture of turning both her thumbs downwards. This was very often followed with the explanation that in Maryport the men wouldn't put out to sea if someone used the word pig in their presence.

As for walking under a ladder this was really asking for it, wasn't it?

Yes, yes it was. Yes, I saw that terrible things could happen by walking under ladders. Cutting your nails on a Friday, crossing knives, saying pig, not to mention when a picture dropped from the wall and you waited day-in, day-out for someone to die. It might be six months later when some aged person in the street came to their natural end, but hadn't there been a warning of it. 'You remember when that picture dropped?' The evidence of a picture dropping could be the two dark frayed ends of string, but this would be entirely ignored for a picture falling meant certain death. I have known Kate coddle me granda with hot whisky and extra care after a picture fell. In her place I think I would have accepted fate thankfully but there was a deep forgiving goodness in Kate, she could forgive and forget.

The same significance was applied to the cricket on the hearth. We'd all be in the kitchen when Kate would exclaim 'Listen'. Everybody would stop what they were doing and listen to the cheep, cheep, cheep, of the death beetle as it was called, coming from somewhere under the hearthstone. If they had known at the time this noise was caused by an insect rubbing its legs together they would have said, I'm sure, that it had been bidden to do just that to act as a warning. So again they would wait for a death, and a death there would be sooner or later. I cannot remember what explanation was given when the ticking went on after the death.

In connection with deaths naturally came funerals and in the

New Buildings when there was a funeral there was always a gathering for a wreath. I was quite young when I knew that this business of gathering for wreaths annoyed me. Sometimes as much as two pounds would be gathered in a door-to-door collection. Two pounds was a lot of money in those days but every penny was spent on floral tributes, when perhaps the widow did not know where her next penny was coming from. There were a number of people in the New Buildings who I knew would have preferred the money to a floral tribute. The stupidity of this practice did not occur to those kind people who went gathering and had something to say about those who would not, or could not, contribute.

But to return to my question 'What am I going to do?' The answer of course was, 'You'll have to go into service.'

Kate had sworn that I wasn't going into service, whatever else she let me do she wasn't going to let me go into service. But I seemed to fall into service quite accidentally. I made friends with a girl who was a daily at a house on the terrace. Although the head of the house was only a foreman-carpenter in the docks their prestige was high because of his wife's association with the mayoress of Jarrow. I think they were sisters. Anyway this family had nothing, and I mean nothing, to do with the other inhabitants of the New Buildings. They were considered very swanky. Some evenings I would go and wait for this girl and Mrs Jobson would ask me into the kitchen. I was very taken with the house and the nice little kitchen which was kept for kitchen uses only. They had a separate dining room, and a sitting room. Well, my friend offended her mistress in some way and when Mrs Jobson asked if I would mind helping out I was only too glad to do so.

There were three sons in the household, all working, and the eldest I liked very much, as only a very young girl can like. I knew he liked me and at fourteen I was ready to fall on his neck. But he was an honourable man and being much older he didn't allow any such thing to happen. He waited until I was eighteen, but it was too late then, for I fancied I had the world of lads grovelling at my feet. And when many years later I thought that I might be able to recapture that girlish passion I found that it was much too late.

There were six rooms in the house, all packed with furniture, two passages, a staircase, a back yard, and a front to clean besides preparing the meals and doing part of the washing. I got ten shillings a week less my stamp. I worked from eight until six each day and for a time was so happy there that I even went back at night and cooked big pans of chips for the men.

But before long I found that I didn't like service, and I feared that if I continued in my post there would soon be a mix-up as to who was the mistress and who was the maid. I dared to fancy that I wasn't made for taking orders or working after other people. As some people in the New Buildings put it: 'She's got ideas about herself has that one,' and as Mrs Waller added, 'She'll end up the same as big Kate.'

I happened to know a girl at the church whose father had been a sea captain, I think their name was Cooper. Kate was very flattered that this girl should want to be friends with me.

The girl and her brother were at boarding school and during the vacation she gave lessons in pen painting and book-keeping at a shilling a lesson. Funds were very low at the time so I asked her if I could have half a lesson for sixpence and she agreed, and as soon as I took the pen in my hand, lifted up a dab of paint and applied it to the pattern on the handkerchief sachet I knew that I could do this kind of thing, and do it right away. And that's just what I did, and on that sixpenny lesson I started a business. Nearly everything was bought by clubs in the North, so why shouldn't they buy painted cushions and tray cloths, and mantel borders on clubs? Why not? They made lovely presents, and to have a hand-painted cushion reclining point upwards in the armchair in the sitting room was a hallmark of refinement. So I went round canvassing and I got my first twenty customers. They paid a shilling a week, which entitled them to two small black satin cushion covers or one large one.

Now began two years of real hard work which was eased by the oil of refinement. Everybody in the house was happy for a time. Kate was glowing. I wasn't in service, I was earning my living at 'art' of all things, and me granda's pride was oozing out of him. I think it was their attitude towards my grand job that gave me the courage to put my foot down firmly at last on the carrying of the grey hen. I'd still had to go for the beer all the time I had been in service but now I felt the grey hen was outside the aura of this elevated Katie McMullen who was earning her living by painting.

Earning my living! I would sit from early morning until late at night, my nose only a few inches from the pen, and I would paint in the transfers of baskets of lilac, irises, daffodils, or gilt cornucopias of fruit. And on the mantel borders, nearly always two peacocks, their nebs meeting and their tails trailing towards the end of the material. And did I work! And how much did I earn? Even in the best of weeks I never cleared more than nine and sixpence profit. I was working much longer hours than when I was in service but as Kate pointed out, 'You're your own boss, hinny, an' you're not dirtying your hands.'

No, I wasn't dirtying me hands, I was only filling me belly with white lead and slowly poisoning myself, but I wasn't dirtying me hands.

I had a friend at this period called Lily Maguire. She was my first real friend and I was very fond of her, as I was of her mother. They lived up in White Leas about three miles from us, and of an evening I would go up to see Lily, and we would talk and laugh, and when we became the proud possessors of bikes we rode miles and for a few hours the world was good and everybody in it was happy.

I used to like going up to the Maguires' house. Mrs Maguire was one of those hard-working, patient women that sustained the mining communities. On my visits Mr Maguire was nearly always washing himself in the tin bath in front of the fire. He was a little man with a big voice who always gave me a loud welcome. And I remember Lily and me standing under the arches one night exchanging our troubles. She herself was seventeen and she was upset, even horrified that her mother was going to have yet another baby. My worries were of a different nature, I was upset because every decent thing I had found its way to Bob's. I can remember saying, 'I can't put up with it much longer, Lily, I'm ashamed to the core, I have no things. As soon as I get them they go.' But when we parted I was filled with regret for having given our Kate away, because Lily, like everyone else, liked Kate, and it was the very first time I had ever said a word against her to anyone.

I lost touch with Lily nearly thirty years ago and tried to

contact her for a long time but succeeded only a few years ago. In her first letter to me she asked if I remembered us walking through the fields, and me saying to her that I would probably marry a rich gentleman and live in a big house, and that she would marry a miner. It must have been said as a joke, but a poor one, but she did marry a miner, and a very nice fellow I remember; as for me marrying a rich man, schoolmasters will never pay surtax, but I did marry a gentleman. She also said that when she heard that I had brought Kate to Hastings she shook her head, saying, 'Poor Kitty. How foolish, she is taking her troubles wherever she goes. She should have learnt by now.'

I was fighting with Kate a lot these days and sometimes me granda would take her part. I didn't mind this in the least; I had realised early on that they could both go for me but that whatever happened they hadn't to go for each other because they had to live together. Come what may, they were tied together for life, and for Kate there were no compensations.

Kate never lifted her hand to me now. She hadn't from the day I hit her back. I can see now that at this particular time she was in a highly nervous state. It was a Saturday dinner-time. She was making a rush dinner of some kind, frying something on the fire. And she had told me to dust the kitchen and get it finished before dinner – all household chores had to be finished before Saturday dinner-time – I had finished the dusting when she said, 'You've never dusted the bottom of the machine.' The Box sewing machine had given place to a Singer's treadle sewing machine and the iron sides formed a sort of lattice work into which you had to poke your fingers to clear the dust.

'I've done it,' I said.

'Get down on your knees and get that properly dusted,' she commanded.

'I'll not. I've done it once and I'm not going to do it again.'

She raised her hand to give me the familiar clout across the ear. I was no longer sent into the bedroom and told to wait, but this raised hand, this hitting of me on the head filled me both with fear of the descending blow and angry resentment at having to endure it. As I saw the hand coming at me I cried, 'If you hit me again I'll hit you back!' There was a stunned silence. Then her hand came down on me but without force, whereupon I retaliated swiftly. And swifter still, me granda cried,

'My God! we've come to somethin' now when you're hittin' your mother. What's come over you?'

Both Kate and I turned simultaneously on him, both denying that I had struck her. But as in the case of me being brought to my senses by Olive Swinburne's blow so Kate never lifted her hand to me again, at least not until I was twenty-seven, and then she didn't know what she was doing.

I had been painting for about a year when David McDermott came off a long voyage. I hated the thought of him coming into the family, yet I had nothing against him, he was a quiet, absolutely unassuming man, and good-natured to the point of fault.

It fell to me to make the arrangements for the marriage. I had to go down to the registry office in Shields and give the names in. And then one Saturday morning, bowed down with a nameless shame and the feeling of betrayal, I accompanied them to their wedding. What followed was cold, soulless, drab. I can't see the scene, but I can recall the feeling, and it was from this day that the longing to find my father became active in me.

When with delicate tact I said I would like to go to Birtley on my bike for the week-end there were no obstacles put in my way and so I left them to themselves. I say to themselves for there was me granda still lording it over his domain, even if in a somewhat subdued fashion. And he had taken on a kind of halo for allowing the marriage to take place at all – I doubt, but for the fact that Davie went to sea for long periods, whether he would have sanctioned the alliance without a fight of some kind. But Davie, being a quiet man, let the fathar have all the saying.

With Davie at sea and Kate drawing the enormous half-pay note of two pounds eighteen a month we settled down into our old way of life, but unrest was deep within me and I would relieve this feeling with spurts of writing.

I was very religious at this time. I would never miss Mass and Benediction on a Sunday, or think of going to the pictures unless I first paid a visit to the Holy Family. So I suppose it was understandable that I should now write a story about Christ coming down in the form of a man and living in a tenement. I called the story 'On the Second Floor'. Years later when I read 'The Passing of the Third Floor Back', I realised that everything has been done before. All our ideas have been thought up before and will be thought up again and again. Nothing is new. But having finished this story and shed bucketsful of tears on to the pages I called in at the little Post Office on my way to White Leas, and Lily's, and asked the man how much it would cost to have it printed – I didn't know anything in those days about typing – and he said,

'How many words are there?'

'Sixteen thousand five hundred and twenty,' I replied accurately. I had counted every one.

'Oh, well, hinny, I think you'd have to pay something in the region of ninepence a thousand to have it typed and if you want a copy it'll be a bit more.'

Ninepence a thousand! Sixteen ninepences. Good lord! I could never rise to that. On I went to White Leas and spilled out my tale of woe. Then Lily saved the day.

'Our Maisie's a good printer,' she said.

Maisie was the clever one, she had got to the High School.

'Would you print my story for me, Maisie?' I asked.

Yes, Maisie said, she'd do it at nights.

So there and then we came to a business arrangement. Maisie was to hand-print my story and on completion I was to pay her the sum of half-a-crown.

After many many months I got my story and poor, poor Maisie got her half-a-crown. Sweated labour, indeed.

At last, at last I was able to parcel my story up and send it to the Editor of the Shields Daily Gazette, who had been waiting for just such a story.

The Gazette had an office on the Dock Bank. I sent it on a Wednesday morning, they received it on the Thursday, and I had it back by the Friday morning. I felt that they must have thrown it at the postman without even looking at it. I was wrong. It was when I had had my fourth novel published that I received a letter from a retired reporter. He had started with the Shields Daily Gazette, which was a penny daily, and he remembered the day my story arrived at the office, and he explained to me the scene. The assistant Editor came tearing out of his room with this bundle in his hand, saying, 'Some so-and-so, so-and-so, so-and-so fool has sent a sixteen thousand word story to a penny daily, can you beat it? Chuck it back.'

When I went silently into the kitchen with my returned – hand-printed – manuscript, me granda said, 'Well, don't you let it get you down, hinny. They're nowt but a lot of soapy sods. You can tell that by the stuff they stick in the paper. Dosey buggers the lot of them.'

This from the man who couldn't read. He comforted me finally by saying, 'They haven't got the brains of Betty.' Betty was a pet hen. She was twelve years old, she had rheumatics and couldn't walk but could still lay eggs. When she died he couldn't eat her, but he wasn't going to lose on her so he sold her to one of the Arab boarding-house keepers in Costerfine Town.

So the irritations mounted and mounted at this time until one night I had a big row with Kate. I don't remember what it was about, but I do remember that me granda took her part, and I was thankful for this. I said to them both, 'I'm finished, I'm getting out.'

I was near the end of a club and had no desire to renew my clients, in fact I felt very tired. There was a great weariness on me and when it came about that I couldn't even talk back to Kate she took me to Doctor McHaffie and the verdict was I must give up pen painting immediately because the white lead was poisoning me. His words were, 'You'd better give it up if you don't want to go up.' Also he said I was very anaemic. Anaemic? That meant not having plenty of blood. Kate couldn't understand this. Why, look at the big shives of meat she got every week. Look at the cabbage and vegetables she cooked; the broth she made, and didn't I have fresh eggs when nobody else had eggs? Yes, I suppose in a way this was all true. The food was there if I wanted it. But I hated brisket. The unending monotony of roast brisket every Sunday, cold brisket every Monday, hashed stews or panhackelty on the Tuesday and cabbage always beaten up with the fat from the meat, or dripping; and meat puddings, never ending. Whereas I always had plenty of home-made bread I never had fresh milk more than a half-a-dozen times until I went into Harton Institution in my late teens. Condensed milk was the order of the day, straight out of the tin during a week-day but put into a glass container for Saturday and Sunday.

Feeling too ill to attack the painting and finish the few articles due to the club-holders I returned the money they had paid in. This left me absolutely penniless, but I was determined I was going to make a break. There was nothing else for it but place again. I wasn't speaking to Kate after yet another row, so I went up to Mrs Maguire early one morning, and I asked her for the loan of a shilling. It was the first money I ever borrowed for myself. I wanted the shilling to go to the registry office to put my name down for a place.

The woman in the registry said to me, 'I think I've got something that'll suit you straightaway. Would you mind looking after a little boy?'

I didn't care much for looking after children but I said, 'Not at all.'

'Well, this lady is going to travel and she wants a nice girl to look after her little boy. He is only four. It's a grand chance for the right person, it could lead to anything.'

Away I went to Westoe. I saw this lady and we took to each other on the spot. She was going to Italy. My sole duty would be to look after the child. She didn't want a trained nurse but someone nice who would be a sort of companion to him, someone still young enough not to have forgotten how to play, but old enough to have sense. She thought I would fill the bill in both requirements.

I was floating on air down the staircase when I suddenly thought of Our Lady and said a little prayer of thanksgiving, and so sincere was this prayer that the essence must have been conveyed to the woman for she said, 'Are you of any particular denomination?'

'I'm a Catholic,' I said.

She stopped on the stairs and I turned and looked up towards her.

'But you're not one those Catholics who wants to run to Mass every Sunday, are you?'

'I must go to Mass every Sunday,' I said flatly.

'But if my husband and I wanted to go away for a day, or a week-end, we couldn't leave the child if we thought you had to go off to Mass. It would be perfectly all right if we were there. You'd be quite willing to fall in with this arrangement I suppose?'

Between the glory of my good luck and me was rising a barrier, and on it was written 'It is a mortal sin to miss Mass.

Those who die in mortal sin will go to hell. The devil takes many shapes and has a smiling face.'

The devil was smiling at me now and saying sweetly, 'But you can't mean it. If through your work you are tied on a Sunday, then you'll be excused from Mass, surely they'll grant you that?'

'No, no,' I said, 'I'll have to go to Mass.'

No small voice said to me, 'You're daft, you're mad, stark staring mad. Go to the priest, explain things and he'll tell you it's all right.' No, there was only black and white in those days. I was a Catholic and under pain of everlasting damnation I must not miss Mass. Father Bradley's voice was booming in my ears, Father Bradley's presence was spreading in front of this woman obliterating her amazed expression from my gaze.

'I'm sorry,' I said, on the point of tears.

'So am I,' she said.

I think she was more amazed than sorry. She was absolutely dumbfounded that the chance she was offering this ignorant untravelled girl could be turned down just because she couldn't guarantee that she would allow her to attend Mass every Sunday.

When I returned to the registry office the woman said nothing for a time, she simply gaped at me, and then on a high sigh she brought out, 'Well, I've heard some things in me time but this beats all. I hope you don't live to regret it.'

Without much interest she gave me the address of a woman in Harton village who wanted a companion-maid. That was the term, companion-maid.

I walked for miles to get to this house, it was well beyond Harton village. It was a big house surrounded by an orchard and gardens. It had large high rooms which were beautifully furnished. It was here that I first saw antique furniture, real antique furniture, not the clumsy Victorian monstrosities, but beautiful pieces with line. Pieces that brought a satisfaction into my being just to look at them, and a strong desire to possess them. These pieces I later came to put names to, Sheraton, Hepplewhite, Louis Quinze, Georgian, Queen Anne, William and Mary. They may not all have been in that house but shape and patina was there, and something inside me rose and recognised it as if an old friend.

139

The lady was in her fifties, small, quiet and very charming. She had, she said, extra help in to do the rough work. I would be required only to help her. She did her own cooking. Perhaps I wouldn't mind helping with the washing?

I took the job, then returned home and told Kate. She was furious.

I wasn't going into any service unless she saw who it was and where I was going, etc., etc.

All right, she could come with me and see for herself. She was very sad about me going into service, she looked upon it as a reflection on herself in some way.

But before I could take up my new duties I had to get rigged out. The lady had said I would need uniform, at least two blue dresses for the mornings and one dark dress for the afternoons. At least half-a-dozen white aprons for the mornings and two fancy ones for the afternoons. And, of course, I would need caps. I did not wonder at the time why a companion should need all this uniform, plus caps. I had never been in this kind of service before. But when I told Kate what was expected she did say, 'Are you sure she said maid-companion? You're just not making it up?'

'The woman in the registry office said that, it's down in the book.' I was indignant. 'I don't tell lies.' And, strangely, at that time I didn't. I felt myself to be above lying. A slight evasion of the truth was one thing, but lying was quite another.

With the kind help of Mrs Maguire I got a five pound club and away I went to Allen's in Shields. It took all of the five pounds for the uniform.

What was my wage to be?

Nine shillings a week, all found.

From under the bed Kate pulled the brown painted tin trunk that had served her through all her places. She turned out the old junk and put into it my uniform and the few bits of underclothing I possessed. Then, she taking one handle and I the other, we left number ten William Black Street and I went out into the world.

The lady was so pleased to see Kate. She also took to her, saying it was so nice for a mother to come with her daughter. It proved that we were so respectable. Not everybody was so respectable, or words to that effect. Kate helped me up to my room with the box. It was a slit of a room but she seemed pleased with it.

Later the master came into the kitchen. He was something in Newcastle. He was very nice indeed and seemed pleased to see me and hoped I would stay with them for a long time.

That evening the lady told me what my duties were. She showed me how I was to do the morning room carpet. I was to sprinkle tea leaves all over it then brush them off – the pile was very deep and there were no Hoovers in those days. Then I had to clean the room and set the table for breakfast. This particular room was bigger than the three rooms in number ten put together.

I could cook bacon, couldn't I?

'Oh yes, of course.'

'Well then, I'll leave it out for you. I'm sure you'll manage,' said the kind lady.

'Then after breakfast you'll do the drawing room, the hall and the stairs. You know how to prepare vegetables, don't you?'

'Oh, yes, of course.'

'And then after you have washed up the lunch things you can do the silver.' – Silver was used for every meal – 'We have tea served in the drawing room at four o'clock, and something high about six.'

This was the Monday. After breakfast on Tuesday the kind lady showed me a stack of dirty linen. It didn't matter if I didn't get it all done that morning – and left me to it. There would be something cold for lunch. I just had to dry my arms, change my apron, adjust my cap and carry it in. I could do that, couldn't I?

'Yes, of course.'

The funny thing about the washing was, although I had seen so much washing done in our house I had no idea of the routine. Kate wouldn't see me in her way, for my tiredness after wielding a scrubbing brush or a poss stick always irritated her. However, I got through more than half the enormous pile of washing, weeks of it I should say.

Every day of that first week the lady told me in the most gentle tones – she never raised her voice and always had a most kindly smile – what she wanted me to do. But she never said, 'Come and sit with me.' She never said, 'What do you read?'

There was no time for that. I rose at six o'clock in the morning, I went to bed at nine at night, almost collapsing with fatigue. It was only my nervous energy that kept me going for I was never physically strong. And then came Friday and the at home day.

In the morning I had to go at the double getting everything ready for the afternoon, and then the lady told me what to do. After getting into my black, donning a fancy apron and new cap, she gave me a silver plate and said in her sweet voice, 'This is for the visitors' cards.' I was to open the door, read the names, then come to the drawing room door and announce the visitor. Did I think I could do that?

'Yes, I thought so.' My enthusiasm wasn't so strong as at the beginning of the week. I had never announced ladies before. I didn't know what an at home was. Our Kate had never talked about waiting on 'at homes'. Nevertheless I was soon to learn.

They came in their ones and twos, and they looked me up and down, and later when I wheeled in the tea trolley I interrupted my mistress talking. Then their eyes were turned on me. Like a cow in the cattle market I was under appraisal.

Not one of the ladies who were surveying the lower animal guessed that the tall girl with the well developed bust and unfashionably thin legs, and the enviable mass of nut-brown hair above a debatable, good-looking face was undergoing a most strange desire. She wanted to stand in the middle of them, and after holding them with the same silence and gimlet eye that she had used on her playmates in an effort to bend them to her will, she wanted, not to say 'Aa feel like a fight' but to question them, and to prove to herself through their answers their inferior intelligence.

With me, to think a thing was to accomplish it mentally, the result of the examination of the ladies was shown in the curl of my lip as I left the room.

The tea over I stood in the kitchen gripping my fancy apron and saying, over and over, 'This is not for me. I can't help it. I cannot stand this.' I shook my head as something within me asked, 'Why?' and answered, 'I just don't know why. I only know I can't stand it.'

As I was getting the evening meal ready the lady appeared

142

and said how nicely I had carried off my duties. Her friends couldn't believe that this was my first real post. I had acted as if I was born to it.

She actually started, so quickly did I turn on her. And although I did not speak something in my face must have warned her, for she left me alone.

Again I gripped my apron. Whatever I'd been born to, it wasn't going to be this. My picture on the wall had come to life, and in it were the so-called ladies and gentlemen and I wasn't to be seen – I had never seen myself as a servant in the picture.

By this time I also had a funny feeling about the lady herself. When was I going to be a companion to her? When was I going to sit with her? Could the companion bit be lies? Oh, no, she was a lady. But there was something funny.

The next afternoon was my half-day and before I went to the station the lady said most solicitously, 'I would put your feet up this afternoon if I were you, Katie.'

I had been on my feet so much during that week that they had swollen up over the tops of my shoes, very like Kate's, and were paining me a great deal.

I went to the station and there on the little platform stood two girls. They eyed me, then said, 'You working in the village or about?'

I hated to admit my position, but then why should I be ashamed of being a companion-maid, so I said, 'Yes, I'm working at Mrs X's.'

'Oh, God!' said one, 'she's done it again,' and they fell on each other's necks and laughed. Then, regaining their dignity, one said, 'Are you her maid-companion?'

'Yes, I am,' I said.

'What companioning have you done so far?' They were laughing again.

'What do you mean?' I asked, but already knowing that they were going to voice my suspicions.

'She's an old bucket and shovel if ever there was one. She just sweeps them up. How she gets off with it I don't know. You're about the sixth she's had this year. Maid-companion! You know, if we all had our rights she should be brought up for false pretences. That agency woman should be told.'

Later, standing in the familiar warmth of our own kitchen,

I related my experiences and the conversation on the platform to Kate and me granda, and their loud indignation warmed me.

'That's them! said Kate. 'That's them! and I never wanted you to go into service. You're not cut out for it in the first place.'

'The smarmy-mouthed deceitful, lying, old bugger,' said me granda, and I laughed and patted his knee.

'She won't deceive me much longer,' I said.

'No,' said Kate, 'you give your notice in the minute you get back.'

'I'm going to,' I said, and then added, somewhat aghast, 'But what about all me uniform? I've got all that to pay for.'

'We'll manage that somehow,' said Kate. 'And you'll get something, don't worry about that.'

It was a very comforting experience being wanted back into the fold, and I did get something. That very night I got a job as a laundry checker in the workhouse.

Although my feet were swollen and the sight of them aroused Kate's anger against 'the lady' still further and she too said I should put them up, I went to the whist drive and dance in the school rooms that evening. I had always attended the weekly whist drive and dance and I didn't want to miss this one. And it was while there that Billy McAnany, Councillor McAnany as he was then, later to be Mayor, came to me and said, 'Katie, how would you like a job in the workhouse as laundry checker?'

It seemed in that moment, as it did often in my youth, that I had only to pray for something very hard and my prayer was answered, with the exception of the one about our Kate.

I'd no idea what a laundry checker was, it might have included scrubbing and possing. I didn't know but I said, 'Billy, I'd love it.'

He said, 'I heard you had to give up the pen painting . . . Now this is what you've got to do.'

He told me I had to go and see a lady on the Monday and she would give me a reference to take to Matron Hill at the Institution. Now I have always given Billy full credit for getting me that job, so it came as a surprise to me when only a few years ago when he was visiting Hastings and we had a talk, he told me that the person who was responsible for getting me the job was Father Bradley, the priest to whom I went when

I was sixteen and asked if he would give me a reference to get me into the same institution to be trained as a nurse. His answer to that had been, 'You're not old enough to train for a nurse. What's more you haven't got the required education.'

My love for him wasn't increased by this remark, and me granda cursed him uphill and down dale. Yet Billy McAnany told me that Father Bradley came to him one day around the time I am speaking of and said, 'I feel something should be done for Katie McMullen. She's a good girl and I would like to see her settled. Do you think we can get her into the Institution?' – Father Bradley was then on the Board of Guardians, as was Billy McAnany – 'There's the post of laundry checker going. It would be quite a good start for her, don't you think? See what can be done about it.'

The lady I was sent to was a power behind the throne. She gave me the note to take to the Matron. It has often puzzled me why Matron Hill, who was a little tartar of a woman, but an excellent matron, should accept me straightaway. Even when I told her quite frankly – if nothing else I was always frank, so frank that it became a failing – that I didn't like being a servant and that I had been worked to death. This was the only time I spoke freely to Matron Hill. She was a terror and put the fear of God into me, but in a different way from Miss Corfield and Father Bradley. She always saw me as a strong individualist and something of a rebel and acted accordingly.

When I told 'the lady' that I was giving a week's notice and that I was going into a laundry she was aghast. As was her husband. They stood over me.

'My dear, you are not cut out for a laundry, you won't last a week in a laundry.'

'You are much too intelligent for a laundry.' This was the gentleman. 'What can your mother be thinking of? It's such a let-down for you.'

'It's a pity your father's at sea, he would surely have put his foot down.'

Davie putting his foot down; poor Davie. He lived to please. Whatever you wanted to do you should do it, was his theory, and this applied to Kate's every wish. Would she have pulled up in the early days if she'd had a stronger minded man? I don't know.

Anyway I stopped being a lady's companion at the end of the week.

About this time there was renewed in me an overpowering desire to see my father. This no doubt had been aggravated by the reference to Davie. I blamed Kate for indicating during her brief meeting with my employer that my father was sea going.

Davie my Father! Davie was the last man I'd choose for a father. Davie was only a stoker, the lowest form of sea-going life. He could never even hope to take the place of my father.

I'm glad that Davie never knew my true feelings for he thought the world of me, and was so proud of me; when there was nothing to be proud of he was still proud. He was a good man was Davie McDermott.

CHAPTER TEN

The following Monday evening Jackie Potts and his pal helped me to carry my tin box through the iron gates of Harton Institution, and so began an interesting period of four and a half years, which was, in the main – happy.

I worked in the laundry checking the dirty linen in and the clean out and keeping the books, from 8 am till 5pm and half-day Saturday. I had every other night off after five o'clock until ten, every Sunday off and every other week-end off. When on duty every alternate evening and every alternate Saturday I usually relieved the infirm ward attendants. Once a month, on a Saturday, I took the unmarried mothers to the Cottage Homes at Cleadon to visit their children. This particular duty always made me think, as I looked at the children, 'But for the grace of God there go I,' and as I looked at the unmarried mothers, 'And there but for her pluck goes our Kate.'

An unmarried mother was kept in the workhouse for fourteen years, that is if her people wouldn't take her out. The child was sent to the Cottage Homes after it left the Workhouse nursery, and the mother wasn't free to leave the Workhouse until the child was old enough to work for itself. Some of the mothers became so used to the workhouse that they couldn't leave it after doing this long-term stretch.

Added to my duties, was the cutting of the bread.

Saturday tea-time was always a high tea with tarts and cakes and such, and this task fell to the lot of the last-comer. My position was at the bottom of the table and the officer next to me was about four years older than myself. There was a great deal of laughter at these teas. They laughed about funny things that I couldn't get the hang of, so I laughed with them. But on this particular Saturday – I had been there about a month – as I stood hacking away at the great loaf to replenish the plates I suddenly realised what the laughter was all about. Somebody had just told a dirty story.

There had always been plenty of swearing in our house, but Kate would have no smutty talk, nor would she indulge in it with the neighbours in the back lane – she had one or two coarse sayings which she considered clever but that was as far as it went. So I had been brought up to abhor this kind of talk. Added to this I was a very strong Catholic. I was also quite fearless in some ways. I turned round with the big bread gully still in my hand, and I startled that whole table, filled mostly with senior officers, by shouting, 'Stop it this minute! If I hear any more dirty talk like that I'll report you all to the Matron.'

The amazed silence was broken by an officer called Morgans. Morgans was a character. I had never liked to hear women swear, and some women have only to say bloody to set my teeth on edge, but Morgans's swearing was an art, you couldn't take offence at Morgans swearing. Morgans on this occasion looked at me, her dark eyes shining, and I think there was both amazement and admiration in her laugh. Anyway she got me over the aftermath of this awful denouncement by saying, 'Come off it, bloody Saint Catherine, and get a move on with that bread.'

I remained 'bloody Saint Catherine' to Morgans until the day I left the Institution, and she was one of the few who didn't send me to Coventry for my sin. But time and time again I would feel like death when, coming back from my night out, I would go to the mess-room, which was also the sitting room, to have a cup of tea and anything that was going – I was always hungry – and would open the door on to laughter and chatter which would fade away on my entering, as would also the people in the room.

There was an officer working there at that time whose home was in Tyne Dock and she knew all about me. My parentage I knew was soon public. She was one of the less refined members of the staff, one of those who put my teeth on edge with her swearing, one of those whom I disliked, and not without reason, because I heard her remark one day, 'Talk about an upstart bastard. And her being in service an' all. Can you imagine where she gets it from?'

Among a number of the officers there was a striving after refeenment rather than refinement, and I soon discovered that our Kate wasn't the only one who pronounced her words wrong and got her sentences mixed up. There were a number of Mrs Malaprops on that staff.

I had been working in the laundry – which job I liked very much at first, even if I disliked the Head Laundress equally so – when I had a return of that mixed emotion which always prompted the question 'What are you going to do now?' I remember I was startled by its re-appearance and I said to myself, 'This is a good job. I've got over two pounds a month and all my uniform found and plenty of off-duty time. What more do I want?'

Well what did I want? I asked myself. I pointed out once again that I hadn't been trained for anything except house-work . . . What about writing? I hadn't been trained for that either, face up to it, my spelling and grammar were atrocious. Yet I could write, I knew I could write if only there was someone somewhere who could help me, give me lessons, who could learn me – no, no, teach me. I was learning by the mistakes of others; one of the officers had said 'Learn me' and another had most tactfully, in front of a full table, corrected her with, 'Only you can learn, others teach.' I wanted to spit in her eye.

Why not aim at an accomplishment, something in music? Why not learn the fiddle.

Yes, that was it, I would learn the fiddle.

I went round the second-hand shops until I found a fiddle for ten shillings and I took lessons at a shilling a time. I have to laugh now when I think about the first night in my room with that fiddle, and the officers coming to view it and have a laugh at my expense, and the chaos in the recreation room where I practised.

The recreation room was above the sewing room and was for the use of the officers, but it was used only for the supper that accompanied the Christmas dances. I came to look upon that great long room as my sole property.

There were eighteen of the staff all told at that time, including the mental block girls, and most of the eighteen threatened what they would do to me if I didn't stop practising that fiddle. There wasn't only my screeching to contend with, there was the assistant matron's dog, which, as soon as it saw me coming down the corridor with the case, would dart to the recreation room, sit under the window and howl to high heaven.

So keen was I to learn that I took the fiddle home with me on my evenings out and the girls used to push up the dining room window and call after me. But nothing deterred me.

When Kate opened the front door to me she would smile ruefully and say, 'Must you bring it with you every night, lass?'

But me granda was for the fiddle. 'You practice, lass,' he encouraged me. 'There's nowt Aa like better than a bit of music.'

Of course he wasn't a great authority on music, having only the box gramophone and our three records to judge by, one of which was, 'You made me love you'.

After spending twelve shillings on lessons and practising for three solid months and still not being able to give a recital I was forced to realise that there was something wrong with the fiddle. So I gave it up and, as my urge, as I came to call the compelling mixture of emotions that would beset me, was going mad again I took up French. Before I could speak English I took up French! But here again I failed because there was something wrong with my accent, the teacher couldn't get it right. I did all I could but it was no use. I went up, she said, where I should go down.

I was very depressed about this failure for I had an over-powering desire for education, for knowledge, and to be thought clever. But people can dislike you for being clever, especially eighteen refeened officers. So I laughed at all my attempts at improvement and made others laugh with me, and at me. I acquired quite an art in this direction. It became the usual question as soon as I entered the mess-room – in my second year after I had been released from Coventry – someone would say 'What's happened the night, Mac?' And if anything hadn't happened that could be turned into something funny and against myself, I would invent an episode to please them. And so when I took up the fiddle I laughed at myself, so with the French, so with the Indian clubs. I practised Indian clubs to make me strong, and I worked so hard at them that at last I was able to swing three in each hand simultaneously and do a sort of dance while performing. One day in the midst of my prac-tice, whirling my clubs, doing a slow waltz and singing to myself, I heard stifled laughter. All the first dinner set, of

150

which I was one, were hiding on the stairs and looking through the banisters at floor level. Supposedly unaware I danced towards them, swinging the clubs, but when I pretended to drop the lot on them there was pandemonium, which all ended in another big laugh.

Nearly always on late leave night – a twelve o'clock pass once a month – I would return to my room to find chaos awaiting me. An apple-pie bed, the whole place stripped; and one time I found the dressmaker's dummy dressed up in my uniform, with the fiddle tied to the sleeves, Indian clubs for legs, a French exercise book on a stand before a face – painted on my pillow with my pen paints – poetry I had been writing pinned over the grotesque chest, and across my window a placard bearing the letters 'Queen of the Arts'.

I took it as usual in good part and slept that night on the floor of my neighbour's bedroom. The next day I gave them the answer to their joke. On the mirror which acted as a notice board in the mess-room I placed a large sheet of paper which bore the words THE QUEEN THANKS HER SUBJECTS and at the bottom in a flourishing hand I signed my name in full. CATHERINE MCMULLEN. Strange, but I used to like writing that name.

One sidelight on this incident was that the assistant Matron asked me to leave the room as it was until the Matron saw it – not to get anyone into trouble, apparently the Matron liked a joke. It was news to me.

It would be about this time, too, that I went into the carnival. I didn't want anyone to know I was going in because I knew that no one would dream that I would do such a thing. Especially the gentleman I was going with and who had ideas about decorum, and the inhabitants of the 'New Buidlings' who thought I was swanky. But at this time there was an urge in me to act the goat – doubtless Kate's humour pushing to the fore.

I got dressed in the house of a friend in Shields and my get-up, a sort of Nellie Wallace creation, made me unrecognis-able. I called myself 'Sailors beware!' During the three mile route a car stopped near me and a gentleman asked my name. Now I had already decided that if I got anywhere in the prize line I'd give a false name. But I didn't know the men in the car were judges so I said, Katie McMullen, and I couldn't believe it when later over the loud speaker I heard 'First prize for causing most amusement on the route, Katie McMullen!'

The following week was very enlightening. Instead of people turning their noses up I was hailed almost as a celebrity. The Assistant Matron had me dress up and go around the wards doing my stuff. People stopped me after church and said, 'Why don't you try for the stage?' and Kate, whom my antics amazed as much as anyone, said, 'The whole buildings are agog, they just couldn't believe that it was you.'

One woman said to me, 'Lass, I've known you since you were a bairn in arms an' you've always had a sad look in the back of your eyes, even when you were tiny you had it, an' to think that you did that on Saturday. I saw you but I still can't take it in it was you.'

Regarding the sad look in my eyes, she was right. All my early photos have it. The first one taken at three years old looks as if I had already known sorrow.

I again turned to writing. I wrote a play about the hospital versus the house side of the Institution. The theme was the snobbish friction which existed between the two. The play was funny and everybody was impressed, well not quite everybody. I had enemies as I was to find out.

I tried to get the younger members of the staff to act the play, but we laughed and larked so much that it came to nothing, yet I felt I had written something worth while at last. So I sent it to a well-known correspondence school who were giving free criticism of manuscripts with a view to judging whether you were eligible for coaching. I waited on a high peak of excitement for weeks and then back came the play, without a covering letter, but written in red ink across the blank back page were the words 'Strongly advise author not to take up writing as a career.'

It was such a blow I stopped writing for a fortnight.

Although we had lots of fun at times there was another side to my years in the Institution, for I was aware of the suspicion that surrounded me because of my birth, and this was not that imagination which is often attributed to illegitimates and their sensitivity to this handicap.

My work as a laundry checker meant checking in all the dirty washing from the main hospital and the male and female mental blocks, and entering each article into a ledger, and when the washing was clean, booking it and sending it out again. Some of the dirty linen was in a vile state as the Hospital catered for men off the ships; it also catered for all kinds of diseases. This thought never troubled me. I rarely handled the dirty linen as I had two inmate helpers to do the sorting, but the stench from the clothes at times made me feel sick. There were periods of time when I felt very much off-colour, sometimes quite ill when I didn't want to do anything – not even to learn. It was about this time that my nose started to bleed heavily. During one such period I broke out in spots. They covered my body from my waist downwards. They were large spots and were very sore and when I told Kate she said, 'It's with all those breakfasts you eat. What do you expect with all that fried stuff.' And of course she was right. I had a great appetite and very often when other members of the staff couldn't face their breakfast at half-past seven in the morning and left it until the ten o'clock break, when the sight of congealed fat tempted them even less, I would gladly dispose of one or more plates of cold bacon and egg. Many a morning I ate three big breakfasts, and it's no wonder I had very little appetite left for the dinners. But I would have a good tea, packing away plenty of bread, so my diet at that time consisted mostly of fats and carbo-hydrates.

Our particular section of the Institution had been raising funds, through dances, to help buy a violet-ray apparatus for the hospital. In return for our help the doctor allowed all the staff to have a free course of treatment. I was sitting in the half-circle of officers one morning, attired only in my knickers and brassiere, when one of them – and she was one of some importance – pointed to my waist and said 'What's that?'

'A spot,' I said; 'I'm covered with them. I must stop eating frys.' This was about eleven o'clock in the morning.

I returned to the laundry at half-past eleven. At a quarter-to-twelve I was ordered to go up to the hospital, and when I arrived I was put in an isolation ward with a special nurse in attendance. What was it all about? She couldn't tell me, so I lay there waiting and wondering, and worrying. It was my spots I supposed, but why this rush? why this ward?

Eventually there came into the room a sort of deputation,

headed by the matron. She stared at me fixedly and coldly, as only she knew how, while Doctor Shanley started to ask me questions. He was a nice doctor and I liked him, and I answered him without hesitation, telling him all he wanted to know. When did I first see the spots, etc. etc., and all the while the matron was staring at me, as was the other doctor, a lady, and the sister and the nurse. Then the doctor examined me. I say he examined me; it seemed to me he started to examine me and then changed his mind, so quickly was the examination over. He took off his gloves and patted my cheek and said with a laugh, 'Come on, we're going to count these' and he counted the spots on my stomach and my buttocks and loins, trying to make me laugh as he did so, but I wasn't feeling like laughing. I looked at the matron and the sister and the other doctor and the nurse and anger rose in me, but not against them so much as against the officer who had reported the spots. And yet at that time I didn't really know why I was angry.

The doctor said, 'Are you constipated?'

Oh, yes, I was constipated I told him, I always had been. I was born with the condition. Kate told me that Doctor McHaffie had had to come to treat me for constipation when I was a month old. At various times during my childhood I was made victim of the crude home-made and scream-inducing treatment of having coarse washing soap inserted into the rectum, after which I was sat over a chamber of boiling water.

The doctor patted my cheek again before he left, as if I were a child, and as he went through the door I overheard him mutter, 'You're mistaken. Never been touched...' And I thought he sounded pleased.

The nurse who was detailed to look after me made a great fuss of me, and my room became the meeting point for lots of the nurses.

You can imagine my pride when I found I could talk to the first-year nurses in their own language because I had been reading up *The Naval Book*. This was a book for sea-going male nurses. Still with the idea of becoming a nurse I had begun some months previously to study anatomy and physiology. I could draw the pelvis and make it look like a nice picture with light and shade. I could talk about the aorta and I knew all the bones of the body. They said, 'Fancy, and you in the laundry

154

and knowing all this. Why, you know more than we do about the theory.' I was very happy in that side ward, I didn't want to leave it. I felt more at home among these girls than I did among the house staff. During the time I was in the ward no one was allowed to visit me from the house.

I had written to our Kate on the Friday night and told her I was in hospital but said I didn't know what was wrong with me except I had spots. On the Tuesday evening I was amazed to see her come into the little ward, and I was also delighted to see her, and because she looked nice I felt a spurt of pride in her and wished that that lot over in the house could see her like this.

'How did you get in?' I asked.

'The Matron sent the maid from the house with me.'

'The Matron? You haven't been to the Matron!'

'I have,' she said with quiet dignity. 'I wanted to know what was wrong with you; you said you weren't allowed visitors.'

'What did she say?' I asked.

At this Kate bent over me and, smiling gently, said, 'She said you're a good girl. You've got a very good daughter, Mrs McDermott,' she said. 'She's a very good girl.'

I could see the Matron's face as she had looked when she entered the ward a few days ago. She hadn't thought I was a good girl then. She must have remembered that only a few weeks previously I had been up before her.

'What is this I hear, Miss McMullen, that you were out until two o'clock on Sunday morning? Is this true?'

After closing my gaping mouth I replied, 'Yes, Matron. I was at a party.'

'What kind of a party?'

I told her what kind of a party. Jackie Potts had taken me to a party at his relatives' house, relatives on his mother's side, people who lived quite close to the Institution, highly respectable people. When I told her their name and the situation of the house, and that I had known the young man since I was a girl she modified her tone and dismissed me with, 'Very well, Miss McMullen, but you should not stay out so late.'

I should not stay out so late.

Christmas parties in the North went on all night. Two o'clock was early for breaking up, and until I left the North I never went to a party at which there was anything intoxicating to drink, except in my own home. I remember bicycling up to Birtley with Lily Maguire for a Catholic dance that started at midnight on Easter Sunday and went on till six o'clock the next morning. All-night parties and dances were nothing out of the common. On looking back I think perhaps the Catholics were more tolerant in this matter, as they also were towards drinking and gambling, and this attitude is not understandable to non-Catholics who consider it doesn't make sense when you take into account the dogma and bigotry. Anyway I wondered, but only for a moment, how the Matron had come to know about me being at the party. And then I thought – I had happened to mention to a certain officer what a good time I'd had at this particular party, forgetting that this lady was the Matron's third ear. She was also a Catholic.

When Kate left that night I was furious. I knew nothing about syphilis or gonorrhoea, but I knew that if you went with men you could pick up a disease. Hadn't the girls in the laundry who had been discharged from the hospital but kept in the workhouse because they had no proper homes to go to, hadn't these girls picked up something through going with men? And they all had a peculiar smell about them. A dirty scenty smell.

So that was why I had been hustled into the hospital. After Kate had gone my rage nearly lifted me out of the bed and over to the Matron's house, but Kate's words came back to me, the words she had said on the day of the party as she stood on the mat looking down on me with pity: 'You'll see your day, hinny, don't you worry. You'll see your day with them all.'

Like the majority of Catholics I was at that time bigoted about my religion, which played a very important part in my life. It sustained me and comforted me, I neither questioned nor probed but accepted it, and therefore was happy in it. And this state of happiness I felt was due to the Virgin and the Holy Family. Never did I pass the church on my way home from Harton but I paid them a visit, and on the journey back I would call in again. Often the church was in black darkness except for the red eye of the sanctuary lamp, but I would grope my way down to the far altar where stood Our Lady, and there, kneeling in the darkness, repeat my desires and beg

156

her to grant my wishes. The ever present wish that Kate would give up the drink; the ever present wish that I would find me da, and the ever present wish to be a good girl, to keep myself pure, a very difficult process, for although, as I understood it, it was not wrong to love, the very fact of loving brought thoughts into the mind that the conscience told you should not be there, and when, fascinated by them, you did not immediately dispel them, this conscience drove you to confession, to grow hot with blushes as you divulged your sins of bad thoughts. I once discussed this business of bad thoughts and the confessing of them with a Catholic girl, one with whom I had been to school. I remember what she said, 'Don't be daft, Katie.' Then she stood back from me, her eyes narrowed and her mouth open in laughter, as she exclaimed, 'By! you are daft, you know. You don't look it, but you are.' Then she went on to tell me that a priest had tried to kiss her mother when she was a young girl. I was aghast, she was lying. I did not speak to her again. Priests did not do things like that. Nor did Catholics withhold any of their sins in the confessional box. Catholics were different. I held this view of Catholics being different for quite a number of years after this incident, and perhaps it was because of this that I made no allowances for a Catholic doing a bad thing. Catholics should know better; Catholics were filled with the grace of God. They were the fortunate and favoured of God; there were a lot of nice Protestants, but, poor souls, they were as far removed from the protection of the real God as it was possible for the human mind to imagine.

Yet on looking back I can't ever remember praying to this Catholic God. I prayed to Mary, the Holy Family and every blessed one of the archangels, saints, and angels, and the ones who did the chores, known as guardian angels. I prayed a great deal to my guardian angel, and even at this stage of thinking when I retain not one belief of those years, I still have a confirmed feeling of someone guiding me. Nobody like a God or a high official in the archangel grade, but just a common or working guardian angel.

I know now that I never prayed to God because I was afraid of Him, of the being in whose likeness I was told I was made. What was God but a male me, of gigantic proportions, sitting somewhere up there, with Jesus on His right-hand and the thief who died on the Cross on His left. But Jesus was minute compared to this being called God. Nor, I remember, did I pray very often to Jesus, as Jesus the man. As Jesus the infant, yes; as symbolised by the Sacred Heart, yes; but Jesus in His many stages of suffering I sheered from.

I couldn't understand a Catholic being petty and vindictive to another Catholic. Yet before I left Harton Institution understanding was brought home to me with considerable force. Get a really spiteful Catholic and the devil couldn't ask for a better advocate.

As my sojourn in the back bedroom of William Black Street had changed my outlook so did my stay in that side ward in the hospital. I returned to the house block outwardly the same Miss McMullen, but inwardly there was a wariness that hadn't been there before, and a stronger determination than ever to show them.

My urge, at this period, nagged at me day in day out. I now began a frantic search for knowledge. I took *T.P. and Cassell's Weekly*. This magazine stirred my mind and sent it groping hither and thither. The magazine was about clever people – writers. I wanted to be clever, I wanted to be a writer, I wanted knowledge. But how? How was I to go about getting it? What kind of books should I read? There was no one to ask. I never thought about going to the library. I was now twenty years old and I had never been inside a library of any kind.

Perhaps concentrated thought is a form of prayer for my desire was granted. I found a tutor.

It came about in this way. I read a book by Elinor Glyn, called *The Career of Catherine Bush*. I felt quite guilty about reading this book because Elinor Glyn was banned by the church. Didn't she write about women lying on tiger skins? There was a great deal of border-line joking at the dining room table about Elinor Glyn and the tiger skins and the repeated phrase 'I did but kiss your little feet'. This always elicited howls of laughter. But there I was reading *The Career of Catherine Bush* by this forbidden writer.

Catherine Bush was a girl of the common people who becomes secretary to a duchess, whose old lover, now a Duke, falls in love with her. The Duchess tells Catherine Bush that if she is going to marry a duke, she must first of all be well-read. She tells

158

her the book on which to base her education. It was *Lord Chesterfield's Letters to his Son.*

When I read this story, particularly the line giving the title of the book that was to turn this girl into a lady, my desires, my craving to be different were compressed into a simple fact. I, too, wanted to be a lady. I flew down to the Library, the only place, I realised, in which I would be able to find this book, and made my acquaintance with Lord Chesterfield, and incidentally with a library.

And here began my education. With Lord Chesterfield I read my first mythology. I learned my first real history and geography. With Lord Chesterfield I went travelling the world. I would fall asleep reading the letters and awake around three o'clock in the morning my mind deep in the fascination of this new world, where people conversed, not just talked. Where the brilliance of words made your heart beat faster. I would see myself beautifully gowned going down a marble staircase on the hand of Lord Chesterfield. At the foot of the staircase great doors would open, and I would enter a salon where would be gathered a selected group of people, waiting for me. And I would converse with them and would astound them with my wisdom, my eloquence, my knowledge, all around three o'clock in the morning, and wake up bleary-eyed when the bell went at seven, step out on to the freezing lino, wash myself in ice cold water, make my way to the messroom telling myself that I was mad to read so late at night, that I was reading far too much because my eyes were becoming very sore. But come dinner-time I would gollop my dinner, dash to my room and there read selected letters aloud, because my tutor said that to be a lady or a gentleman you must, simply must, ARTICULATE CORRECTLY, and I knew only too well that I did not articulate correctly. I didn't talk Geordie but I had something wrong with my voice. I didn't know then it was my inflection, I only knew as the French teacher had said, that it went up when it should have gone down.

The end of this reading aloud came one day when the laundry bell rang and I had been so engrossed in the letters I had forgotten that I should be already at work. It would take me all of three minutes to get to the laundry and so I threw the book down and dashed to the door, and when I pulled it open I fell into a huddle of inmates – all mental

159

defectives, who had been gathered round the keyhole – and one, not so mentally deficient as the rest, turned to her pals and said, 'An' they pay hor to luk after us.'

Lord Chesterfield became very real to me. Was he not writing to his illegitimate son? And did he not say in his fourth letter to the boy: 'Although I now love you dearly, if you continue to go on so, I shall love you still more tenderly: if you improve and grow learned everyone will be fond of you, and desirous of your company; whereas ignorant people are shunned and despised. In order that I may not be ignorant myself I read a great deal. The other day I went through the history of Dido which I will now tell you.'

Dear, dear, Lord Chesterfield. Snob or not I owe him so much.

Never for very long during this period of my life was the thought of my father out of my mind. I felt that I had only to see him and he would take me into his world – which of course was the upper class world. So much did I long to find him that I enlisted the services of a young man I was going with at that time, promising to marry him if he could get me any information concerning the man whose name I gave to him. I was not in love with this young man and had he succeeded in finding my father and had my hopes of a different way of life materialised through his research, he would have stood less chance than ever of me becoming his wife.

In those days I didn't blame my father for walking out on Kate. How could you expect a gentleman to accept anyone like me granda or me Uncle Jack, or even me homely grandma. And these were the people he had seen, the only time he had visited the house.

There must have been long periods between his visits to the public house at Lamesley for when Kate found herself pregnant she had come home, and he, sometime later going to the inn and not finding her there, had asked for her address. It was me Uncle Jack who had come to Kate and said, 'There's a fellow outside asking about you.' I have a hazy memory of being told that me grandma went out and spoke to him, but it was Kate herself shortly before she died who told me that she went with my father to Newcastle for the day and he was greatly disturbed about her condition and said they must be

160

married at once. When they parted that evening he gave her his address in Newcastle. Then, not hearing from him for some days she made her way to this address; no one of that name was known there.

Life in Harton Institution wasn't, I think, far removed from the time of Dickens. The female inmates all wore a hideous uniform, the dress reaching down to their strong boot-tops, over which was an apron, and they all wore starched caps. They fed in the hall, which also served as a chapel. It was furnished with long white wooden tables and backless forms. The sight of the food they ate and the way it was served up used to make me sick, and filled me with guilt when, in the messroom, I was presented with a plentiful meal. The kitchen was overrun with thousands of cockroaches, which appeared in hordes at a given time each evening, when the staff went off duty.

The kitchen staff consisted of inmates, headed by a cook who had herself been an inmate. Whether she had suffered from the system which tied a woman for fourteen years because of a misdemeanour or she had to come in because she had no one to support her family I am not quite sure, I wasn't interested enough at the time to find out, I only knew she had been an inmate. What interested me more was that cockroaches, from time to time, found their way into the inmates' porridge.

There were three infirm wards besides a nursery in the house side. Infirm One was where the chronic patients were kept. This ward was divided by a main corridor along which I had to pass to get to my room, and the stench of urine from it always stung my nose, even though the place was kept scrupulously clean. I became closer acquainted with Infirm One and two of its inmates from doing evening duty there. The two women were both in wheel-chairs. One was called Mrs Henagan. She was under thirty and suffering from a chronic form of arthritis, as was the older woman whose name I forget, but who was not much older, yet both looked aged with pain and despair and they instantly aroused my compassion.

Of my four nights off a week I always went home at least on two of them and my visits were looked forward to with eagerness both by Kate and me granda, for I would entertain them with stories of the happenings in the Institution. I think

I took a pride, more so in bringing them to tears than to laughter, and I achieved the former with Kate when I described to them the plight of Mrs Henagan and her friend. From this time I never returned to the Institution on a Sunday night but that I brought something for them. It might only be a piece of cake but often it was a cooked chicken. Kate was nothing if not generous.

If anyone was sorry to see me leave the Institution it was these two women, and in the years since I last saw them – they must be dead now – their plight has become clearer and more terrible to me; a young woman tied for ever to a wheel-chair in that foul smelling atmosphere, surrounded by painted stone walls and without friends. I think I am right in my recalling that her husband left her when she became chronically ill.

One of my duties that I really hated was to take the hall during Saturday visiting. As in prison, an officer had always to be present when the inmates had their visitors. It was while doing these duties that I discovered a new part of myself, a part that was vulnerable to the pain of others. This part would come to the fore as I watched a girl begging her parents to take her home – she was likely there for some misdemeanour and had been considered by the Courts as being out of control. Today she would have been put out to foster parents. Or to watch a simple-minded girl who had a baby being visited by the man who had given it to her, he probably already married and with a family. Or to watch a husband, who was on the men's side, visiting his wife, and see them sitting silently together in wordless misery. Often these cases were the result of a family having had the 'bums' in, and, having nowhere to go, had to come into the workhouse, the man to the male side, the woman to the female side, the children to the Cottage Homes.

Saturday afternoon duty in the hall did not come often for me, it would usually be as a stand-in for some officer who was sick, and I was very glad that it wasn't my permanent duty for nearly always after the bell rang I went to my room and had a little weep, and I would realise with painful clarity the fear that had always been in me granda and in most poor people, the fear of the workhouse.

I became very fond of certain inmates, particularly my deaf helper in the laundry. I had two helpers, one was an old woman of over seventy, her name was Mary Gunn, yet she was still sprightly with a good figure and beautiful skin even at that age. She was in the workhouse simply because she had no home. The other was also called Mary. She was much younger and deaf, and she had been brought up in the workhouse. She had a violent temper but she could make me laugh and would go out of her way to do so by relating one of the several times she had left the Institution to take up service outside. This girl had become so 'institutionalised' that she could not settle in the outside world and invariably returned to the workhouse from her several places. Being deaf she spoke in a quaint high tone and would relate to me why she left her last place in Shields.

'Because of the butcher boy, you know,' she would say. Her butcher sounded like boot-chair. 'The boot-chair boy, he came to the door and he said, "Mary, Aa you comin' out?" '

'Goo way boot-chair boy,' I said.

'Aw, Mary come on out. Come on in the wash-house for a minute, Mary.'

'Goo away, boot-chair boy, goo way.'

'I'll give you a bit of meat if you'll come into the wash-house, Mary.'

'Aa know what you'll give me, boot-chair boy, an' Aa don't want it. Fourteen years is a long time, boot-chair boy.'

This relating of the butcher boy episode would go on in her high squeaky voice while she mimed the butcher boy's expression with her thin face. I have seen me granda and Kate double up when I have done Mary and the butcher boy to them. Often me granda would greet me with 'Goo way boot-chair boy, goo way,' and we would all laugh.

There were many characters among the women who worked in the laundry, but a good percentage of them were mentally deficient in some way or another. I remember the day when one young woman got her hand caught in a calender. She got it entwined in a sheet, and it was dragged on to the hot steel bed and crushed by the rollers. I was assistant laundress at the time, having been promoted from laundry checker, and was coming out of my store when I heard the screams. I knew what had happened and the next minute I found myself running out through the main door. Quickly I pulled myself together and dashed back into the place and helped to support the screaming creature.

This girl was in hospital for some time, and when three months later and presumably better, with a much mangled hand, they put her back into the laundry I thought it was the most unfeeling thing I had as yet come across.

The thought that turned my steps that day of the accident was, if you want to manage you've got to face up to things like this. And I did want to manage. My aim then was to manage the biggest laundry going. If I wasn't fit to do anything else, I told myself, I was going to get to the top in this business, and so when the head laundress left to get married I asked the matron for her post.

'No, Miss McMullen,' she said, 'you are much too young and inexperienced.'

Not to be beaten, I waited a while, then asked her again. And again it was, 'No!' but much louder this time. On the third time of asking she bawled, 'If you approach me again I will have you thrown out of the gates.'

There was some difficulty in finding a suitable person to manage the laundry, none of the applicants seeming to have the required experience. Then they took on a young girl who had been running a small hand-laundry. I was indignant, but nevertheless put a good face on it. The girl and I became friendly and she admitted to me she was terrified of the responsibility and that if she stayed on – she was merely on trial – I would be doing the work and she would be getting the money.

I was sent for by the assistant matron the following week, after the girl had given in her notice, and told she had left because I had said that I was doing the work and she was getting the money and it was quite unfair. Although I stated exactly what had transpired between us, and in no meek terms, I knew I wasn't believed.

The assistant laundress whose place I had taken the previous year came back as manageress and I determined to get another post. This was only one of the reasons that made me decide on a move; I was very unhappy and there had scarcely been a night during the previous two years when I hadn't, in some measure, cried myself to sleep – even while reading Lord Chesterfield. The trouble was that I was very much in love, and had been since I was fifteen, with the gentleman who wanted a lady. Although I had many other boy friends this man was always prominent in my mind, and although I eventually kept company with him for nearly two years it was a painful and humiliating experience because I was aware that I was merely being used and hadn't the strength of will to make a stand against it. When eventually I did, it was like performing an operation on myself without an anaesthetic, and although the wound healed the scar remained.

Kate was very kind and understanding to me at this period. When I was leaving after my visit home, having kissed me granda's stubbly cheek and passed a last joke with him, she would accompany me to the front door, and there we would stand on the step and talk. Often as not the moon would be shining over the cornfield and should I make any reference to it she would invariably say, 'Leave it alone, it's not touching you.' It was one of her jokes and she would laugh. But some nights we just stood saying nothing, until she would ask, 'Got the blues, lass?' and I would nod, for my heart would be sore and my throat full of tears, and she would say, 'I'm not going to interfere with your life, lass, but you'll never be happy with him. He's not for you. You think he's above you but he's not. My God, you could leave him at the post; you've more brains in your little finger than he's got in his big body . . . Handsome is as handsome does, lass. You know what the fathar was saying last night, he said, he'd rather see you take' – she mentioned the name of a boy I'd been going with – 'It's true he wouldn't be able to give you much more than sixpenn'orth of block ornaments' – scraps of meat from the butcher's block – 'but he'd make you a damn sight happier than this one would.'

She was very comforting at times was Kate.

So it was that in the spring of 1929 I left the North, sad yet hopeful; sad because I told myself I was never going back. I had finished with the North and all it stood for. Hopeful, because I was going to make something of myself. In my case I carried notes from Lord Chesterfield and a page torn from a cheap magazine. I think it was called *The Happy Mag*. I still have that page, and the words on it I learnt by heart.

I will succeed I simply cannot fail,
The only obstacle is doubt.
There's not a hill I cannot scale
Once fear is put to rout.
Don't think defeat,
Don't talk defeat,
The word will rob you of your strength.
I will succeed, this phrase repeat
Throughout the journey's length.

The moment that I can't is said,
You slam a door right in your face.
Why not exclaim I will instead,
Half won then is the race.
You close the door to your success
By entertaining one small fear.
Think happiness, talk happiness,
Watch joy then coming near.

These words I repeated daily with my prayers, and long afterwards when I stopped saying prayers I still said them.

I hadn't heard of Samuel Smiles's *Self-Help* then, and the meaning of philosophy was yet to come, but these simple words were what I needed at the time.

The morning that I left 10 William Black Street for the last time is like an etching in miniature, every line is distinct, but I see it from a great distance. Kate was crying. We kissed and held each other tightly. I loved her deeply in that moment. Had I ever prayed she would die? It was unthinkable. I loved her so much and I could love her more and more now because I was being set free. Never would I again have to wonder if she was all right as I walked up the street. I wasn't only saying good-bye to Kate, but to the sick, sick dread that had lived with me from my earliest memory.

'Bye-bye, Kate, Bye bye. Yes ... yes, I'll write twice a week.'

'Bye bye my love. God bless you and take care of you.'

I wouldn't let her come to the station with me, and she was too overcome to see me to the bottom of the street where I was to get the tram; or was she leaving it to me granda to escort me on his own. Did she have a feeling it would be the last time he would see me? Perhaps.

He kissed me. His chin as usual was rough. His eyes were wet.

'Bye-bye, Granda.'

'Bye-bye, hinny. Bye-bye me lass . . . Bye-bye. God go with you. Bye-bye me lass . . . Mind how you go. Bye-bye. Bye-bye me bairn.'

Part Three

LIFE EVERLASTING

CHAPTER ELEVEN

When I left the North it was to take up the post of Head Laundress in a workhouse which I understood was quite near Clacton-on-Sea but which I found was ten miles out. After eight lonely months there I got the post of laundry manageress in the workhouse at Hastings. Here I only intended to stay a year before moving on to a bigger and better post – if my fate was to work in a laundry then I would one day manage the biggest in the country.

It happened that almost from the time I left the North up to my fourth year in Hastings, I was pursued by married men. This state of affairs created in me another fear: Was the stamp of my birth evident in some way, that these types should think me easy bait? During these years I met five men, four of whom were introduced to me as single. One of these gentlemen introduced me to serious music. Night after night he would take me to hear the Municipal Orchestra in the White Rock Pavilion in Hastings. I was delighted about this, it was all part of the education plan. I liked this man – love did not enter into it but the night I discovered he was married I turned on him so wildly that one could imagine that I was again suffering the effects of a deep passion.

He had been away for the week-end and had not told me

where he was going, but on the Sunday evening he called at my lodgings in an excited state. He had something to tell me, so we went for a walk over the East Hill. We were actually walking along the edge of the cliff when he told me he had been to see his wife with regard to getting a divorce because he wanted to marry me. What prevented me from pushing him over the cliff I never knew. He was number three on the list.

It would appear that I was only attractive to married men, in fact, when I had the same experience again I really became afraid. It was as if the scales were tipped too heavily against me. What was I to do? I had a great deal of Kate in me – I had a warm nature. After all my striving to be different was it going to be a hole and corner affair with a married man? No. Definitely no. I came to the sad decision – I would never marry.

Meanwhile I became the owner of the house of my imagination. The Hurst, Hoadswood Road – a fifteen-roomed gentleman's residence.

You might wonder how a laundry manageress earning £3 a week – although this was a big wage in 1930 for a girl of twenty-three – could buy a fifteen-roomed house, but I had been preparing for this from the days when I had carried the grey hen instead of taking the tram, and so saved a ha'penny. This was hidden in the rafters of the lavatory where the plaster was broken, and if Kate knew about it she never raided my bank, although if she were very hard up she might say 'Ee! I don't know what Aa'm going to do, Aa haven't a penny for the gas,' and she would shake her head and then ask, 'Have you anything, hinny?'

My reply was nearly always the same, 'Mind, I want it back our Kate,' and I usually got it back.

Although I was a saver I was never mean. Once I gave two shillings to Tommy Richardson – I was ten at the time. The first Kate knew about it was when Mrs Richardson came to the door.

'Did you know that your Katie has given our Tommy two shillings?'

'No,' said Kate. 'But if she has its her own money that she's saved, it's not mine so you needn't worry.'

I liked our Kate that day.

'Why did you give him two shillings?' she asked me later.

' 'Cos I was sorry for him,' I said. 'He never gets to the Crown.'

'But you can get in the Crown for a penny.'

'I know,' I said.

She shook her head. 'Have you any coppers left?' she asked.

I stared at her: 'I gave him the lot.'

When I first went into service and received ten shillings a week I would turn it up to Kate and she would give me two shillings back, which was quite generous pocket-money. That she wanted to borrow a shilling on the Monday didn't matter, I could have spent it all on the Saturday. And when I started my pen painting business and made a profit of nine and sixpence a week I managed to save enough to put down for a bike. This, too, I eventually paid for. I've always had a horror of debt and I can remember fighting with her when the instalment was due and she wanted me to let it slide. I never knew any peace until that bike was paid for.

But I didn't start to save properly until I went into Harton Institution. And I knew then I had to save for a purpose. Me granda was now becoming an old man and I was well aware that when he died there would be no money to bury him, so I put five shillings a month into a South Shields Building Society; I also insured Kate in the Prudential at a penny a week.

Taking all things into consideration, Kate was very lenient with me with regard to money. She must have remembered what it felt like always to have to tip her pay up, and never once did she enforce this on me. But nearly every pay-day, on the last day of the month, she asked if I could lend her a pound, almost half my wages. Sometimes I stuck out because I knew what would happen to it. At such times she would get me granda to appeal to me, and somehow I could never refuse him anything he asked for, for he never asked much of me. If I hadn't been sure that what I gave them would go mostly on filling the grey hen and getting a drop of hard I would have willingly turned up the whole of my pay, and have been happy to do so, feeling their need of me.

When I left Harton Institution in nineteen twenty-nine I took out my first big insurance. This was a tricky affair because I thought I could not produce a birth certificate. Being illegitimate I was under the impression that either I wouldn't have one, or, if I had, it would state the true nature of my birth. I couldn't ask anyone about this, least of all, Kate, so there was a lien put on the certificate in case I should die from some congenital disease. When I arrived in Hastings I raised the insurance to a thousand pounds. And I met the added weight of the premiums by taking the bonuses as they fell due.

I remember going for an exaimination to a doctor in Hastings who was acting on behalf of the insurance company and he, looking at me very funnily, said, 'What does a young girl like you want to take out such big policies for? Are you thinking of committing suicide? Or if you're saving what are you saving for?' In answer to this I could have told him that I was now under the impression that in my position I would never meet the kind of man who would be able to give me the way of life and the things I craved, so I was saving to supply my own needs.

Yet this was not the sole reason I took out the policies. When I was eleven and making my first train journey alone from Tyne Dock to Birtley I insured my life at the booking office – I think it cost tuppence for a fifty pound insurance – because I always felt that I wanted our Kate to have something of her own. This would appear to be in complete variance with the feeling that I was only happy when there was no money in the house to buy drink, but I worked it out in those far off days in a very unchildish way: if I were dead I wouldn't feel about her drinking would I? But when she got the money she would know that I thought about her – I didn't phrase it: she would know that I loved her. So, with the larger policy as with that first one, I made it over to her in the event of anything happening to me. And it did occur to me on this occasion that she would drink herself to death. The mind is a strange mixture of contradictions.

But that is how I came to have the securities to offer a building society in return for the gentleman's residence, which was, even in those days, dropping to bits with dry rot and woodworm.

Why did I want this house? Well again there were two main reasons; one concerned Kate, the other is evident in all I have written. This was the goal I'd aimed at for years. This was the picture come down from the wall, the picture that housed the ladies and gentlemen. This was the other way of life.

Also I realised that I wanted this house because of the piece of ground on which it stood as much as anything else. I never wanted to walk in public parks or through someone else's wood, I wanted a square of ground, shall we say, leasehold from God. Outside my square, nations could rage, governments could fall, but nothing would be able to touch me. It was a sort of faith with me that once I had acquired a piece of ground for myself I'd know happiness.

My experience of living in a number of furnished rooms – I seemed to be unfortunate in picking landladies who had a way with orange boxes and could convert them into dressing tables and cupboards – I decided was a poor exchange for what I had left in the North. During a sojourn with one such orange box landlady, I lived for a time in the Institution, taking the Assistant Matron's place in an emergency during a flu epidemic, and I found that the good lady was letting my room while still drawing the money for it. This decided me to follow the advice of a friend and take a flat.

The flat was in Westhill House and had one large room and a kitchen-cum-bathroom.

Having been brought up among old furniture, everything being second, third, or fourth-hand, I determined I was going to have everything in my flat new. The room cost me a hundred pounds to furnish – I did it on the instalment plan – and the result was something that I have never been able to achieve since. When describing it now it sounds awful, even to me; it had to be seen to be appreciated. The walls were papered with a dark blue paper, the woodwork was black. On the long window I draped dull pink satin curtains; in front of them were two jewel boxes, on each of which stood an eighteen inch figure of a snow-white octaroon, these were the only second-hand things I bought. The carpet was in Chinese design, being plain grey with a black spray. The Put-U-Up suite was in another shade of blue, and there was one picture entitled 'The First Piano Lesson'.

I loved this flat and was so proud of it – but not proud of the job that provided the money for it.

I think I felt ashamed of working in a laundry from my first week in Hastings. Although I was managing and had an assistant and ten outdoor staff, besides being in charge of any number up to twenty-five mentally defective inmates, and two to four different men every day from the casual ward, I felt it was an inferior type of work and inwardly resented the fact that I was wasting my brains and energy on it, for as always I gave everything I had to the job in hand. It was not up to the standard of the two previous laundries I had worked in, yet everything outside it seemed to be on a much higher level. I remember being shown old Hastings – and the slums. Slums? Where were the slums? There didn't at that time seem to be any real poor in this town. The conditions of living were far above those which I had left, not in the New Buildings – these remained static throughout the years – but in Shields and Jarrow, and Hebburn, and Pelaw and all the towns along the Tyne, and far inland too into mining districts. Perhaps it was the atmosphere of this town that was swept so closely by the sea breezes and where everything appeared so clean which helped with the higher level impression. Yet I remember Kate remarking during her first holiday, as she pointed to some litter lying in the High Street around seven o'clock in the morning – we were on our way to watch the sun rising from the East Hill – 'By, this wouldn't happen in the North, the streets would have been clean before this time in the morning.'

In spite of this feeling of being ashamed of my work, when I was asked out by what seemed to me in those days the better class people, I lost no time in telling them where I was employed. I didn't want to pass under false pretences.

I remember one old lady asking me how I had become educated since I had apparently been working from an early age and was now working in a laundry. I was flattered that she should think that I was educated, and replied that I had been taught privately. Well, was not Lord Chesterfield my tutor?

This particular old lady was known as a gentlewoman. She had run a tiny house-school and was not only without a degree of any kind but had had no education that qualified her for teaching. Her only accomplishment as far as I could gather was a natural refinement of manner.

It is hard to believe now but up to a few short years ago a town such as this had many such schools, and the pupils left them with the privilege of looking down their noses at the lesser female world, and very little else. In those days I envied the lady-like veneer that covered their ignorance, and wished that I could have attended such an establishment.

It was when I first came to Hastings that I learned too that doctors, like priests, didn't know everything. I had been brought up with the idea that they did. Doctor MacHaffie was a very clever man, me granda said so; and then there was Doctor Shanley in Harton Institution. The verdict on Doctor Shanley was 'He's ever so nice' and 'He'll put you right'. But from the first doctor I met in Hastings – an eye specialist to be correct – I learned they weren't infallible; nevertheless it was from this man I also learned how I appeared to other people.

My eyes had been giving me great trouble. For years now I had been doing ledger work. Managing, I shouldn't have had to continue with this task but I had, the result being that my eyes, which had never been good, began to get worse, and when I could no longer see the figures I went to the oculist. He took one look at me and said, 'You had better go to the hospital.'

The specialist at the hospital, after a very short examination, said, 'You must have glasses right away. You should have worn them from a small child. Come to my house tomorrow morning and I'll see they are ready for you.'

This was indeed very good of the man and when I went to his house the next morning – a very posh affair – I realised that I was being treated as a private patient, and when I offered to pay for his services and he refused I thought, what a nice man.

'You'll have no more trouble now,' he said, 'except that things may appear on different levels for a time. But you must always wear glasses, remember that.'

Whereas I couldn't see figures before, now I saw them not only enlarged but rising out of the page and almost hitting me. This distortion became worse when I was walking. The pavement moved, and steps disappeared from under my feet. I put up with this for he had warned me of it; but he hadn't warned me about the spots.

These spots in my eyes became very painful. After a fortnight I went back to the hospital. The doctor – Mister he was called, which gave him an added distinction – seemed slightly surprised to see me but told me that this condition would pass.

After another fortnight, and it hadn't passed, and I was in real distress, even more so than before I had been given the glasses, I again went to the hospital and sat on one of the wooden forms in the out-patients' department. There were about ten patients before me but the doctor, when coming in, happened to catch a glimpse of me and sent the nurse to tell me to come into the surgery first.

'What do you want?

'I've got these spots, doctor; they are very painful.'

'Sit down.'

I sat down.

'Now . . . Do you mean to tell me that you think you can still see spots?'

'Yes, doctor, even at night.'

He stared at me for a long, long moment; then rising abruptly, he said, 'Come here.'

In the dark room he almost took my eyes out and laid them on my cheeks. Then we returned to the office again, he marching ahead. Sitting down and facing me now he stared at me for another long moment before he remarked, 'There's nothing wrong with your eyes other than the need for glasses. But you are the kind of woman who, if you want to see spots, you'll see spots.'

No one had ever spoken to me like this before, least of all a doctor.

As I stood at the dispensary window waiting for some ointment, and feeling terribly low, I couldn't control my tears and a man and woman came from among the waiting patients and spoke to me. When I told them what had happened they looked at each other, and then the woman said, 'It's a repeat of five years ago. I thought I was going blind. They sent me to London because of the spots and there they found out it was nothing to do with my eyes. I had stomach trouble, and once that cleared up I didn't have the spots any more. My eyes are all right now but my husband's need attention . . . I was always troubled with constipation,' she finished.

The spots soon disappeared. But I always remember that man for he showed me a side of my character of which I hadn't been consciously aware. My insistence and persistence annoyed him. If I wanted to do a thing I would do it.

To this day I say to myself, 'If you want to see spots you'll see spots. Go to it.'

*   *   *

176

At one period during my first year in Hastings I experienced a feeling of great loneliness. I was afraid of making men friends, and I couldn't seem to get to know any girls of my own age with similar tastes outside the institution. Inside it I had two good friends in the Master and Matron who kindly looked upon me as a daughter, but as they already had one of their own, and of my age, this wasn't actually a good thing. This also was a trying period physically, for I was bleeding from the right nostril almost every day and it sapped my energy, and what I needed most of all in my job was energy for I was trying to inoculate a phlegmatic staff with a northern approach to work.

One Saturday night, returning from the pictures to my current orange box bedsitter, in the attic of a tall house on the West Hill, when the landlady was away, as were all the other tenants, I climbed the endless stone steps up to the house, and the four flights of stairs, saying to myself 'I can't stand it, I'm going home, I'm going home.' I had been brought up among friendly people, people who would stop and speak to you in the street whether you wanted them to or not. Here you could die and no one would even know; and this could have come about quite easily within the next few hours.

All the loneliness in the world was wedged inside me, it had to come out. It swelled, and swelled, threatening to choke me. I began to cry as I'd never cried before; the tears seemed to gush out of every pore in my body and the blood flowed from both my nostrils. Reaching my room, I threw myself on to the bed just as I was. I couldn't stop my crying, I couldn't stop the bleeding. Sometime in the night I fell asleep, and when I awoke at twelve o'clock on the Sunday morning I thought I was dead and had gone to Hell. Eventually I got on my feet but I couldn't recognise myself, or the bed. Everything was covered with blood.

The following week I saw a specialist, whose main question was did I pick my nose. He kept using the word epistaxis. So that's what I had epistaxis. But what was epistaxis? The dictionary said – bleeding from the nose.

I was told I must go into hospital. I waited weeks, I waited months. When at last I received the notification it was dated for December 23rd. I had made arrangements to go and spend Christmas with Elsie, my northern friend. She had relations in Hull and we were going to have a grand time. I went to Hull. What was a nose bleed or two compared to being with friends.

During this lonely period I made a friend of a temporary worker in the laundry. She was eleven years my senior, Irish and full of blarney and charm; she was married but had left her husband and child in Ireland. I was breaking a rule here, for I had made up my mind never to make friends with members of my staff. It just wouldn't work. But once again I took this happening as an answer to a prayer. In my loneliness I had prayed for a friend; and God said, take your pick and pay for it. But I hadn't to pay the price for Annie for some years.

And now I come to the other reason why I took 'The Hurst', the reason that concerns Kate.

It was in the August 1931 that I went home for my first holiday. The house seemed strange and empty. Me granda was no longer in it; he had died on Holy Thursday of the previous year. I had not come home for his funeral. Logic told me it would be putting the money to a wrong use. Far better send it to Kate with the twenty pounds I'd saved to bury him. This I did. I felt guilty about not going to me granda's funeral, and I knew really that the logic concerning the money had nothing to do with my absence, the truth being I was afraid to witness how the money would be spent, and its effects on Kate – I remembered me grandma's funeral. My fears were well-founded, as my Aunt Mary piously informed me later. 'She was rotten with it,' she said, 'and she only paid half the bill'.

The last thing me granda said was, 'Is there word from her?' I had written home at least twice a week, and until he took to his bed he had always met the postman. And it was because he was no longer in the kitchen that I knew a phase of my life had ended.

Of course I spoke glowingly about Hastings, and my flat.

'Oh,' said Kate, 'wouldn't I just love to see it!'

At this particular time she had been married to Davie McDermott for eight years. The slump was at its height in the North and he had been out of work for over a year and they had been living on the dole. And she said to me that they had lived better, and happier, on the dole than at any other time of her life. The dole was regular, at least for a period, and they had passed the means test.

Anyway Kate knew that if she got into debt it would be fatal, so for about the only time in her life she planned her spending, and a good fifty per cent of it went on food. Then there was the rent and the gas and the coal, which left very little out of a pound for drink.

At this time she looked happier than I'd ever seen her. Davie and she had the house to themselves, life was quiet. But as I talked of Hastings and my flat she expressed an urge to get away from the mucky North and all it held, and kept saying, 'Aw! lass, I'm glad you made the break.' So why should I not say to her, 'You must come for a holiday.'

She looked at me and her eyes clouded as she said, 'Aw! Katie, I would love that. I've had but one holiday in me life and that's when I went to the Lake District when I was looking after the Patterson bairns in me teens.'

So Kate came to Hastings for a holiday and she charmed everybody she met. The day I took her round the laundry she was dressed in black silk and lace. It was a dress she had come by in a second-hand shop and it suited her to perfection. She looked a regal figure; her skin was still good, her nose, at this time was not red and blotched, for being deprived of spirits had benefited both her figure and her looks, and she could carry herself well.

In the eyes of my staff, right down to the most mental defective of the inmates, my stock went up.

Aye, they said, didn't she look a lady, every inch a lady. But she wasn't stiff, not like you'd think of Miss Mac's mother at all, if you know what I mean, because Miss Mac was straight-faced, Miss Mac hadn't that pleasant kind look her mother had. Oh, she was a real lady, you could see that.

I kept close to Kate all the time and guided her through the departments, being careful that she didn't stop to chatter to anyone, for I dreaded her starting to joke. More still, I dreaded her bringing out a malapropism, which as likely as not she would do once she got going. She liked to impress company, did Kate.

The visit was a success; everybody thought she was wonderful – with one exception, the Matron. The Matron had taken me under her wing. Matrons had a habit of doing this with me. By this time she knew about my birth, because she had asked for my birth certificate and I had told her I hadn't one, and she had said it wasn't any surprise to her. And when she saw my mother she said to me, 'You have nothing of her in you, and you should thank God for it.'

Kate did not take to the Matron either. I had written to her earlier telling her that I had to explain the circumstances of not having a birth certificate. It was then, for the first time, in a long letter, she told me that I had a birth certificate. What made me think I hadn't? And my father's name was on the birth certificate. She was angry that, as she said, I should have given myself away.

I had always been under the impression that because I hadn't a known father I wouldn't have a birth certificate. It was as if I'd decided that the law which labelled me as illegitimate, which state, as everybody knew, was a bad thing, was not likely to give me anything to prove that I existed. Of course I had never dreamed of enquiring into this matter. The subject was one to steer clear of. It was taboo except in the depths of my mind where it was continuously active, forever churning itself in a morass of shame.

Anyway the holiday was a success. Kate took a liking to Hastings, a greater liking to the flat and my way of life. She didn't once go near a bar during her visit and when I got her a bottle of beer in and she said, 'I don't want it, lass. I don't need it any more.' I think that was the happiest moment of my life. She didn't need it any more.

Annie was absolutely charmed with Kate and she said to me, 'Fancy having a mother like that and living apart. She has no ties in the North, why on earth don't you have her to live with you? She's a wonderful woman, and a wonderful cook, and so cheerful, so good, so kind.'

Annie knew nothing whatever about Kate's drinking or the trials of my early life, so I suppose I must not blame her, but she it was who said to Kate in front of me, 'Why don't you come and live here, mam?' And she it was who first called Kate, Mother. And Kate turned to me, I can see her look now, beseeching, as she said quietly, 'It's up to Katie.'

What could Katie do?

When we were together I said to her, 'You know I can't stand the drink; it nearly drove me mad before,' and she answered, 'Aw, lass, that's in the past. I've never touched a drop since just after fathar died, not until you bought it for me.'

'Is that true?'

'Honest to God.' She blessed herself.

And so she came to Hastings.

I took a larger flat in the same house, a five-roomed flat. It cost me twenty-five shillings a week.

And then came the day that she was to arrive. I left work early to meet the five o'clock train, but she had arrived at four-thirty and was sitting outside the station on one of her cases, and I stopped dead some yards from her, petrified.

A great sickness was sapping the soul of me. I was crying loudly inside, 'What have I done? What have I done? Oh my God not again, not in Hastings, not in this new way of life.' The face I was looking at was bloated, the blue of the eyes almost opaque. I knew the signs, she had been on the bottle for some days, and, as always, she was aggressive with it. Where had I been? She sitting in a strange place all this time and nobody to meet her. Fine thing. Well, wasn't I going to take a case?

Now began a period of strategy and cover up, and Kate, being no fool, knew herself that this was necessary. There were, on the next floor to us in Westhill House, three sisters. They were gentlewomen of the first water. Their name was Harvey, and it was in their drawing room that a man rose to his feet for the first time in my presence. This was significant to me and it had happened before my mother came on the scene; it seemed all part of my new way of life. But they, too, liked Kate. 'Oh, Miss McMullen,' they said, 'your mother has such a happy disposition. She is such a dear person.'

I told Kate. It was a gentle warning not to let herself down in front of the Misses Harvey. For a period she didn't; and for a period, too, she did all she could to help me. Davie was on a weekly boat at the time and nearly every week he would send her five pounds. This was a very good wage in those days, and constituted quite a lot of overtime. He would have been wise to send her half that amount, but Davie adored her and could see nothing wrong in anything she did. She bought the food and we lived well, and with my money I furnished the remainder of the two-floor flat. The idea was to take in summer visitors.

Every Friday night I would visit the antique shops of Mr Cracknell, Mr Reeves, and Mr Papworth, in the High Street, and there pay on some piece of furniture I had put aside. I was learning that all second-hand furniture was not junk. Why, in those shops I saw pieces like those in the house of the lady in Harton, the one I had been companion to. It was enlightening.

As yet I steered clear of sale rooms. This was because of a bargain Annie had got me earlier. I had, when I furnished my little flat, everything but a small kitchen table. I would have to wait for that, I couldn't run up any more bills. 'Nonsense!' said Annie; 'I can get you one at Dunks for five shillings.'

One night I returned home from work, opened my door and fell back. I thought I had come into the wrong flat. I looked at the number on the door. It was my number all right. Annie had got me the kitchen table, plus the entire contents of the kitchen and hallway of a decrepit hotel. For eighteen shillings she acquired seventeen aspidistras in great china pots – one was two foot six across – two mighty gas stoves, in comparison with which the one in the kitchen of No 10 was a pup, a seven foot kitchen table, now up-ended in the middle of my lovely room, and three wash baskets of filthy kitchen utensils, among which was a box holding forty corkscrews.

It was five years before I entered a sale room.

With one thing and another it's no wonder my age was never believed. I was twenty-four at this time and looked every hour of thirty. I was holding down a tough job, and managing the staff of that laundry was a tough job, for nearly all the women were married and much older than myself. Moreover I had my own ideas about how a laundry should be run and the finished articles appear. I was nothing if not efficient. I was known among my staff as a nigger-driver, and among some as a bugger.

One happy period Kate and I did have, and this was her first Christmas in Hastings. Funds were low and I remember that together with Annie we went out shopping late on the Christmas Eve and managed to get a fifteen-pound turkey for seven and sixpence. And we laughed and we ate, and I relaxed for three whole days.

But this was too good to last. There was a public house at the bottom of the street, too near for anyone as weak as Kate to resist for long. She had managed to keep out of it for a longer period than I had thought possible, but now it became a daily occurrence to pay a visit to 'The Hole in the Wall'.

The red light was shining brightly again and I was worried sick in case she would let herself go. There was only one thing for it, I should have to get her right away from the bars. It was at this time that I saw the advert: 'Gentleman's residence for sale'.

On the day the agent took me to view the place it was pouring with rain. But as soon as I saw this house beyond the big red gate I knew that it was for me. Here was the picture come down from the wall. Here was the setting I had dreamed since I was a small child. Here was the place I had bragged about in the school yard at Simonside. And here was the actual court-yard with the stables going off. Inside the house was a twenty foot half-panelled hall with a stained glass window. A beautiful drawing room with skirting boards two feet high, and mouldings round the ceiling. A big windowed alcove leading into a domed conservatory completed the charm.

The house had a funny smell. I knew nothing about dry rot at that time and it wouldn't have mattered if I had. I noticed here and there in the woodwork lots of little holes. I had never heard of woodworm. Again it wouldn't have mattered. And had I hesitated one moment about taking that house that agent would have prevented me for he was a psychologist. There was a butler's pantry going off the hall and during our excursion over the fifteen rooms, which included a glass observatory giving a magnificent view, he kept reminding me how handy that butler's pantry would be, how near the kitchen – it was only thirty feet from the stove. But that man knew that a Katie McMullen from William Black Street could not resist a house that had a butler's pantry.

So the building society took my Sun Life of Canada policies and I took the house in Hoads Wood Road, the general idea at that time being to make it into a guest house, but at the back of my mind I wanted to run it as a home for epileptics and mental defectives. And if Kate suspected that one of my reasons for taking the house was that it was a long walk to the first bar, she said nothing, for she too was enamoured of the place and worked wholeheartedly to get it into shape, for it had been empty two years and badly neglected before that.

There was one snag about leaving the flat. I had signed an agreement for three years and unless I could sub-let it I would have to pay the rent of twenty-five shillings a week. I couldn't let it, and the twenty-five shillings was a dreadful drain on my small resources. But it seemed it had to be this way, for eighteen months later Kate returned to the flat.

What led up to this is better left undisturbed, sufficient to say that I had not only to fight the drink at this time but a dominant woman who felt that because of the house I could not do without her. I was in a cleft stick; I had to put up with the drink – which was now delivered – or find myself with this great place on my hands, so she thought.

The picture on the wall had turned sour on me. I would have willingly lived in a garret full of orange boxes to be rid of the mental torture.

There were fights, reconciliations, promises. Fights, reconciliations, promises over and over. But she would not leave me until one black day, almost dead black for me, it was forced home to her that but for the intervention of Annie she would have had a corpse on her hands.

Annie was no longer living with us. Quite a while previously Kate had laid the blame for taking to the bottle again on the effect that Annie's daughter had on her. Annie had brought her seven year old daughter from Ireland. The child was not normal, but she was an innocent clinging thing wanting love. Kate had never had anything to do with mentals of any kind so the child got on her nerves. The result was Annie left, taking Maisie with her, and that's what Kate wanted for she had been jealous of her. I was very upset about this for in spite of Annie's constant blarney and the difference in our natures and approach to life I liked her very much because she had come into my life when I was lonely and had been kind to me.

After Kate had gone I had a very denuded house for I had refurnished the six rooms of the flat to enable her to take guests right away and I had to start from scratch again and build up. But the torment was less, although it was still in the background.

When the lease ran out on the flat and she was now called upon to pay the rent she made a move, and to a large house. She had got the taste for big houses in The Hurst. She was now going to show me what she could do. She was going to run a guest house, a select guest house.

Her first boarder was a master from the Hastings Grammar School. When this young man left he was replaced by a Mr Cookson.

Her letter telling me this reached me in Paris. I was at this time taking foreign guests and I became friendly with a family who insisted that I go and visit them at least for a week-end. That week-end was my second trip to Paris, the only times I was ever abroad; and with the exception of a fortnight in Gilsland and a week in Belfast, the only holidays I'd had up till then. I returned from Paris feeling very ill, physically because of the journey, I am no traveller, mentally because of Kate. She was living not half-a-mile from me now and was rarely, if ever, quite sober. So painful was it to me when I went to visit her that I would stop going for periods until concern for her would bring me to her again, sometimes to find her crying with loneliness, sometimes to meet the force of her tongue.

I called this night and could see she had a small load on, and when she asked me to go into the front room to meet the new guest I refused. Yet as she preceded me through the passage to let me out she pushed open the sitting room door and exclaimed in a tone which held deep pride 'Mr Cookson, this is my daughter.'

A fair young man rose from behind a table. He had beautiful hair and a kind face and a quiet voice.

It was done. In that first second of meeting fate was fixed for both of us. It happened as quickly as that.

My greeting was, 'Do you fence?' – this was said out of sheer nervousness. No, he didn't fence. Apparently we had nothing in common. Fencing was my only recreation. The lessons at the Bathing Pool were cheap and with a foil in my hand I struck out at life.

It was on the Wednesday evening that Kate made the introduction. On the Friday evening Tom Cookson called on me. For a timid young man, and he was timid in those days, he showed a great deal of courage, for I wasn't an easy person

185

to approach. He wondered if I would like to see the evening paper? Also he wondered if I would care to go to the pictures. I did care. It had begun.

My mother was pleased, Annie was pleased, but both only for a very short time. They couldn't either of them imagine that there could be anything serious between this young schoolmaster and me. It was ludicrous! If I had liked, couldn't I have married this one, or that one, or the other one, great big strapping men? From experience I knew all about great big strapping men. Right from my teens I had known great big strapping men and, mostly, I had found them – boast inside – a very explanatory North-country phrase for empty.

Now began a war, a siege. If I had made light of the matter nothing would have happened, but I did not feel this thing lightly. I was really in love for the first time in my life. In temperament and character, at least outwardly, Thomas Henry Cookson and I were at opposite poles, yet beneath the surface of flesh and bone, in the channels where the intangible but real life runs, we were one and we recognised this. I had what he needed – strength. Besides the physical attraction I had strength of purpose. He had what I needed, kindliness, a loving nature, a high sense of moral values, and above all he had what I needed most – a mind.

I had always wanted a man who could speak my language, not my verbal language but the one which I felt. I had known for a long time the reason why I hadn't married any of the men I had met, the eligible men; it was because mentally I felt they were inferior and I had the wisdom to know it is not a good thing for a woman to feel mentally superior to a man.

The fight I had to put up for Tom against my mother and Annie would fill a book of another kind.

It was not until two years later when they had managed to separate us that Kate decided that if I would pay her debts – for she was now surrounded by real debts, and in a dreadful state of health through incessant whisky drinking – she would go back to the North, back to the New Buildings. This decision was a great blow to her pride for she knew people would say, 'I told you so'.

I had not seen her for some weeks for I had told her I was finally finished. This was after I heard she was maligning me.

The only thing I really valued, my good character, she was aiming to destroy.

In all her stages of drinking I think this was her lowest.

We parted on Hastings station one Saturday morning at nine o'clock. She was crying so much she couldn't see me. She was sober and sad. She was the Kate I loved. How could I let her go back to the New Buildings and humiliation. She was my mother. I had a duty to her because she was ill. What did it matter what she had done to me, perhaps God meant that I should suffer in this way . . . 'DON'T BE SUCH A BLOODY FOOL!' The voice seemed to spurt up from the depth of my misery-filled bowels and explode in a screech which filled the station. I was startled by the train letting off steam.

There was no word of good-bye. We held hands. The train moved away and I groped blindly towards a seat and sat down. Sadness, pity and guilt were playing their usual havoc with me. Poor Kate. Poor Kate; but thank God. Oh thank God, it was over. I was free again. And I must never, never, never, let her live with, or be near me ever again in my life. But of course I wouldn't, I wasn't mad altogether. Or was I? A few minutes ago I had nearly said 'Stay.'

I made my way to church. I had not been to church for some time, for my mind, in spite of the fear this engendered, would probe and question the dogma of my faith. But this morning I wanted to thank God. I did so, and finished humbly, 'Help her, oh Lord, for I can't. And forgive me, for I know that never as long as I live will I be able to stand her near me for any length of time.'

'Never is a long time,' said God.

Before Kate left Hastings she asked me would I take Tom as a boarder. He was on his summer vacation and was abroad. She hadn't told him she was leaving, and she didn't want to put him to the trouble of searching for new digs. She suggested this only because she felt absolutely sure it was well and truly over between us. He now had other interests, and wasn't someone interested in me, a big man? What did it matter if he was married.

I had, at this time, in the Hurst two epileptics, two T.B. convalescent patients, and a retired Army Captain whose pension was swallowed by a maintenance order which left him with about twenty-five shillings a week on which to run a car – a Captain must have a car – breed dogs, and pay for full board and lodgings. But he had great charm, and it worked – and not only with Annie.

Annie was now running the house for me, as only an indolent Irishwoman can. She was helped by a cook-general who was deaf, vile tempered and incompetent, and as neither of them had any idea of time, or organisation, or, least of all, the staggering rapidity with which bills mounted, I had, on the side so to speak, another daily source of worry.

So to join the household came Tom, with Annie's approval, for she too was backing the big fellow.

As soon as Tom entered the door and we looked at each other, it was done again. It had never been undone, there had only been a forced separation.

Now began open warfare, Annie, like Kate, thought she had me in a cleft stick. How would I manage if she walked out? I had to keep on my job? Since it was the only sure source of income – guests came and went, except Army Captains who knew when they were on to a good thing. For nearly two years this particular battle raged. I was tired and weary.

Why didn't I throw the lot of them out? Incompetent cooks, possessive friends, sponging Army Captains, patients, whose people had money to burn but who would beat you down to the last penny – I would never argue about money and always let myself be touched by a sob story. But I couldn't make a clean sweep because anyone who does me a good turn has me for life. I always want to repay a good turn tenfold. Annie had been good to me when I was lonely, and although it was pointed out that she had been repaid a thousandfold, with my friendship, that didn't matter. I don't forget easily; moreover, she wasn't well. As for Mrs Webster, the cook, she was handicapped by deafness. She was alone in the world. Where would she go if I put her out? To the Salvation Army home in London. And then the patients themselves. They seemed to like living at The Hurst, and the timetable didn't bother them. But it bothered the summer guests, and me.

I was tied now by different loyalties.

By 1939 I had been working at the Institution for ten years.

I had actually been doing an average of a sixteen hour day over those ten years, for when I returned at half-past five in the evening to The Hurst, there was always planning, arranging, and worrying and work of another sort. And not a little section of this was the pampering and the nursing of this decaying, tender house, and I mean tender, because that is how I felt towards The Hurst.

Every penny I had left after paying the bills went into patching up the house; the floors, the stairs which fell through, the roof, which leaked every time it rained. The Heath Robinson water system which gave us, one Christmas Eve, a total of twenty-six bursts at one go and practically left us afloat. The garden, in which I turned navvy and made tons of concrete in the construction of a pond and crazy paving. I had a little help with this at first but funds wouldn't allow for continuous paid labour, so for two years I struggled with my pond and paths, and this I took as a form of recreation.

But in the beginning of 1938 there came a showdown. Things could not carry on as they were for I was near breaking point. So, as a solution, I mortgaged The Hurst and bought another house for thirteen hundred pounds so that Annie could start up in business on her own. She borrowed a £100 which went towards the purchase. Within a week part of the adjoining land was sold for more than £600, with half of which I paid off the house, the remainder going to Annie. I must have been barmy, for I hadn't a penny myself at the time. When, after the War, and amid bitterness, I transferred the house to her as a deed of gift – my return for this was £250 – she sold it for a substantial sum – as a result of that deal Annie was to become the owner of many houses, and to make a great deal of money, only to lose it all, together with her friends. We didn't meet for some years and when we did her first words to me were, 'You always said you couldn't buy friendship'.

So once again Annie is back in my life; but a different Annie now, one who almost adores the man she hated, for his kindness in her need reduced her to shame.

But with Annie leaving The Hurst I was at the mercy of Mrs Webster. Temper and bad cooking were the least of my worries. I knew that I would have to make a go of The Hurst, for so much more depended on it, so I decided to run it entirely as a home for mental defectives and epileptics, and so began planning to leave the Institution.

For some months after Kate went North I knew a feeling of release, and then Davie died. Drowned one night when he was returning to his ship. They had been having a night out, as was usual when his boat made its weekly docking, and in the dark he fell into the river, and the bottles in his pocket helped to weigh him down.

Her sorrow at this time was terrible. Davie had not only loved her, he had adored her. To him she could do no wrong, and she had known the only real happiness she'd had in her life through him, and now he was gone.

The only thing that would ease the pain was whisky.

She was living in a flat in Larkin's house, the big house on the terrace in the New Buildings. I stayed with her for a fortnight and it was a continuous nightmare. When sober, her anguish tore at me until I was even glad when it was hushed with the drink.

She hadn't a penny coming in and I put in some work to get her a sum of money from the company Davie had worked for. They weren't obliged to give her anything, but they allowed her something over two hundred pounds. I asked if they would give it to her at the rate of two pounds a week and this was arranged.

I think it was in the May when she received her first payment, but by the first week in August there was nothing left. Annie came to me to say she had been sending her money for the past fortnight – Annie was always good like this – apparently Kate had gone to the company with a tale of setting up a business, and they had given her the lot, and she had spent every farthing. She couldn't have drunk all that amount herself in that short time and still lived, but you can always get friends when you have money. She could never keep money. Perhaps that's why she survived until she was seventy-three.

I left the Institution in the August 1939 and was glad to do so for they had not been happy years. I always seemed to be at war with someone, from the Matron downwards. She, too, wanted to dominate my life, and pick my friends, and so we would quarrel and make it up, and quarrel again. The strain of running the laundry at my standard was wearing and I thought my staff would be glad to see me go; so it was heartening when, meeting one of them later, she said, 'Oh, we wish you were back. We thought you the very devil at first but we all grew to respect and like you. You see, we knew exactly how far we could go and where we stood with you.'

Even the Sister Tutor asked me if I wouldn't consider going back, that is if I wasn't married. They all thought I'd been married on the quiet, for who would be mad enough in 1939 to give up a job with three pounds a week plus dinners and a pension unless to pick up a bigger pay packet.

For weeks afterwards I too wondered if I wasn't a little mad for I had only two patients, but I thought, let my private wars settle a bit and then Tom and I would get married quietly.

A few weeks later war started, and I was turned into one of the minute cogs in its wheel.

As I had fifteen rooms in The Hurst I was told that I had to fill them either with children or blind people. Children were out of the question, with mental defectives, so I took the blind, and for a year, with the help of Gladys – the antithesis of Mrs Webster who was now managing Annie's house under my supervision, for Annie herself was in the Army – and Tom, after school, I coped with twelve blind men from the East end of London. I received a pound a head for each man, out of which he had to be fed, nursed – some were bed-ridden – shaved, hair cut, and entertained. Like the wireless, I had a Monday-night at-eight during which they had a sing-song and dance, and beer and extras. All out of a pound a week.

I was always a very good manager but even so I couldn't make that pound cover the cost. But what was money anyway, I thought; just take a day at a time, we might all be dead tomorrow. So I went on cooking, cleaning, nursing and washing. Whereas I had never wet my hands in the laundry, I now wet not only my hands, but my feet, because some of the men's underwear would be so filthy I wouldn't handle it but tramped it out in the bath.

A year of being on duty for twenty-four hours a day, together with the previous years of hard work and anxiety was now beginning to tell. I was under the doctor for what he termed nervous debility, and I was bleeding from the nose every day. This he looked upon as a safety valve.

It was on the 1 June, 1940 that Tom and I were married. They were evacuating Dunkirk. The country was in a state of chaos. My blind people were going to be re-evacuated. Everybody around me seemed in a dither all except me. At two o'clock on this Saturday I was going towards something that from being a mirage had turned into solid reality. The master of the Institution, Mr Silverlock, was to give me away. And as I walked down the aisle of St Mary Star-of-the-Sea on his arm I silently rejected my childish image of Doctor McHaffie as me da, and substituted this fine man in his place; and strangely, from that day the master, as I always called him, referred to himself as my adopted father.

The marriage service was short, even ugly. The priest seemed to throw it at us. Tom had not become a Catholic, although he had signed a paper to say the children of the marriage would be brought up as Catholics. This particular priest had visited my house for two or three years, as had the nuns from the Convent. I was at that period clutching at all outward signs to hang on to my religion, trying to shut my mind against all criticism. I had, since my second year in Hastings, twice given up my religion, but now I was back in it praying that it would hold me, praying that it would not deprive me of its particular form of security, and peace. The priest used to visit the house weekly, stay to tea, play the piano, sing, and later cause me to chastise myself and ask what did I want, why couldn't I see my religion through the eyes of this priest who was jolly and broadminded?

The priest had every hope that Tom would come into the Church. For my part I wasn't pressing Tom openly, but I was praying that he would, for once in he would be a stave to which I could tie myself.

It was on the Monday morning previous to the Saturday on which we were married, that I received a letter which caused me to make the sudden decision. It came to me with lightning clarity that if Tom and I did not marry, and soon, still other elements would now drive a wedge between us. So I remember running to the gate and calling after him down the road, 'Tom! Tom! just a minute.'

When he came back I said to him, 'We'll be married on Saturday.' Just like that. He stared at me for a moment, clutched my hand, then turned and ran down the road. He always ran when he was happy, or excited. So I had gone to the priest and said, 'Father, we want to be married on Saturday.'

'Nonsense!' he said. 'Saturday? Oh, no, my dear, he'll have to come into the Church.'

'We want to be married on Saturday, Father.'

'Well . . . well, you can't be married in church without a dispensation from the Bishop and that will take some time.'

'I'm going to be married on Saturday, Father.'

'What if you can't?'

'I mean to Father.'

'Oh, now, now. Now!'

'We'll go to a Registry Office, Father.'

If you want to see spots you'll see spots.

Yet I find it odd when looking back that, being the type of person the oculist suggested, my life should have been so shaped by my emotions, for they have been as strings for certain people to play on, and once they discovered this weakness in me they twanged them all the harder. Yet every now and again I can see myself making a stand, as against the priest; and I won't play down the courage that it needed for a Catholic to stand up to a priest, especially twenty-nine years ago.

So we were married on that Saturday, and by the priest, in the church.

We told no one except the Master and Matron until the last minute. Yet there were quite a number of people in the Church, and it was said afterwards that never had so much laughter been heard in a vestry as on that day.

We came back to the house, to a wedding cake and refreshments. And there were a few telegrams awaiting us; one from Kate, who was holding her own kind of wedding reception.

'Well,' as she said to Mary, who passed it on later, 'whoever heard of a dry wedding.'

Going up to London the train stopped at Tonbridge. The station was full of Frenchmen, dirty and tired, the remnants of Dunkirk, and I sat in the carriage and cried.

We spent the first night of our married life in the Charing Cross Hotel, and the following day went to Grays, to Tom's people, who welcomed me most warmly. The same evening we returned home.

The house, and all in it seemed changed. As I stepped through the door I thought, Katie McMullen is dead. Miss McMullen is dead. Long live Catherine Cookson. Mrs Catherine Cookson.

Within a month The Hurst was empty, at least of people, and with the Grammar School I went to St Albans and sat on my cases in a sorting room waiting to be allotted lodgings.

A few weeks later we were very lucky to get a tiny little flat in the main street in St Albans, and there Tom and I spent the happiest year it was possible for two people to experience, and this in spite of me being ill all the time, and bleeding from the nose every day, which increased with my pregnancy.

I was five months pregnant when I received a letter from a friend to say that Kate was ill, and if I wanted to see her alive I should go North. I was always impulsive, and although I was in bed at the time I said to Tom we must make the journey, for if she died I would have her on my conscience all my life.

Why I should feel this way I just didn't know, I owed her nothing in the way of duty, or anything else, yet there was this bond between us pulling me towards her. And so on the Friday night we went up to London, on our way North, and ran into a big raid. I will never forget my first sight of an underground station packed, with horizontal humanity. The experience was devastating in itself, and later we sat in a train that crawled through inky blackness all night. The warnings were still on when, at nine o'clock the following morning, we arrived in Brinkburn Street, South Shields, at the very outdoor beer shop where I had come so often for the beer, and above which Kate was now living. She opened the door to me looking better than I'd seen her for a long time. She couldn't understand why I had come. 'Nonsense,' she said, 'I've never been bad, I've only had a cold.'

But I was glad I had come anyway. Everything was so uncertain; we might never see each other again; there was a war on, and what was more she was pathetically delighted to see us, for now she accepted Tom. And as she said on the quiet, she had always liked him but she hadn't liked him for me, but there it was. Many years later she confessed to loving him,

194

so much so that before she died she thought there was no one to equal him.

She had, at this time, found work with a doctor and Mrs Carstairs, but this only after trailing the streets of Shields for weeks in search of it. Time and again she had been turned down because, being so fat, no one could imagine her skipping around and doing a full day's work. As she herself often said, she could do a ten hour stretch and come up for more. And she did, often with the flesh of her ankles almost touching the floor.

For ten years she worked at the doctor's, right up until I brought her back home. Mrs Carstairs was good to her, and in return she repaid her in the only way she knew, with hard work that knew no limited hours. The Carstairs' household became her main interest, and twice a week I heard of their joys, and their sorrows. Until Kate died Mrs Carstairs wrote to her and never forgot her birthday. This brought Kate a great deal of happiness.

Doctor and Mrs Carstairs had known of Kate's weakness, but like most other people they were fond of her in spite of it, and, as Mrs Carstairs said, 'That was Kate's private life. She never let it intrude on her work.'

And there was another reason I was glad I had braved the raids and come North. I could now show them, indeed I could, that I was no longer Katie McMullen. I had a name. At last I had a name of my own. Moreover, I hadn't married a nobody; I had married a Grammar School master, a man who had been to Oxford.

I would have married Tom if he had been another Rooney, a dustman, from around Eldon Street. But he wasn't a dustman, he was a Grammar School master and I had married him. Yet the miracle was that the Grammar School master had married me. And yet I told myself, this is what I had been leading up to for years. This is why I had been educating myself. It had been tough going but I had made it.

During that visit as I was going through the arches towards East Jarrow, I met a woman. And she stopped me and said, 'Why, Katie, it's you! How are you gettin' on?'

So I told her how I was getting on: I was married, I was married to a Grammar School master.

'Aye, lass, it's just like yesterday that you used to go up and down this very road with a sack on your back catching the droppin's from the coke carts, remember? Aye, an' the trails you had up and down this very road with that grey hen. An' to Bob's ... mind Bob's? Aye, lass, you had a life of it. An' now you're married ... an' to a Grammar School master? It's hardly believable. Aye, you've done well for yourself; you've fallen on your feet, lass.'

Yes, I had fallen on my feet.

But it was brought home to me that day that you cannot get away from your early environment, you cannot get away from yourself, from the members of your family, the family of your townsfolk, the people you grew up with. They know all about you, and they will never see you but as they remember you when you lived among them.

The result of my trip to the North was that on the seventh of December I lost my baby. After nine days and nights of labour an exhausted nurse, with the help of Tom, delivered his six months old son, an exact, and minute, replica of himself, and I felt I was about to die.

Later, I was devastated afresh when I learned that the baby could not have a grave of its own but had to be buried in a general grave. Later still, when I went to the cemetery the attendant told me he had buried it with an old woman from the workhouse who had no one belonging to her, which gave me strange comfort.

In 1942 I lost my second baby in Sleaford. When in 1943 – we were now established in Hereford, Tom being at Madley R.A.F. Station – I lost my third baby, and was warned strongly that there were to be no more, I was faced with the fact that it was a sin to prevent life. There still remained in my mind the voice of the priest in the pulpit at Tyne Dock saying. 'It is less of a sin to take a new born child and dash its brains out against a wall than to prevent it coming into life.' I took my problem to the priest and the answer he gave me sent me out of the confessional box mystified. If there was sinning to be done, he said, then let it be done by my husband. I was to take no part in it.

No part in it?

The transubstantiation was worrying me too. I was willing

to accept it as a symbol, but I had been told flatly by the priest that this was no symbol, the bread and wine were actually the flesh and blood of Jesus Christ. The thought was repulsive to me; I couldn't go to Communion. The bread, as I've said, was always repugnant to me, but this conception of flesh and blood was rejected by both my stomach and my mind. This led a step further. At the exposition of the Host I no longer believed that Christ was alive on the Altar, and although I said, 'As the heart pants after the fountain of water so does my soul pant after thee,' in which I recognised beauty even when a small child, it was no use, I no longer believed what I was saying.

There was at that time in Hereford a priest who was a convert. He was kind and understanding. He was so because, being a convert, he saw my troubles primarily through the eyes of a Protestant; so sensible was he that Tom began to take instruction under him. This in a way terrified me, for I could now see Tom inside the Church, and me out. But I need not have worried on this score. Tom, I found, was merely trying to do this to help me solve my problems. And one of my problems was, that every Catholic was supposed to do everything within his power to bring his non-Catholic partner into the Church. This, he thought, might be the source of my trouble.

At this time I was becoming annoyed, and angry, and voiced my anger against some of the stupidity, and bigotry, of my religion. One thing in particular that angered me was a notice within the Church door dealing with mixed marriages. It seemed to my mind to place the Protestant partner in the marriage union on an animal level. The non-Catholic party was, in the eyes of the Church, damned, and the only hope for him was to come into this all-knowing, meticulous and God-presided fold.

But I didn't want to leave the Catholic Church. I loved Our Lady. I prayed to her constantly. I went to the convent and talked to the nuns. I wanted above all things, even more so than having a child, to remain a Catholic. I could have, like thousands of other Catholics, just lapsed, perhaps gone to my duties once a year, or when the priest raked me out. But I wasn't built that way, that was a form of cheating, of fear, and I, who was afraid of so many things, feared fear, and fought it.

CHAPTER TWELVE

After the loss of my first baby in St Albans I discovered, while forced to lie in bed, that I could draw. It was a great discovery. By the time I reached Hereford, via Leicester and Sleaford, I knew that I had unearthed a hidden talent. I could draw architecture. I took one of my drawings to a printer to see if it could be turned into Christmas cards. Indeed it could, he said, I had the art of texture.

What was texture with regard to art? I didn't know.

I was to learn that texture was the knack of making stone look like stone, or velvet appear like velvet with the simple aid of a pencil. I discovered academy chalk and carbon crayon. The printer said to me, 'You should go to the Art School. If you've done this without a lesson you have a gift that you should use.'

And so said the master of the Art School. He could not believe that I had achieved these drawings without a lesson. 'You must come when you can and take lessons here,' he said; 'you are capable of taking a third year exam and there is no reason why you should not eventually get to the Slade.'

I didn't know what the Slade was.

So much faith had Mr Milligan in my work that he had hung, in the yearly exhibition, two of my cathedral studies, and to my amazement and delight they got a mention in the Press.

I was an artist. Moreover, I was selling some of my drawings at five pounds a time. These were copies of photographs which the firm would send me, some as small as two inches by one and half inches, and these had to be enlarged to eleven inches by nine. I learned a new trade the hard way. Five pounds appeared like a fortune for a drawing until I realised I was back on the basis of my pen-painting days. It would take me a fortnight to do a drawing, and I would sit from the time Tom left for camp in the morning almost until he returned in the evening. Among other things now, my eyes began to suffer greatly again and I had to attend the hospital.

Then there was music. Hadn't I passed with honours in that first exam? Now was the time to take it up again. When I hadn't any orders in for drawing I was practising two, three or more hours a day. My teacher said, 'You know, you could be quite good. You must practice and take exams.'

I wanted to take exams for everything. I wanted to have something to show, something to prove that I could do things. I longed for exams.

During all this I was bleeding each day. But what was more, every moment of every day, and every second of every moment I was filled with anxiety and worry over Tom. He was, it could be said, in a comparatively cushy job instructing at Madley. A cushy job that he hated, and loathed, and which he tried to get out of time and again, but one at which I prayed that he would be kept until the end of the War.

I was obsessed at this time, too, by a feeling of guilt that I wasn't doing my duty. I offered myself for part-time work at the munition factory – although I was exempt through ill-health.

After five weeks packing cordite, I got cordite poisoning, and that was that.

Right from the beginning of the War I had a weird feeling that I wouldn't see the end of it, and in a way I didn't.

I had been ill for a long, long time and should have had medical attention. Continual loss of blood from my nose had made me anaemic. I was as thin as two laths. And I found now that I was becoming overwhelmed by the shame of my birth. The strange thing was that no one was aware of this. Not even Tom. I was a lively spark. I always made people laugh, I always talked and chatted. I always felt it was my duty to make a party go, there must never be a dull moment. People liked to be with me; I liked to be with people. And then I got phlebitis.

My condition was diagnosed in a surgery by an elderly doctor. I was told to go straight to bed. I was attended at the house the following day by a young, harassed, foreign doctor who had shown marked impatience with me before. On the third day he ordered me out of bed; on the sixth day I felt desperately ill and he came and ordered me back to bed again. I was in the house alone all day except for the father of my landlady, who was a very old man, and a nurse who came in to wash me. But most of the next six weeks was spent lying rigidly still, because of my leg, and looking out at the towering stone wall of Bulmer's Cider Factory that rose straight up from the bottom of the little garden, and thinking – when I wasn't practising my drawing for the exam – of all the things that had happened to me, but mainly about my birth, and Kate; and my thoughts weren't loving.

Then one morning, after Tom had gone to the camp, I was overcome by a weird and terrifying feeling. My heart raced, my limbs trembled, I felt sick and I was sure I was going to die. It was my first experience of nervous hysteria, but I was not told what it was.

I was now full of terrifying fears which I couldn't sort out or place in any category, and I found, when the time came to get up, that I couldn't use my legs.

A specialist was brought and advised that I should have a week or so in hospital, just for a change of scene. I had never minded going to hospital, I always got on very well in hospital. But on this occasion, unfortunately, I was put in a small ward where there was a patient who ruled the roost. I was in no state to combat an ignorant, stupid woman, but I knew after a week that if I didn't get out of that place, and away from her, I would go mad, really mad. Her technique was to inform all and sundry, in a loud whisper, 'That one across there has nerves. There's not a thing wrong with her, she just thinks there is. She's one of that sort, you know. It would do her good if she had something the matter with her. That would show her. There's me been in here . . .'

I thought when I arrived back in our room everything would be all right, but it was merely the beginning of the end. I couldn't get over the fact that I had nerves, that people thought that I was a bit funny. I, who was so sensible, and level-headed, with such a sense of humour – people with a sense of humour didn't have nerves.

When it was suggested that perhaps I should see a psychiatrist, the boil burst.

When, during my visit to him, this man further suggested that I should go for voluntary treatment, fear ran riot. Seeing this, he said it was up to me. I could either handle the situation myself, or have help. He was a very wise man in putting the onus on me for I knew I was no longer capable of handling this situation. It had now grown to such a gigantic form that even when in the state of deep depression, when nothing mattered, fear still held domination.

I went as a voluntary patient for treatment.

I cannot speak too highly of the kindness shown me by the Matron, nurses and staff of this particular place.

There were about twenty beds in our dormitory, classed as the light cases. One of the light cases was a big Catholic woman. She slept next to me and cried and screamed out her agony of mind most of the time. Another was a young girl, a pretty girl who had been there for years and was always walking out – they didn't call it running away – and always being brought back again. There was the vivacious good-looking girl who thought her husband had been going to poison her. And many others. The only one who seemed comparable with my own case was the woman who, when she lost her husband, couldn't face up to life.

In this place I could see myself becoming any one of these patients, for I was open to negative suggestion like a sieve to water. At times I felt I was a bit of every one of them. Yet the Matron and nurses took my case very lightly. It was just a passing thing they said; as i knew all my symptoms and the reason why I was in this state, half the battle was already won. Of course, I felt aggressive. Of course, I wanted to hit back at people and life. That was natural after what I had been through; it would all pass.

Once again I made myself useful to a Matron, by assisting her in the storeroom, and under occupational therapy I made gloves, and wove cloth, and suffered the torments of Hell, and not a little because all feeling of affection had left me. I had to confess to my beloved Tom that I no longer had any feeling for him whatever. It could have been that he was an inanimate object.

Tom, at this time, proved just how right I had been in my first judgment of him. No man could have been kinder, more loving, more patient than he was. Every night he rode fourteen miles on an old bike to see me for a few minutes. This after finishing a day's work in camp, the double journey to and from which entailed another fifteen miles.

It is hard for me to believe now that my main recollection of this place is the smell of urine. The house itself was magnificent. There was a large hall in which we ate very well; there were wide corridors, and a simply magnificent staircase. At an appointed time, we light cases went for electric shock treatment. I have an impression of going down stone stairs and sitting on wooden forms around a room which was adjacent to lavatories. The smell of urine that pervaded this place was worse than that in the infirm ward at Harton. And there we would sit, waiting our turn to go in and be shocked into unconsciousness. I remember, as I sat in this room, thinking of the lavatory in William Black Street that had been my haven, but that lavatory had never smelt like this. And then there came to my mind a forgotten memory from the past, and with it the intense feeling of disgust, and shame, that I experienced one day as I was crossing the road from the last arch, near the dock gates, and in my line of vision was the men's urinal, and out of it came two women accompanied by two men, and they were hanging on each other and laughing. The depravity of that moment was in the smell that was around me.

Under one electric treatment the machinery must have gone slightly wrong for I bounced up on the couch under the force of a terrific shock, but I was still conscious. This frightened me still further. The weird thing about the electric treatment was that you walked back to the ward. You were conscious of walking as if in a dream. Your feet lifted heavily over small objects that had turned into huge obstacles.

When I had been in the place five weeks I went into Hereford on my own for the day. It was a test. The test proved to myself that I was still mentally ill. On the following Sunday I decided to go to Mass. The priest was coming out from Hereford, the nice priest. I was clutching once more at the God I was denying, anything to use as a life-belt. I never forget the look on the priest's face when he saw me coming into that room. He came towards me, saying slowly, 'What-on-earth-are-you-doing *here?*'

A condition such as mine is difficult to explain at this distance. I can only say that I wouldn't wish the devil in hell

202

to have a breakdown. And if I had the choice of having a crippling, agonising physical disease, or that of a breakdown, I know, without hesitation, which I would choose.

Fear had been my companion since a tiny child. Hardly ever a day went past but I feared something, and the accumulation of all those fears was with me now.

Fear of drink . . . . of Kate in drink.

Fear of God.

Fear of not living a good life.

Fear of dying an unhappy death.

Fear of the priest and of his admonition from behind the grid in the confessional.

Fear of loving and of slipping the way of Kate.

Fear of people . . . even behind my gay laughter fear of people and what they might say about me having no Da.

Fear of losing Tom in the War – a great consuming, agonising fear.

Fear of doctors.

Fear of operations, of blood spattered floors and blinding arc lights.

Fear of swear words; this was with me always.

Fear of going mad.

FEAR . . . FEAR . . . FEAR . . . On with the years, mounting, swelling, until my laughter and small talk could not stretch to cover it, until I laughed too much. Then for a long period I laughed not at all.

I turned into a solid block of fear.

It would, at times, paralyse me, and I would lose the entire use of my legs; at others, it would make me retch for hours on end.

For twenty hours of each day I was in a wide-awake state of trembling terror, and the worst part of the state was the fear of what I might do in retaliation. The aggressiveness of my childhood period had returned. Indiscriminately it was turned against all mankind, but in particular, and powerfully, it settled on Kate.

One thing I knew for a certainty. I must face this thing and fight it. But how? The answer was that I must get back to The Hurst. In that house I would know a resurrection; at least so I thought. And in a way this proved true.

I had been in hospital just over six weeks when I discharged myself. They thought it was foolish of me, but I knew that I would only become worse surrounded by those poor people, who were, in a way, in a much worse state than I, for they were beyond being able to recognise, or analyse, their own symptoms.

The Hurst was in a dreadful state. For five years – except for a few months when it had a tenant who left it much dirtier than a herd of pigs would have done – it had been empty. It had received the slanting blows of two time-bombs, and the roof, never good, was now in very bad shape. It had taken a great shuddering, yet all we could claim for war damage was the removal of the tower.

But it didn't matter, nothing mattered. I was home once more. I almost knelt down and kissed the floor. Tom had a fortnight's leave, and with the help of his mother, who was most kind to me, we tackled the cleaning of the house.

An odd thing happened when I entered The Hurst that bright July day in 1945, for I was assailed by a strong filthy smell of urine, and I thought, My God! I am always going to smell urine. But when we went upstairs and into the bedrooms we found overflowing chambers under all the beds. We found full receptacles even in the long linen cupboards on the landing. On top of this the tenant had flitted, owing us the rent.

But what did it really matter, I was back home. I would get better; the War was over, and Tom would soon be home for good.

Not more than two or three people knew I had been ill, and even these saw that I was quite well now. I reinforced the façade with an armour plate, and this, too, was held together with fear; no one must know that I was still ill. If you set a pattern for yourself you become like that pattern, act well and you became well; so I read in the books on psychology and auto-suggestion. I worked on myself all my waking hours; I very rarely got more than four hours sleep and those only with the help of drugs. So realistic did my façade become that it deceived almost everyone. I met a person down the town who knew I had been ill. We had coffee together, and after chatting and talking for some time, apropos of nothing that had gone before, she suddenly said, 'You know, Kitty, some people are wicked. You know so-and-so? Well, she said you had been in an asylum.

I wouldn't believe this, and now . . . why, I've never known any-body in my life so down-to-earth and less like going into an asylum than you are. People are wicked, aren't they?'

I reached home with another fear added to the rest; people knew about me being ill. Yet at the same time I was indignant that they should have thought I had been in an asylum – I hadn't been in an asylum, I had been a voluntary patient and had private treatment in a home for nerve cases.

My illness entered another phase. I rejected completely all idea of a God, even while part of my mind was still begging the Blessed Virgin for help, still appealing to the Holy Family. When I look back now I think that the terror that filled me when I dared deny the existence of my catholic God was the nearest to madness I reached. Never once did this thought attack me but I vomited with it. I haven't the power to translate this feeling into words; only those Catholics like me who have lost God, consciously lost God through thinking him out of their lives, know what I'm talking about. There is a great difference between this way of losing God, and that of the lapsed Catholic; it is usually laziness that creates the lapsed Catholic, and nearly always they recant on their death bed, but to people such as myself, the thought of recanting is only another means of giving in to fear again.

Up till recently, when I have been asked the reason why I left the Catholic Church, I have had difficulty in explaining. The only definite statements I could make were that I didn't believe in the transubstantiation, or that I would go to hell if I purposely missed Mass, and died without confessing my sin.

Then one morning I received an envelope in which was a small book entitled 'A letter to a lapsed Catholic'. And I had not read two pages of it before I had the answer to why I was no longer a Catholic. Here was the narrowness, here the bigotry, here the fear that had been engendered in me in my early years.

I pick out a few quotations:

Shall we put it down to ignorance? Are you really con-vinced that the Catholic Church is different from all other Churches? That the Catholic Church was founded by Jesus Christ, who was God Himself, whereas all the others were set up by men? That the Catholic Church teaches you, pardons you, guides you, makes you holy and leads you to heaven by the authority of Christ Himself, who is God?

God does not want to have to damn you. He died to save you from damnation. If you do go to hell – which God forbid – it will be through your own deliberate fault, through rejecting the graces He offers you, possibly through refusing the appeal of this letter.

I say God does not want you to go to hell. He died to save you from that. He gave Himself to the very last drop of His precious Blood. How are you repaying that infinite generosity?

YOU WILL GO TO HELL POSSIBLY THROUGH RE-FUSING THE APPEAL OF THIS LETTER.
To a trained, logical and educated mind it's ridiculous, but only a small percentage of Catholics have trained, logical and educated minds. Only ten years ago that sentence would have filled me with fear.

God does not make laws without helping us to keep them. He is not a slave-driver, threatening us all the time with punishment. He is a Father, infinitely wise, kind, good and loving. He wants us to save our souls infinitely more than we do ourselves. He wants you to resolve now to come back to your Church.

Think of what He says to us through His Prophet in the Bible: 'You shall be carried at the breasts, and upon the knees they shall caress you. As one whom the mother cares – so will I comfort you.' Have you ever thought of it that way before – of yourself as a little child being carried through life like a tiny baby being loved in its mother's lap or upon her knee?

What level of mentality is this supposed to appeal to?

'Crucifying Him?' Yes, indeed. Mortal sin, like missing Mass or your Easter duties, is just that – crucifying Christ. The Holy Spirit tells us so through St Paul, writing to the Hebrews: Grave sinners, those who 'are fallen away'

206

are 'crucifying again to themselves the Son of God, and making him a mockery.' That means, in everyday language, that when you deliberately and without an adequate excuse miss Mass on Sunday, instead of watching at the foot of the Cross with Our Lady and St John, you join the Roman soldiers or the Jewish priests, help to drive the nails into Christ's flesh and add to their mockery of Him.

I have never yet met any person whom I could believe would consciously wish to crucify Christ again. I cannot believe that a person of that sort would read this letter of mine. I do honestly believe that most lapsed Catholics are being unworthy to themselves for just as long as they refuse to come back home. The consequences to themselves of every week's delay are so incalculable that, did they but realise it, they would never afflict themselves so.

Perhaps you were married out of the Church. I have met many people who have done what you have done. Very, very few of them were not, deep down in their hearts, worried and anxious to come back home. *PROBABLY YOUR MARRIAGE CAN BE PUT RIGHT;* (my italics) do please see a priest about it as soon as you can. You will be the first to agree with me that it is foolish to go on living in sin. Sin never pays. Why delay? Why deny yourself all the graces you might so easily be receiving through Confession and Holy Communion?

There is more and more.

Time and again I have asked myself, would I not like to return to the church? and the answer from the bottom of my heart has been, yes, for I want God. I want something to hold fast to. But, when I read things like this, I say, never, for here is the core of my problem, this archaic threat of everlasting Hell.

When I discussed the above with a Catholic he said, 'Good gracious! you don't take any heed to that, that's written especially for the –' he paused – 'well, you know, the rabble; it's the only way to get through to them.'

I was once of the rabble.

CHAPTER THIRTEEN

I look back now and cannot understand how I came through that time. Perhaps Kate's innate stamina was fighting for me. I was alone in that big house for seven months during which time I had another miscarriage.

I wrote out a schedule of work that took up every hour of the day, and on the wall of the kitchen I pinned a graph, like a hospital chart, and on it I marked my mental progress each night. I have the charts before me as I write, and I see in three places where the dots touched the bottom line. One of the dots represented a time when I decided to take all my pills at once. I could not go on living with this torment any longer. It was around two o'clock in the morning and I was alone. I went into the bathroom and collected the contents of three boxes, but instead of going into the bedroom again I went into the lavatory and put them all down the pan. After I had pulled the chain I thought, there, now you're on your own, and miraculously for a matter of about three or four minutes I came up out of the depth, and I took it as a sign.

According to my chart it was a whole year before I knew one complete day without being overcome by the sickness of fear. And in my godless world I was attributing my then state to my denial of Him. The effect of this was renewed terror. How dare I question God, I would be punished still further for the sacrilege.

One person I dared not think about was Kate. She wrote twice a week but I did not answer. I was finished with Kate. For the last time she had brought me near to madness.

While waiting for Tom to be demobbed, I started to write again. All my other little accomplishments were dead. I knew I would never draw again. The thought of those intricate, finicky designs that had kept my nose to the paper for days on end now filled me with resentment, and the sound of a piano being practised brought my hands up to my ears and my nerves jangling – but I could still write. This seemed odd to me at the time. It was like being washed up after a shipwreck and finding that you had brought ashore with you a locked shelter, in which, once you got the door open, you could live. So I transferred my tortured mind into a make-believe world, and began to write plays in which my cardboard characters worked out a nice ordered existence.

Then Tom came home.

For a week before his arrival I counted the hours, and in the last hour I counted the minutes, and when at last he held me in his arms I thought, if I don't come alive now I'm in for a long waking death.

Tom encouraged me to write. He was wholeheartedly for anything that would help me.

After writing three plays I knew I wasn't on the right track, so I started on short stories. I intended to do a number to form a book. The first was about a little North-country girl; she hadn't a father and her playmates revealed this to her and she wanted to die. She went to confession and told the priest that she wanted to die.

'Why?' said the priest.

'Because I ain't got no da,' said the little girl.

The priest, a kind understanding man, made her, in defiance of the schoolmistress, head of the May Procession and dressed as Our Lady.

I gave it the title of 'She Had No Da'.

About this time I forced myself to join the Hastings Writers' Circle. I wrote other stories about other children, and read them to the members, and they were quite well received.

Then one very bad Friday, it was not only Friday, but the thirteenth, I dared to make a stand against superstition, against fear, against God. I had, on this day, unthinkingly taken up a pair of scissors and stood cutting my nails. Then, as on that far Friday in the kitchen, the scissors went hurtling from me. Hadn't I had enough without asking for more? What was I thinking about? Yes, what was I thinking about. Slowly I felt welling up in me what I can only describe as a great anger, an anger directed against fear, against the cause of it, and I dived for the scissors and chopped off my nails. Then going to the window, and looking upwards over the top of the trees and into the sky, I sent tearing heavenwards words that made me tremble with fear even as I forced them out. But I was saying them, saying them aloud and defiantly. I was answering back my fears for the first time. What the hell does it matter! To blazes and bloody damnation with it all! ... God, dogma, the Catholic Church, the Devil, Hell, people, opinions, laws, illegitimacy ... and fear. Bugger them all. I was crying out aloud to the sky, 'I'll fear no more! Do you hear? I'm telling you I'll fear no more, I'm vomiting for the last time. Do what you like. Everlasting torment! Ha! I've had it.'

It was a brave show, that much could be said for it. It would be nice to say, too, that at that point a miracle happened and I feared no more.

This was three years after my breakdown, and had I known that another ten years would have to pass before I could go a full week without fear of some kind, I might not have felt so confident.

Later, on that particular Friday, as I sorted among my stories to find something to take to the Writers' Circle, a section of my mind seemed to open on to the past, but in a different way. All the past had held for me during the previous three years was fear, and mixed-up intangible, terrifying thoughts, but now, out of this same past stepped a child. She seemed to take shape before me. She was the little girl I had put in 'She Had No Da'. She had long nut-brown ringlets, a heart-shaped face, round blinking eyes, a pert mouth and an uptilted nose with a little cut on the left side. And she stood looking at me, and I at her. And I realised that a great deal of my mental trouble was that I had been over sorry for this child. I had forever compared her with those in a more favourable position and I had bestowed on her what I hated to receive from other people, pity. Yet the pity for her was embedded in my system and I couldn't eradicate it by just willing it so, it would have to be worked out.

Later that evening, at the Writers' Circle, I read this short story. I read it while seated; I had rheumatism in my legs. No one would have believed me if I'd had the courage to tell them that I couldn't stand on my feet and talk, or read, for any length of time because of nerves. The reception that this little story received astounded me. It was clapped and clapped, and one or two members at the back of the room even stood up while clapping. I cried on my way home. I knew now that the way to get rid of the pity for this child was to write her out of my system, and so began the 'Mary Ann' stories, although they didn't take shape in book form until almost eight years later.

I had read extensively for years, starting with Chaucer, in the original – I knew no better. I didn't know there was a translation, and the original read very much like Geordie language, anyway – Erasmus, Donne, Gibbon's *Decline and Fall*, and had even struggled with *Finnegans Wake*.

I never read for pleasure, only instruction, and I could talk of books; but here again, I found the same stumbling block that I had met with in Harton Institution. One was suspect if one showed off one's knowledge. Hadn't she worked in a laundry? When I sensed this attitude it was hopeless to try and discuss anything; in fact, it stripped me of what learning I had acquired and reduced me at times to shades of Kate, and Mrs Malaprop.

Up to a point I was well read; and so, being well read and knowing that I was a natural writer, what more did I need? Nothing; nothing at all. And this is where Tom's criticism came in and was very hurtful to me.

What I did need apparently, what was essential to good writing, was good grammar. I knew that a noun was the name of anything; I knew what an adjective was, but did I know anything about clauses? did I know anything about prepositions or conjunctions? did I know anything about direct or indirect objects of the verb? did I know anything about subordinating a clause?

No, I knew nothing about the intricate depths of grammar, and it was a known fact that few writers did.

So I said to Tom there was no need for me to learn that kind of grammar, I wanted to write natural dialogue.

But he said I couldn't fill my books with natural dialogue, I must use some prose. So I must learn grammar.

All right I would learn grammar.

Tom thought I was being very sensible. Often his criticism was harsh and reduced me to painful tears. This kind and thoughtful man, who was known never to say a rough word to anyone, would slay me with a sabre-edged sentence. North country people might think like that, and talk like that, but I had to put it over grammatically, so he said.

From this time on, each day, he set me a lesson. I learned slowly, with the result that in my second year of writing I was writing slowly, and thoughtfully, and correctly, about North country people who spoke grammatical dialogue – and it lacked guts.

After many months Tom was forced to realise that if I was going on with my writing it had to be in my way of thinking, and not academically. Not for me the chewing over of the perfection of a sentence, but getting down the sense of it as I saw it through the character.

But Tom's help was invaluable; I was born to write, I knew that now, and that I would have reached my goal I also know, but I was fortunate in having in my husband a harsh critic, and a kind man. At this time, too, I had to face another fact and this was that I wouldn't write a word that anyone would really want to read until I threw off the pseudo-lady and accepted my early environment, me granda, the pawn, the beer carrying, the cinder picking, Kate's drinking, and of course my birth, for it was these things that had gone to make me. Also, to own to being a Northerner and all this implied.

It was this cathartic outlook that set the pattern for my first novel.

I was in the middle of writing the novel when Major Christopher Bush gave a lecture on 'How to write a novel' in the Hastings Library. It was a bitter winter's night and everyone with sense was indoors. There were only about a dozen people at the lecture, and when the Major, talking to his all-female audience, told them that any woman who could write a laundry list could write a novel, I dared, when after the lecture the questions were being put to him, to disagree with him on this point. Then, feeling that my attack had been a little out of place, I spoke to him alone just before I left the room. I found him most kind and interested in the fact that I was writing a novel. He gave me his agent's address and told me to send the first chapters to him.

In a high state of excitement I followed Major Bush's advice, and within a short time had a reply from John Smith, of Christy & Moore, to say I must let him have the finished work as soon as possible.

Kate Hannigan was accepted by the first publisher Mr Smith sent it to. I was on my way.

I knew that I was going to make money out of this book, thousands and thousands. You read in the papers about the money authors made, look at Somerset Maugham. Why not Catherine Cookson?

My agent had told me in a letter that he would get me what he could, no stated sum, just what he could. Being a member of the Writers' Group I should have had some vague idea what one got for a first novel, but I cannot remember a novel being discussed. The readings and discussions all concerned short stories, articles, and poems. I think most of us at that time came under the heading of, Art for Art's sake. So my ignorance on the money question can be understood.

Anyway, I knew I would receive a substantial amount. I'd even thought in the region of a gardener, a car and a fur coat – my hands were like a navvy's with working both inside and outside the house. To keep fifteen rooms shining took some doing, besides all my other commitments.

I had made myself into a working machine. Apart from wanting to fill my every moment and keep my mind occupied, we hadn't the money to employ anyone for even a short length of time. During our years in The Hurst Tom learned to be an efficient plumber, decorator and convertor, but he still could not cope adequately in his limited time with this large decaying house.

So we needed money badly especially for the roof.

Then I received a letter from Mr Smith, or John as he soon became. In it, he said that the publishers were offering a hundred pounds advance against royalties on *Kate Hannigan*.

A HUNDRED POUNDS! Ten pounds to the typist, the agent's fees. A year's solid writing. A HUNDRED POUNDS. Bang went the idea of outside help, the dream of a car and a fur coat.

I did not realise then that a hundred pounds was a generous offer to a nonentity, because that's what you are, as a writer of a first novel. You are a horse who hasn't run.

It was Tom who said wait until they get into the shop and start to sell. We did not know then, the most a bookseller will take of most first authors is three copies, sale or return.

I survived the disappointment and leaned more heavily on the glory of being in print, of being a novelist. There is a certain particular and special madness attached to having a novel published, a first novel.

The madness was strong on me the day I received a letter, through my agent, asking if I would go to London and have lunch with my publisher. He was no longer the publisher, he was my publisher. It was a wonderful feeling to have a publisher. Funds were very low at the time; Tom, a Grammar School master, with a good honours degree, was earning the vast sum of forty pounds a month. But I must have some new clothes to go and meet my publisher. I had made do and mended for so long that I had nothing presentable in which to descend upon London, so, taking a little from the rate box, the coal box, the electric box – all our commitments had a box to themselves – I got rigged out and was prepared for the great adventure.

I took the Parker Road bus into the town. This bus I used two or three times a week when I went shopping, and early in the morning it was full of women on the same bent, or going to work, many of them looking weary. This morning I sat among them, but I was not of them, I was Catherine Cookson going to London to have lunch with her publisher. I had the greatest desire to nudge the woman sitting next to me and say, in very refeened tones, 'I'm going to London to have lunch with my publisher; I have written a novel.' Had I done this, she would, without a doubt, have turned to me and said 'So what!'

I remember I sat in the corner of a compartment all the way to London opposite an old man who sniffed. Any other time I would not have been able to bear this. Apart from anything else I hated travelling in company, but this morning I not only sat opposite this old sniffer but we talked nearly all the way to London, for was I not a novelist going to town to have lunch with her publisher. The oil of success was flowing over me like warm butter. I discovered that morning that you can always be charming when you feel successful.

I think I was a little taken aback when I arrived at Victoria not to be met by the Mayor and Corporation. But still, there was the taxi driver. I had a long talk with the taxi driver. This is not quite accurate – it would be more correct to say that the taxi driver had a long talk with me, and during our conversation I acquired a lot of new words. I thought I had heard them all in the docks, but no, this London taxi driver taught me many more during the course of our conversation. It took place on the edge of the kerb, while two cars, a bus and a lorry untwined themselves. No damage had been done, not really, just a little concertinaing together. Of course, what that taxi driver didn't know was, that I was a novelist, and up in London to have lunch with my publisher, and, unlike the mass of ordinary individuals. That was why I had walked in front of his cab on a corner.

After escaping from the taxi driver I went up a side street and composed myself; eventually, I arrived at the offices of my publisher and was shown up to the top floor, sanctum sanctorum, and there I met a very surprised man. I had come on the wrong day.

Dear John had made a mistake in the date.

I went out to lunch with the secretary, a charming woman, and the person, incidentally, who was the first to spot ability in my novel and point it out to Mr Murray Thompson. But, she wasn't my publisher; the glory of the day had vanished.

I was on my way but I was, mentally, still very much in the breakdown. Although the chart was showing now more dots above the middle line than below, I still had frequent bouts of retching, and trembling. These were always the result of fear. And the fear was at its height when Kate paid her first visit to The Hurst after many years. She wanted to see me, and in a way I wanted to see her. I wanted to see what effect she would have on me. It was disastrous.

In my waking hours I could control my thoughts and what they prompted me to do, but what I was afraid of was that the force of my dreaming would compel me to walk in my sleep, for never a night had passed since I started the breakdown but I dreamt of her, and the dreams all followed the same pattern. She was in a state of drink, and I was beating her with my fists, or choking the life out of her. Always I was struggling with her. From these dreams I would wake up trembling, sweating, and exhausted. The night before she arrived I made up my mind to ask Tom to tie me to the bed, so that, should I try to rise while still asleep, I would wake up. But then I told myself not to suffer this humiliation.

Kate came. She was shocked by the sight of me. I was very thin. I wasn't shocked by the sight of her, she was as I had expected her to be. Yet during the fortnight she was with us not once did she have a drink. The days in her company were like me granda's salt in a raw wound, and the nights were nightmares, when all I wanted to do was go across the landing and kill her.

The following year she came for a month, and I knew she was happy to be with me. During this visit she said to me it was a wonder I hadn't had a breakdown much earlier, for if a child was affected by the condition of the mother during pregnancy then it wouldn't have surprised her had I been born mental. I'm sure she was absolutely blind to the fact that it was her continuous drinking, and its power to change her character, which largely contributed to my breakdown.

CHAPTER FOURTEEN

If it wasn't for the terrible torment endured through a break-down it would be good for everyone to experience it, for no state is so self-revealing.

All during this time of trial Tom had been wonderful with me. I wanted sympathy from no one else but him, and this was bad, and we both knew it, but it seemed that I had only him in the whole wide world. So, feeling like this, I don't know from where I dragged the courage to tell him not to sympathise with me; and when he took me at my word, being a woman, I blamed him. I felt, once again, lost and completely alone. But now he had hurt my pride, and this acted as a spur to make me fight all the harder against my condition. To be beholden to no one, to do it on my own.

I knew by this time, too, that I was not alone in my mental agony, the War was beginning to take its toll on nerves, and so I wrote my second broadcast, calling it, 'Putting nerves in their place'. My first broadcast had been called 'Learning to draw at thirty'.

It was strange how I first managed to get on the wireless; it all happened because I was annoyed. A lady made a remark, in public, half in fun and whole in earnest, about the carrying quality of my voice. And as I was going home the thought came to me: I'll get on the wireless; I'll show her where my voice can carry me. And that is how it started. Each morning for three months, when Tom had gone to school, I took the script that I had written, about learning to draw, into the study, and, sitting opposite the electric light switch, I waited for it to turn red, because, I understood that's what happened in a broadcasting studio. When I thought I could read the script well enough for the BBC I sent it up, and to my surprise was asked to go for an audition. And I was on.

And now, I thought, I'm going to kill two birds with one stone. I'm going to get rid of the fear of anyone knowing I've had a breakdown by speaking of it, and in doing it I well help others, because I realised that many people were suffering as much from the fact that anyone should know that they had had a breakdown as from the trouble itself. But even knowing this, the result of the broadcast was astounding. I had letters from all kinds of people, all suffering. Moreover, many people came to see me, people who couldn't believe that I was in the same state as themselves. They imagined that I could, at one time, have felt as terrible as they did, but they could not believe that I was still feeling like this, for a good part of the time anyway.

So, on the days when I hit bottom again and felt I just couldn't go on, I would remember certain people to whom my apparently peaceful mental condition was as a lodestone, and they, in their turn, would help me to go on with the fight.

I was helped, too, at this time very much by the writings of Leslie Weatherhead. So much did he help me that I wrote him a letter of thanks and was amazed to get a reply by return of post, thanking me in turn for giving him a bright start on a dull Monday morning. I was puzzled by this until I learned through his further writings that he too knew all there was to know about breakdowns.

I look back now on the years between forty and fifty as on a painful nightmare. Not only had I my mental state to contend with but the inevitable attack on all sections of my weakened system by an early menopause. Add to this, neuritis of the arms and legs, a skin allergy, and the capacity for picking up anything that was going, even mange from my bull terrier, to say nothing of my nose, which, if possible, was bleeding more at this time, and had also taken on to itself a painful antrum.

My doctor used to infuriate me, for, no matter what I went to him with, he would say airily, 'Oh, Mrs Cookson! you've got to expect this, it's your temperament, you know. You've got to pay for being a writer.'

In 1948, 49 and 50 I had three operations on my temperament. I may say here that these were the first operations for which, before I went down to the theatre I was given an injection to quieten the system. Four out of the previous six times I had been in an operation theatre I had lain on the table while they cleared up the gore from the last patient. It's odd how people always thought I was tough.

Following this, my temperament gave me, with the help of some tree shears, mastitis of the breasts. Then my temperament, with the help of my pen, gave me writer's cramp, and neuritis which caused a frozen shoulder. Some temperament.

CHAPTER FIFTEEN

I don't know when I first started my flying dreams. Perhaps it was at the beginning of puberty. Somewhere in Freud it explains these dreams as being connected with the awakening of sex. Be that as it may, I looked forward to my flying dreams. I would go down to the bottom of the street, stand with my back against the telegraph pole, shout 'Go!' and I would go. First of all, I would scoot up the long pole until I reached the wires. Then I would pause a moment, look along the thin sparkling strands and fly to the next pole, where I would stand on the top for a second before sliding down to the ground again. Why did my subconscious choose telegraph poles? I didn't like telegraph poles. There was a family called McLaughlin who lived up Bogey Hill. The brother and sister were much bigger than me and always went for me, and I was scared to death of them. They were strong Catholics, so why did they pick on me? I wore my green on St Patrick's day, yet it was usually on this day, or around this time, when young pious and ardent members of differing denominations were making innocent looking paper balls that held flint stones in their middle, ready to do battle for their respective beliefs, that this couple would waylay me; they would hold me against the telegraph pole and knock my head repeatedly against it by the simple procedure of shaking me violently by the shoulders. So I didn't like telegraph poles. Yet the dream went on for years.

I never remember having any dreams that I enjoyed except this one. Sometimes, even now, I find myself flying. I am walking along a street and I suddenly say to myself 'Go on, fly,' and I will rise from the ground, and no one around me thinks it is in any way extraordinary.

I have at times found myself in the sea in my dreams, swimming, but this was never a pleasant dream because I couldn't swim. Having nearly drowned on my first attempt in the Shields Baths when I was nineteen, I had an inordinate fear of the water, which, try as I might, I couldn't overcome. My experience on the slacks didn't help me at all.

My holidays each year became another form of nightmare, through having to spend them on a boat, for Tom is boat mad. Each morning I was surprised we hadn't sunk, and each evening I was amazed I hadn't fallen overboard. After seven years of such holidays I just had to make the big effort. I was fifty-two and it seemed a little late, but thanks to Mr Ryker, the instructor in the Hastings Baths, I accomplished the impossible. I think I look upon it as my greatest achievement. I have never had my swimming dream since I learnt to swim.

Then there were, and still are, the dreams of being naked. Dreams have always played a great part in my life, and although I have now thrown overboard most of the superstitions which plagued me, and would very much like to reject the applied significance of all my dreams, I find, from experience over the years, that to do so would be rejecting a form of truth. The dreams and their significance I don't pretend to understand; I only know that certain dreams signify certain things for me, and even at one particular period when I said firmly, 'I'm taking no more notice of dreams,' they still went on, and the happenings that would follow them proved conclusively that, ignore them how I might, they would remain the negative to the print.

The naked dream, like the dream of the black robed priest, who popped up in all odd places, but mostly on the altar with his back towards me, started with the loss of my first baby, and dealt exclusively with my physical health. Sometimes I dreamt I was naked to the waist, at others, there might just be one arm bare, or my feet bare.

There has been only one time when I dreamt I was completely naked. Two days later I developed a cold; it turned severe, but I refused to pamper it. I had learned not to run to the doctor with any slight illness. In fact, not to go to the doctor unless I was absolutely forced; also, not to put myself to bed, which often in the past I had done. So when my dream only resulted in a cold I said to myself, 'So much for being stark naked . . . a lot of bare flesh for a running nose and a headache.'

The following week I still had a cold and it forced me to

221

bed, but I still went on working, croaking into my tape recorder. I knew that I had to be right for the following week, and the week after. I had been asked to speak at a Conservative luncheon. I was also due to go North. The South Shields Lecture and Literary Society had done me the kindness to make me their President. I must just get rid of this cold.

When I eventually sent for the doctor I had double pneumonia. But this wasn't the worst. Being rhesus negative, and also allergic to all kinds of drugs, my reaction to the drug that checked the pneumonia was worse than the disease itself; so much so that I thought, this is it.

Now out of this arose the question: 'Do you want to see a priest?'

Pushed at the back of a drawer was the crucifix, the holy water font, and the statue of Our Lady, and St Joseph, that used to form my altar. I had bought these in the porch of St Peter and St Paul's in my early teens, putting a few coppers away each week on one or other of them. I had set up my altar on the little iron mantelpiece in the corner of the bedroom, and night and morning I had said my prayers beneath it – provided there were no lodgers in the room. Even when I went to Harton Institution I set up my altar, but this didn't stop them thinking the worst of me, or reporting me for having indecent pictures in my room, which on inspection the Matron found to be: Minnie-Ha-Ha, hanging at one side of the altar, and a reproduction of Paolo and Francesca at the other. Since coming South, however, I had never set up my altar, yet I hadn't the heart to throw the relics of my religion away. Now my inner eye was on them. This is what people meant when they said that Catholics always recant on their death bed. Well, did I want a priest? Did I want the last rites?

What for? God, if there was a God, knew exactly how I felt. He knew that I didn't want to deny Him. He knew that I had struggled against denial for years. If there was a God, then He knew every facet of my thinking. Would He think any more of me if I was to placate Him now by submitting to certain rites in which I no longer believed? What, after all was a priest but a man? I knew all about ordination, which is sealed by the laying on of hands by a bishop, who after all is another man, subject to a pope, who is another man, successor, we must

222

believe of Peter; but with a difference. Peter was not magnificently housed in a city set apart, nor was his belly well filled four times a day. I don't know the intake of popes in this matter, but I do know that of priests, at least some priests. But this carnal matter, although not beside the point is going off at a tangent and that's what always happens when you touch on this subject. Anyway, could a priest's mumbled words have any effect on the mind of God? Could they alter God's attitude towards me in the eternal second between life and death? No, if I believed that, I was in for more mental torment.

I didn't want a priest. I lay and waited. Death didn't come.

Perhaps the Catholic view of my reprieve would be that I was being given another chance. This view had been presented to me before. It was while I was in St Helen's Hospital in 1952. I had lost a lot of blood during some weeks, and was feeling very low after the operation. It was a Sunday afternoon and I was dozing – I opened my eyes to see the bright shining faces of two nuns bending over me. My heart again leapt up to my mouth. I had told Tom to say I was of no denomination, but apparently he had been worried at the time and stated my denomination to be Catholic. The nuns were sweet but I had to tell them the truth. 'I am no longer a Catholic, sisters,' I said.

Talk about the persistent attack of angels.

'You have had an operation. You have got better only by God's grace. He has given you this chance in order that you may see your error. He'll not do it again. You can test Him too far.'

'You wouldn't want to spend your eternal life in Hell, my dear, would you?'

On and on it went.

When Tom came in, as he said later, I had gone back almost to the breakdown. 'Get me out of this.' I cried at him. 'I don't care how you do it, but get me out. They'll come back.'

An hour later I was carried to a taxi, and carried out of it, and then I was in my own bed. Physically I was in a very low state, mentally I had really gone back years.

On the Monday I sent for my doctor. He did not come but sent me a pamphlet on rehabilitation – the main theme was to keep oneself busy. I looked from the letter through the window and into the sky, and asked why had it to happen to me. I wanted

223

help. Why was I always refused outside help? Perhaps it was after all God's way of showing me I was wrong, perhaps those nuns were right.

I was retching again.

But the other side of the coin, as regards dreams, is the one I have about lavatories. Perhaps because in my childhood I found peace when I escaped to the lavatory, and had my earliest dreams there, now in the time of my success the lavatory should stand as a symbol to me. Whatever the real explanation of this I do not know, for as I've said I cannot stand the smell of lavatories, but I do know that the lavatory dream arrived just about ten years ago when I first began to earn real money by writing. The lavatory dreams always portend what the fortune teller would term, good fortune. And according to the number of lavatories and their condition, so the amount of money that comes to me.

One night, about two years ago, I dreamt of a long line of lavatories which, one after the other, I refused to enter because of the state they were in, and when I came to the last one and my necessity was great I still would not deign to enter it, and then, as happens in dreams, the whole place turned into one huge lavatory and there was I in the middle of it with no clear path out.

I awoke only to find it was a dream within a dream. Still asleep and dreaming, I said to myself, 'What a frightful dream!' I was now looking in a mirror, my lip was curled back from my teeth, my nose was at an upward angle, and I asked of my reflection, 'Why have I to dream about lavatories?'

When I did eventually wake I remembered my dream within a dream, and said to myself, all things being equal that could mean something. Two days later I received an offer to do work that brought me in the fattest cheque I had ever received.

It is interesting to recall that the lavatory dream started when the climbing dream stopped. From when I began to write seriously in 1945, until about 1955, I frequently had a dream of climbing mountains, of a rock face that presented me with a jutting overlap. I was always clawing my way up, hand over hand, trying to get footholds here and there; I was always exhausted when I came to this overlap. It would take a mighty effort to climb outwards and on to its top. Always, with one exception, I reached my objective and lay there spent. No wonder I woke up tired in the morning, so tired that I could hardly crawl out of bed.

The one time that I did not succeed in climbing the mountain was when I found myself in a dark valley with the rock faces going straight upwards, so steeply that they almost obliterated the light. There was no way out, the only thing was to go back the way I had come. I stood still looking upwards to the un-reachable summits, and in this position I woke up, and I said to myself, 'What now? I've got to face something, or go back. What is it?' The answer was, Kate. I had to conquer my feeling towards her or retreat into myself by way of the dark road I had come.

For six years Kate had been visiting me, and each year her visits grew longer, until they lasted for three months. Always during her stay I got her her daily beer, and never once did she ask for or mention, whisky. This spoke plainly of her power of control, which she could use if she liked. I know now that there were times when she was staying with me when she must have gone through hell, so great was her craving.

Following each visit, I always got a letter saying, 'Oh, lass, only four walls to look at and no garden; and no you, or Tom.' She had by this time become very attached to Tom.

Twice during her long stays she was ill and in bed for six weeks at a time, and strangely I enjoyed nursing her. When her dominant character was low and I knew there was no possi-bility of her slipping out, she became Our Kate to me, the nice Our Kate.

But as the years went on, and although there were three hundred miles between us now, the burden of her still weighed on me, for I was living in dread of the day when, not being able to look after herself, I would, to use her own phraseology, be saddled with her.

When the final day of testing came in 1953 and I went North, I found her in a deplorable state. She had swelled to enormous proportions. She had heart trouble, dropsy, and cancer of the stomach, the latter she was unaware of, and she had been drinking heavily, paying someone to bring it in for her. Dr

Carstairs gave her a short time to live. Like me granda, she had a fear of hospital, so there was nothing for it but to bring her back with me.

What strengthened and helped me during this time was Tom's moral support. Although he knew to what depths of mental distress she had brought me, and the daily irritations in store for himself – one of which was her cooking, for she took it as an insult if her great stacked plates of gravy covered food weren't eaten – he said, 'You must bring her home.' And I knew I must, and for good, for my conscience was loud in me, telling me that whatever I went through with her now would be nothing to what I would suffer if I didn't make this final effort.

After a journey by train sleeper, and ambulance, I brought her home for the last time. She was ill, very ill, and when at last I had her in bed in her old room and I looked at her, I thought, thank God it won't be for long, then was immediately horrified that I could think this way. I stared pityingly down at the great balloon of water that her body had become, at the faded blue of her eyes, and the colour of her nose, bulbous now. There was no beauty left, not even the beauty of age. And then she took my hand. With the tears running down her face she held it to her cheek as she said, 'Aw, lass, thank God I'm home. I'm home, I'm home. Aw, me lass. Aw, me lass, God's good. He's brought me home to die. Every night when I've said me prayers I've asked him to bring me home.' Strange, but she did say her prayers every night, and stranger still that she should consider her home was wherever I was.

I had wanted her dead for years. Only by her dying could I be released from the burden. I was nearing fifty. I had stood enough, I wasn't physically, or mentally strong enough to stand any more, yet it was in that moment, when I told myself these things, that I knew she must not die, that I couldn't let her die, that she had to live and we had to come to know each other. I, too, had to have my chance. I had to sublimate this feeling of hate with another feeling, with the feeling that had always been there, this passionate, and compassionate love for her, this had to rise to the top. I, too, needed saving. I, too, had to live with myself. I said to her, 'You are not going to die . . . Mam, you are going to live to be happy.' I had called her mam for the first time.

226

And she did live, and she was happy. For three years we lived together, and for most of the time there was happiness. There were the ordinary irritations of life, more so when she was getting about as she did sometimes in the morning – she had to be in bed most days by two o'clock – because she always wanted to do the cooking, and the name of Gayelord Hauser affected her like a red rag to a bull, for our eating habits for some years had been guided by his cookery books.

There was one thing in her that never weakened until the moment she died, and that was her dominant character. Yet during these last years she fitted in with our life and tried in every way to please us, I say us, because she wanted Tom to think well of her.

Only twice did she express any desire to go out, and on the first occasion she stopped abruptly outside a bar door and said as abruptly, 'I won't be a few minutes, I just want a half, just a half.' Sickness overwhelmed me again, and bitterness. I knew she would down a couple of doubles and have a flat flask in her bag and all within a few minutes. But following this I realised the agony the craving caused her, and decided that I must get her some spirits, at least once or twice a month. And so, on the quiet, I would bring her in a quarter bottle of whisky, saying, 'Hide that,' for Tom wasn't supposed to know anything about it. And very often he didn't for he was strongly against her having it; beer yes, and brandy, which the doctor had ordered, but not whisky. She hated brandy. Oh, the look on her face when I would give her the bottle. 'Aw, thanks lass, thanks lass.' She would be happy, and laughing, and gay for days.

But the most important thing during this last period was that we came to know one another. We talked openly about the past for the first time in our lives. And once she said to me, 'I've never understood you, lass. It's come to me that I've never understood you. Years ago I used to think you had the making of an upstart, and funny, I wanted you to be an upstart, because it proved to me you were different. But you were different from the day you were born. You were like him, you didn't belong to the North or anything in it.' Here she was wrong. 'But you were no upstart, you were too straight and honest for that, and you never rejected me.' (If she could only have seen into my mind and heart) 'I once heard tell that

Taggart Smith said to you in the New Buildings when you were leaving home to go into place that time, that you should make a clean break from us an' that you would never make anything of yourself if you kept in with us. It was me she meant. I've never born malice to anybody in me life but I found it hard to forgive her for that. But you did make something of yourself. There's nobody in the place risen like you have, an' you didn't disown us to do it.'

How often did I want to, Kate. How often.

Kate was overjoyed at this time with my writing success, and when the news came that J. Arthur Rank wanted to turn my latest book, *A Grand Man,* into a film, she held me in her arms and cried, 'I'm happy for you. Aw, lass, I'm happy for you.'

It was odd, but her demonstrations of affection always embarrassed me now. I wasn't used to them. They had come too late as it were. But I, too, was happy and excited over the news. *A Grand Man* was my fifth book and it had been written merely as a try-out. After finishing my fourth book I was wondering what theme I should use for the next one, when I thought of my short stories about the child from the Tyne which had started with 'She Had No Da' and I decided to have a shot at putting them in novel form, pathos and humour mixed. And so *A Grand Man* came into being.

In 1954 I was sent by the film company to Belfast, there to set the location and do the the first script for the film 'Jacqueline', the title given to *A Grand Man.* I should have enjoyed this but I was ill all the time. When I returned I went straight into hospital, and I was physically ill for the next two years, which was a pity, for this was the period when exciting things were happening. There was the première of the film in London. A great night for me, and Tom. Then greater excitement still when we learned that the Queen had the film shown at one of her private parties.

Then came the offer to film *Rooney,* and the request again to do the first script. It was difficult going, but I have to feel very ill before I stop writing; when I have no urge to write I know things are in a bad way with me.

It was during this time that I was asked to go North to open a sale of work for the Polio Fund, and I stayed with a Doctor and Mrs Anderson, whom I had met once before and who from this visit, were to become my very dear friends; but the out-standing incident of this trip for me happened as I stood on the platform looking down on the crowded hall. There was a man and woman standing staring up at me. The man had a child in his arms, and the woman kept smiling broadly as if she knew me, as I thought doubtless she did, for many in that Hall remembered me that day. After I had said my piece this couple made their way towards me.

'Hello,' said the woman.

'Hello,' I said.

She looked blankly at me for a moment before asking, 'Don't you remember me?'

I racked my brains quickly. I have a good memory for things that happened years ago but I can forget a name that I heard only yesterday. But this woman was from the past; I had a vague feeling that I should have remembered her. I hesitated too long, and then the man put in stiffly, 'But you must remember her. Why, you must. You picked tatties together in the cornfield.'

There I was, dressed up to the eyes, Catherine Cookson, the writer, seven books to my name, two of which had been filmed. Booked to give talks here and there, asked to open garden parties, fêtes, and make after-dinner speeches, and the reporter from the Shields Gazette had just paid me the compli-ment of saying I looked more like a model than a writer, and here I was being reminded that I had picked tatties with this woman.

I had forgotten I had picked tatties in the cornfield, but now I was remembering. It was after I'd had the hip injury, and had left school. Funds were very low. Bella Weir, from up the street, was picking tatties in the cornfield; but then Bella was a big strong hefty lass. And there were others from Bogey Hill who were picking tatties and did so every year, but I had never picked tatties before. Wanting to earn some money to help things along , I said to Kate, 'I'll go and pick for a day or so.'

It came back to me that Kate had protested strongly, but I went, though only for two days, because I became dizzy and had that funny tired feeling. And now, vaguely, I was recalling this woman, and understanding why I hadn't been able to remember her; she wasn't from the New Buildings where I could recall every face, and every name, she was from the Bogey Hill end. Half-a-mile is a long distance when you are a child; I couldn't remember playing with this girl although she now reminded me that I had. The atmosphere was very strained; I could see what the man was thinking. Bloody upstart! They get on and forget what they were. Brought up along of old John McMullen, and Kate, her that would drink it through a dirty rag. God, don't they make you sick.

If ever before there had been a doubt in my mind about the hold that my early environment had on me this incident shattered it.

I was no longer coming North to show them what Katie McMullen had become, there was no need now. I was established as Catherine Cookson, the writer, yet to my ain folk I would ever remain Katie McMullen of the New Buildings. But wasn't it as Katie McMullen of the New Buildings that I saw myself from inside? The truth was, I was still her; I had always been her and would ever remain her, and that with her, and through her I still lived in the past because that is where I belonged. I had spent a lifetime trying to get away from my past, not realising the impossibility of getting away from oneself, for I was the North, through my early environment I was the epitome of the North. Its people were my people.

I was Katie McMullen. Resolutely, unashamedly. Now I recognised my inheritance, and it centred round the name I had claim to, for that name was not even my mother's, but that of a drunken, bigoted, ignorant old Irishman. God bless him, for who would not bless a man for loving a child as he did me.

CHAPTER SIXTEEN

Kate had been with us for nearly three years now, during which time we had moved from The Hurst, to a charming house in a wood situated about a mile away.

The move was in a way painful to me and I didn't really get over it for a year or more, for The Hurst had been the realisation of a dream. I had bought The Hurst when it was old, and had nursed it. Then Tom came and he nursed it, but he, not tied by my sentimentality saw the futility of working like galley slaves to keep a fifteen-roomed house, and large garden, for two, at most three people.

Kate loved the new house. She had a room on the ground floor with two large windows at which the roses tapped in the summer, and when she looked out, she looked at walls built of larches, and rowans. But above all, the kitchen with its Aga cooker was a never ending joy to her, and it was a job to get her to bed after lunch each day. Even when she could hardly stand she would get up in the mornings and come into the kitchen.

'Now don't you do those dishes, lass; I told you I'd be up. Go on an' get on with your writing.'

But there were times when she couldn't struggle up and she would be in bed for weeks, but not without protest.

More and more now she hated me out of her sight. Sometimes at night when, nerves very taut, I would go into the drawing room to look at the television and would fall asleep from sheer fatigue, she would say later when I went in, 'It's been a long night, lass,' or 'You been out to the pictures?' She would make a joke of it, but I always took it as a reprimand.

For a full year I never left her except for two hours every Friday when I went into town to the Bank, and to the Library for her books, and try as I might to hide it the strain was beginning to tell, and also on Tom. So it was arranged that a friend of mine, Mrs Chapman and her husband and son, should come and stay and see to the house and her, while we had a week's holiday on The Fenland Rivers. She didn't like this. She hated anyone else running the house. Moreover, I noticed at this time, that she seemed very irritable, and she was also afraid of me being in a boat in case anything happened.

We left on the Saturday morning at nine o'clock by taxi to the station, and as my friend wanted to do some shopping she came down in the taxi with us.

I learnt later it was at five past nine that Kate telephoned the shop from where I got her weekly supply of beer, and ordered a bottle of whisky, asking them to deliver it straightaway. And with this last gesture she certainly precipitated her end.

I phoned her every day from some part of the River Cam, and she always said, 'Aw, lass, I miss you.' One day she was excited because my Cousin Sarah, and Jack, her husband, had broken their holiday journey South to see her. She was very fond of Sarah, and Sarah, like all her nieces and nephews thought a great deal of her. Besides, Sarah had never criticised her, she would only say 'Eeh! poor Aunt Kate.'

It was her birthday on September the fifteenth, and this was the day we were to return home, but not until the evening, so I had made arrangements for a basket of fruit, of which she was very fond, and other presents to be delivered early in the day. Her reaction to the fact that I had thought ahead, and hadn't forgotten her birthday, was pathetic.

She was in bed when we arrived home, and I will never forget the look on her face when she saw me, and when she got her arms about me she would not let me go.

'Thank God! Thank God you're home safe. I've prayed night, noon, and morning. Never leave me again, lass. Promise you'll never leave me again.'

'I'll never leave you again.'

'Promise.'

'I promise. Why, I'll tell you what we've done. We've booked a boat from Banhams for next year. Flat-bottomed and straight all through. No steps. We booked it so that you'll be able to come with us.' – And we had – 'And it's got big windows, and you can sit with your feet up and look out. How's that? A life on the ocean wave!'

'Aw, lass. Aw, lass.' She was crying. 'I had the feeling I would never see you again. Don't ever leave me, will you? Will you?'

'There now, no more, no more. I've told you. I'll never leave you again, not even for a day.'

On the Sunday she got up but she looked ill, and was very irritable. On the Monday, and Tuesday, she was the same, and on the Wednesday morning she rose at nine, saying, 'I'm going to do that ironing.'

'Oh, leave it,' I said. 'There's plenty of time for that.'

'What do you want me to do, sit and pick me nails? All you want to do is keep me in bed. I'm sick of bed.'

At twelve o'clock she was just finishing the ironing, standing – she would never sit down. Only lazy bitches sat down – when suddenly she exclaimed, 'I feel so sick. I'm going to be sick.'

When she vomited blood I sent for the doctor. Our own doctor was away at the time and another local doctor came, a Doctor Cutler. He was big, and bearded, and as soon as she saw him she took to him. She was in bed by now and she joked and chaffed him as he sat by her and held her hand. I left them together.

Later, when he came out of the room, he said, 'She's a grand old girl, as plucky as they come.'

'How long has she?' I asked.

'A few days, a week at the most. As you know her heart's bad, and her kidneys must be in a shocking state, but it's the cancer of the stomach that's going to see her off. She must have had a constitution like a horse. Did she eat well?'

'Like a horse,' I said.

'Give her ice, and a drop of brandy,' he said. 'I'll be back in the morning.'

I didn't know how I was going to meet her eyes with this news in my face, and my whole being wanting to burst asunder with pity, and love, and remorse. But I needn't have worried; she had the situation in hand, for she greeted me with, 'Now don't try and do me out of it, he says I can have what I like. Have you a drop?' She was smiling.

'Only brandy,' I said.

'Well, I'm in no position to argue am I?.' She was actually laughing now. It was too much. The tears burst from me like a rain storm and brought her up in the bed, crying, 'Oh me bairn, don't, don't. I'm not worth your tears. I know I'm not. Aw, lass. Don't, don't.'

Tom and I sat up that night with her and she was sick many times, but when the doctor arrived early on the Thursday she greeted him with a smile, saying, 'Aw, lad, I'm glad to see you.'

He was a long time with her, and when he came into the kitchen he seemed moved. 'She's a brave woman is your mother,' he said. 'A brave woman.'

I don't know what had passed between them but I think she must have told him she knew she was dying, and rapidly.

On the Friday night she held my hands, and it was at this point she said that she had been a wicked woman. She was in great pain now and obviously sinking. Just before she lost consciousness she said, 'Will that lad be coming the night?'

'Yes,' I said, 'he'll come.'

She woke up later to see him bending over her, and she smiled and made an effort to wisecrack about his beard, but it wouldn't come.

On the Saturday morning she regained consciousness for a short while and looked at me lovingly, but she could no longer smile, then she drifted away again to wake no more.

She died at one o'clock on the Sunday. And 'that lad' who had only made her acquaintance four days before, and whose week-end off it was, came at twelve o'clock, because, he said, he kept thinking of her – besides good priests, and good dustmen, there are good doctors.

When she was nearing her end he led me from the room, saying, 'Come on, you've had enough.' Tom and my mother-in-law were with her, but I knew she was already gone. She had been gone since yesterday morning.

Sitting on the terrace, the doctor said, 'Now you are going to feel awful, full of remorse because of the things you haven't done.' I stared at him. How did he know? How did he know that already I was torn inside because I hadn't openly shown affection to her, returned her embraces, stayed with her in the evenings instead of falling asleep in front of the television?

I did not know that the doctor was speaking generally and that

234

this reaction was what most people feel on the death of their parents.

In my case I should have felt little self-condemnation, yet I was weighed down by it. The days following her funeral, my mind became a battleground for conflicting emotions. I was free, free. I was fifty years old and for forty-five of those years I had been carrying the burden of her. Oh, the countless times I wished that she was dead; and now she was dead and I was free of the worry, the fear, the anxiety, but I was lost. I missed her. I wanted our Kate back. Drunk or sober, I wanted her back.

This feeling did not lift to show what was behind it until the first time Tom and I went out together to an evening entertainment, for then, in spite of my sorrow – which was very real – I felt like a young girl being let out of school. Or a more fitting description would be, a middle-aged woman being let out of prison.

It wasn't until sometime later that it was proved to me that Kate had been an alcoholic. If I had thought of this it was to dismiss it, for I said to myself that she could go for weeks without whisky. I thought an alcoholic drank all the time. This limited knowledge of the subject was because I wouldn't go into it. But even if I had known years ago what her trouble was it would have been more than my life was worth to suggest treatment. I once, during her stay in 'The Hurst', got her to a doctor after she'd had what appeared like a slight stroke, and lost the use of her arm. She would not let me go in with her, and when she came out she said, 'I haven't got to eat so much meat.' And that was that.

Anyway, everything from now on must be plain sailing. I was really free. There was nothing more to worry about. This being so I would get really better now.

But the past hadn't finished with me. It was to haul me back right to the beginning.

When I returned home to Hastings after the War, I had on my left cheekbone a small red mark, not a spot, and this developed a halo round it, the whole taking up about an eighth of an inch of the skin. It didn't disappear but was practically unnoticeable under make-up. Within the next two or three years there followed six of these marks on the left side of my face, one on the lip, and I was surprised to find that my tongue also was covered with them. I had frequently bled from the tongue, which was worse than bleeding from the nose, but had never associated the bleeding with these marks. The marks on the tongue didn't have haloes round them like those on my cheek. When yet another one showed itself on my neck I went to my doctor. He did not say it was my temperament this time, but heartened me by remarking that they were a sign of age creeping on, a sort of disintegration, and I was to expect this kind of thing. I was then in my early forties.

Then about twelve years ago, shortly after my mother died, when I could no longer completely cover the marks up with make-up, I went to a doctor again, a different doctor this time. And she thought I should see a specialist.

I saw the specialist in a general hospital. He took one look at the blemishes, then sent for a number of students. 'Do any of you know what these are?' He pointed to the marks on my face and neck, but none of them seemed to know.

'This patient is suffering from Telangiectasis, a hereditary form of a rare vascular disease.'

I was back on the table having an electric shock. I could smell urine. My heart had leapt up into my throat and was checking my breathing. I heard his voice as from a distance saying, 'This patient has bled from her nose since she was eighteen, she's had it cauterized numbers of times but cauterization is no use here ... Do you bleed from the stomach?'

'I beg your pardon?'

'Do you bleed from the stomach?'

'No.'

'Were there any bleeders in the family?'

'Not that I know.'

'Think. Did you ever know anyone on your mother's side to have this trouble?'

'No.' I could say this for a certainty.

'What about you father's side?' He stared at me and I stared at him, and the students stood waiting for my answer. Should I say no, or, I didn't know? Should I fumble and lie out of this awkward situation? I looked back at the big, broad figure of the man sitting opposite to me, waiting, he represented the entire world. He was the children in the back lane saying,

236

'You haven't no da.' He was the girl who wouldn't let me into her party. He was the people of the New Buildings who had pitied little Katie. He was some of the girls in Harton; the one who would have taken from me my good character, and especially the one who had thought she had spotted syphilis. He was the man who had turned me down.

'I am illegitimate.'

There, I had said it, aloud and in public, this frightening word, this word that had bred fear, that had brought shame into my life, this word that had started all the trouble. Not bastard, or fly-blow, or side-shoot, but the dictionary word, illegitimate, which meant 'Not authorised by law, improper, not born in lawful wedlock – bastard wrongly inferred, abnormal.'

'Yes, yes, er . . . yes.' The thick lids blinked twice before the head turned away. The students left; we talked a little more and then I went out.

It was a bitterly cold day but I was sweating. It was running freely between my breasts and down my legs. Fear was once more in command. I had a blood disease, an inherited blood disease. My God, this too. After all I'd gone through I had to have an inherited blood disease.

'Come off it!'

The woman who had reasoned and fought for ten years was speaking for the first time as a mature adult. She said, and with chilling saneness, 'If you've got an inherited blood disease you've had it since you were born. You are now fifty. You haven't died with it so far, so why the panic. And we'll waste no more sympathy because of what you've gone through either, as child, or woman. Katie may have been entitled to sympathy but she never wanted it. And don't forget, a minute ago back in there you shot your bolt, you admitted the shame publicly . . . it's done; you'll never feel it in the same way again.

And now you can write it all down.

I have written my tale in the room where Kate died. The roses are tapping on the window again and her presence is strong about me. I look towards the corner where her bed stood and she is smiling at me.

'You'll feel better now lass.'

'You think so?'

237

'Sure of it.'

'I've tried to be fair.'

'You were always fair, lass, always. And you haven't put down half that happened, you never need worry about not being fair. But because you've learned to forgive things will settle in you now.'

'I don't know. I've still a long way to go . . . and, well there's my religion. I want a religion, something that I can believe in, not a denomination, a religion.'

'It'll come, lass, never doubt. Remember that piece of poetry you read to me once by somebody with a name like, like ammonia.'

'You mean Aumonier.'

'Yes, that's him. Well, say it now, and say it every day and it'll come true. Believe me lass, it'll come true.'

I will seek Beauty all my days

Within the dark chaos of a troubled world I will
    seek and find some Beauteous Thing.

From eyes grown dim with weeping will shine a Light
    to guide me, and in Sorrow's Hour
    I shall behold a great High Courage.

I shall find the wonder of an infinite Patience,
    and a quiet Faith in coming Joy and Peace.

And Love will I seek in the midst of Discord, and
    find swift eager hands out-stretched in welcome.

I will seek Beauty all my days, and in my quest
    I shall not be dismayed.

I   SHALL   FIND   GOD

Good-Bye, Kate, and thank you for giving me life.

Catherine Cookson
'Loreto'
Hastings
December 1968